Ending
the LDP
Hegemony

Ending the LDP Hegemony

Party Cooperation in Japan

Ray Christensen

University of Hawai'i Press
Honolulu

05 04 03 02 01 00   5 4 3 2 1

Library of Congress Cataloging-in-Publication Data
Christensen, Ray, 1960–
    Ending the LDP hegemony : party cooperation in Japan / Ray Christensen.
       p.   cm.
    Includes bibliographical references and index.
    ISBN 0–8248–2230–7 (cloth : acid-free paper) —
    ISBN 0–8248–2295–1 (paper : acid-free paper)
    1. Political parties—Japan. 2. Jiyū Minshutō. 3. Opposition (Political
science)—Japan. 4. Japan—Politics and government—1989–   . I. Title.
JQ1698.A1 C485 2000
320.952′09′049—dc21   99–045572

Designed by Kenneth Miyamoto
Printed by The Maple-Vail Book Manufacturing Group

Contents

Acknowledgments

I HAVE HAD the privilege of working and studying at several universities while preparing this book. The Reischauer Institute of Japanese Studies at Harvard University supported my research as a graduate student by purchasing a data set of Japanese elections. The National Science Foundation provided assistance for work in Japan and during graduate school. Two Fulbright grants supported me during my stay in Japan and made it possible for me to conduct research at the Faculty of Law of Tokyo University. The University of Kansas, Brigham Young University, and Daito Bunka University have also supported my work.

Along the way many have helped me to refine my ideas. I am particularly indebted to Susan Pharr, Jim Alt, Brian Woodall, Steve Reed, Sasaki Takeshi, Takabatake Michitoshi, Igarashi Akio, Kan Naoto, Doi Takako, Kunihiro Masao, Gary Cox, Ron Francisco, Paul Johnson, Sven Wilson, and Jay Goodliffe. Patricia Crosby at the University of Hawai'i Press has been kind and patient in explaining the publishing process to me. I reserve my greatest expressions of gratitude for the many Japanese politicians, academics, journalists, and union officials who have taken time to explain the obvious and instruct the floundering foreigner in their midst.

1

Stereotypes of Success or Failure in Japanese Politics

HISTORY IS THE STORY of winners, and of the inevitability of their triumphs. Rarely is a losing candidate noticed, much less praised, after an election; the virtue cited, if any, is usually graceful defeat. Governments that lose wars, are unstable, or suffer an economic recession are soundly condemned as incapable. The more competitive the arena, the more intense the ritual castigation of the loser. Perhaps this explains the extreme invective heaped on losers in war, politics, and sports, areas of intense competition.

Losers are, most likely, responsible to some degree for their loss. A curious bias enters into the postcompetition analysis, however. Often in the rush to explain the loss, commentators focus on all possible mistakes, ignoring the loser's achievements. A losing candidate may have done extremely well in fund-raising but lost the election because he was not telegenic. A government may have taken seemingly appropriate measures at the beginning of a crisis, only to discover, with the benefit of hindsight, that its actions were inappropriate or insufficient.

This bias of seeing only fault in the actions of losers and only merit in the actions of winners can have serious consequences. Mancur Olson (1982) argues that the winners of World War II were the least innovative after the war, because their victory reaffirmed the status quo in those countries. In the electoral arena, the failure of Germany's Weimar Republic and France's Fourth Republic reduced the attractiveness of those republics' proportional representation electoral systems for a generation. Critics seem to view every aspect of the Weimar Republic as bad because the republic itself failed. The Weimar Republic example is even more curious because of the unrivaled popularity of the post–World

1

War II German electoral system, a system associated with the successes of the postwar German state. It is questionable that the electoral systems of the Weimar Republic and of post–World War II Germany had anything to do with the success or failure of these regimes, but the electoral systems have inherited the aura of their regime's success or failure.

An even more comical example of the bias in favor of winners was the 1970s American trend to indiscriminately copy attributes of Japanese companies in order to recreate their success. Some commentators believed that part of the secret of Japanese productivity was employees' performance of morning calisthenics in company uniforms, or the lack of such management prerogatives as separate cafeterias or parking lots. Early on, Chalmers Johnson ridiculed this belief by suggesting that United States companies force their workers to endure a one-hour commute standing in a crowded subway car and feed them room-temperature fish and rice for lunch, to see if these practices did not also boost worker productivity.[1]

The bias against losers is nowhere more manifest than in electoral politics. In each election campaign, pundits explain to the public the hopeless incompetence of the loser. It seems impossible to run a competent campaign and still lose the election, because loss is equated with error and inability. In the long United States presidential campaigns, this tendency leads to the curious phenomenon of the eventual winner having been previously castigated at some point for running an incompetent, error-prone campaign. The loser can do nothing right, and the winner has the political equivalent of the Midas touch. This bias hinders a balanced, analytical approach that examines both the strength and strategic victories of the losers, and the failures and foibles of the victors.

This lack of balance likewise exists in the postwar analyses of Japanese politics. Japan's four former opposition parties—the Japan Socialist Party, the Japan Communist Party, the Democratic Socialist Party, and the Clean Government Party—were seen to flounder helplessly under the complete domination of the ruling Liberal Democratic Party (LDP).[2] From its founding in 1955 until 1989, the LDP won every national election and selected every prime minister and cabinet member.[3] Other democracies have had similarly dominant parties, but none of them come close to the LDP in terms of its longevity in power and its complete dominance of the political scene.[4] In contrast, Giovanni Sartori's (1990, 333) term "irresponsible opposition" seems to precisely describe the behavior of the Japanese opposition, especially the Socialist Party.

The early 1990s seemed to have finally brought vindication to these perennial losers. In 1989, the LDP lost an election and control of the House of Councillors (upper house) of the Japanese Diet (Japan's national legislature). This was followed in 1993 by defections from the LDP, by the LDP losing control of the House of Representatives (the lower house), and by the first non-LDP government since the party's formation in 1955. The latter half of the decade, however, saw the gradual reassertion of LDP power and control. The party came back into power in 1994 in a historic coalition with two opposition parties. Though the LDP failed to win majorities in subsequent elections, the disintegration of one of its competitors led to the readmission to the LDP of enough former defectors for it to regain its House of Representatives majority in 1997. The 1990s ended with the LDP back in the position it occupied a decade earlier; though it still lacked a majority in the House of Councillors, the LDP appeared strong and confident, while the opposition was in disarray.

After a brief moment of success, the Japanese opposition appeared to be back to its ineffectual ways, with a record of apparent failure that deserves explanation and analysis. Existing analysis overlooks the successes of the Japanese opposition, however. The explanations of failure can be grouped into three categories: the rigid ideology or inflexibility of the opposition; the party leaders' lack of desire to take power, or their bad leadership; and the parties' lack of resources.

Otake Hideo's (1990) contrasting comparison of the failed Socialist Party in Japan with Germany's successful Social Democratic Party is perhaps the best example of the rigid ideology/inflexibility explanation. He describes how the Social Democrats in Germany moved to the center at the historic Bad Godesburg party congress and asserts that this ideological flexibility made it possible for the party to come to power. The Japanese Socialists failed to make a similar transition, he contends; their stubborn clinging to outdated ideologies relegated the party to permanent status as an opposition party in decline.

Terry Edward MacDougall's (1982) excellent study of leadership in the Socialist Party argues persuasively that party leaders were thwarted at every turn in their efforts to reform the party. MacDougall avoids simplistic arguments that opposition party leaders were indifferent about taking power, or that these leaders were incompetent. His careful arguments, however, ultimately lead to the conclusion that the opposition failed to take power because of other leadership shortcomings.

Gary Cox (1996, 1997) makes a strong case for a resource explanation of opposition failure in Japan. As the party in power, the LDP has access

to the largesse of government. It can steer government projects and
money to supporters and home districts in classic "pork-barrel" fashion.
It can raise large sums of money from businesses and other interests that
hope to augment their access to the government by currying favor with
LDP politicians. Though Cox recognizes that the opposition parties may
have resources of their own, the success of the LDP in elections points
to his conclusion that the LDP must have greater or better resources at
its disposal.

I do not dispute the conclusions of any of these authors. The Socialist
Party did remain attached for much too long to an outdated, inappropriate ideology. Party structures have thwarted the aspirations of innovative leaders, and the opposition lacks the monetary resources and governmental access of the LDP. These are only partial explanations of the
opposition's electoral failures, however; they have left out crucial information that is necessary to understand the record of the opposition. In
their analysis of why the opposition has failed, these and other analysts
have missed the areas in which the opposition has succeeded.
Furthermore, their analyses miss an important explanation for opposition behavior: the strategic dilemma for the opposition created by the
relatively large size of the LDP, and the effect that this size has on
the strategic options of the opposition parties.

The opposition record is much more mixed than the assessment of
abject failure that seems to be the norm in most accounts of these
parties. These parties have overcome significant barriers and have cooperated in many of Japan's elections. Their efforts in the realm of electoral cooperation have borne fruit, depriving the LDP of seats and
parliamentary majorities. For example, Cox (1996, 1997) presents evidence that the opposition does not coordinate its electoral efforts as
well as the LDP. Upon reexamination, however, this same evidence
shows that when the opposition parties decided to fully cooperate, they
actually coordinated their efforts better than the LDP. The only short-
coming of the opposition parties that needs to be explained is why they
eschewed cooperation in some elections.

Another success of the opposition is its ability to draw support away
from the LDP and to keep the LDP from winning majorities in elections. The LDP vote declined steadily until the 1980s, when it became
much more volatile. In the 1990s, the LDP failed to win a majority of
seats in the four national elections held from 1993 to 1998. The movement of defectors back to the LDP that began in earnest in 1997 could
set the stage for the LDP winning a parliamentary majority in the lower

house election scheduled for 1999 or 2000; however, these moves could also help focus the anti-LDP vote on a more unified opposition, an outcome that would be to the LDP's detriment. Analysts of opposition failures rarely note how successful the opposition has been in reducing the LDP vote.

A third significant success of the opposition is its brief record in government. Many felt that the Japanese would never trust the reins of government to the inexperienced, untested leaders of the opposition parties. Their brief stint in power has given the opposition the credentials it has needed to mount a credible challenge to LDP policies, however. In the mid-1990s, the most popular politician in Japan was opposition leader Kan Naoto, who gained his popularity precisely because of his handling of a scandal in the Ministry of Health and Welfare, which he headed during the opposition coalition government.

Besides an account of the successes of the opposition, I hope to contribute to a better understanding of opposition failure by describing the strategic dilemma that the opposition faces, a dilemma that better explains why the LDP so often wins at the expense of the opposition. The crux of this dilemma is the size of the LDP and the splintered nature of the Japanese opposition. Because of this difference, it is easy for the LDP to entice an opposition party to defect from the opposition, joining the LDP either in a formal coalition government or simply in a parliamentary alliance to pass a crucial piece of legislation. The LDP has a bargaining advantage that it has used repeatedly and successfully.

An analysis of this dilemma casts new light, for example, on the negative evaluation of the Japanese opposition by Herbert Kitschelt. In his insightful analysis of social democracy in Europe, he makes tentative observations about the failings of the Socialist Party in Japan:

> The JSP remained an intellectual's party inspired by different brands of extreme antiparliamentary and anticapitalist radicalism and never made it out of its political ivory tower. At the same time, MPs running uncontested as the party's sole candidates in their districts had little incentive to change the terms of the party discourse. (Kitschelt 1994, 294)

Kitschelt's critique cites two of the three common criticisms described earlier. The Socialists are in an ideologically extreme "ivory tower." Their leaders aren't just ineffectual; they lack a desire to change. No wonder Kitschelt subtitles his discussion of Japanese Socialists "The Logic of Self-Destruction" (Kitschelt 1994, 292).

Though I disagree with some of Kitschelt's conclusions with regard to Japan, his comparative analysis of social democratic parties is enlightening and useful. Specifically, he counters claims by Adam Przeworski and John Sprague (1986) that socialist parties face a trade-off in votes—varying with country in its degree of harshness—if they try to reposition themselves more toward the center of an ideological spectrum. Kitschelt sees a much greater potential for parties to successfully change their ideological orientation, constrained only by internal party preferences and organizational attributes, the external constellation of other parties, and the preferences of the electorate. Thus, Kitschelt sees three possible paths for socialist parties. They can maximize their vote in the short term by moving their party into emerging areas of public opinion, typically more toward the center in what Kitschelt calls a "left libertarian" perspective. Another option is to move to the left to decimate a leftist rival and take up an "oligopolistic" position as the premier party of the Left. Finally, a party can move to the ideological center, not to win more votes but to position the party in the "pivot," the place where no governing coalition can be formed without the party's participation.

Neither Przeworski and Sprague's nor Kitschelt's analyses capture the primary reason for opposition failure in Japan, nor do their analytical frameworks describe what has occurred in Japan. Both works focus primarily on the prospect of an opposition increasing its size by enhancing its electoral appeal. Kitschelt goes further, in that he allows for an opposition to pursue the goal of office seeking, but he does not fully appreciate the potential of this option, because of his emphasis on the ideological continuity of governing coalitions. Perhaps in the European setting the ideological continuity of governing coalitions is of paramount concern, but in Japan the ideological composition of a coalition can and does take a variety of forms.

I agree with Kitschelt that the opposition in Japan could pursue an electoral or an office-seeking path to success. I differ, however, in considering the electoral path to success, the focus of Przeworski and Sprague's and of Kitschelt's research, to be less important to Japan's opposition parties. These parties' efforts have been primarily in the arena of building coalitions. Thus, I posit the following three paths that are available to the Japanese opposition. Each opposition party can go it alone and try to become a majority party by enhancing its electoral appeal. Alternatively, the opposition can work together, trying to deprive the LDP of its majority and building an opposition coalition government. A third option is for the opposition parties to compete against each other to become the junior coalition partner of the LDP when the LDP loses its majority.

Kitschelt is correct that Japan's Socialist Party has utterly failed to increase in size and take power from the LDP. It has failed to enhance its electoral appeal. However, his analysis ignores opposition efforts to take power through cooperation and the strategic dilemma of following this path because of the bargaining advantage the LDP can bring to any coalition negotiations. Kitschelt analyzes the preferred route to power, but for much of the 1970s, 1980s, and 1990s, the opposition parties had given up on this option, instead focusing their efforts on cooperation and coalition governments, an area only briefly covered in Kitschelt's analysis.

I argue that the opposition has been successful in some areas, and that its failings can best be explained by the strategic dilemmas of cooperation in the Japanese context. Further, I hope my work contributes to a different conception of the overall nature of Japanese politics. My analysis of the opposition focuses on cooperative efforts between the opposition parties and on the relations between each of these parties and the LDP. The long, varied history of these interparty relations largely has been ignored in those studies of Japanese politics that focus on the LDP. I use the opportunity created by the LDP upset of 1993 to turn the spotlight on this underexamined arena of Japanese political behavior—the cooperative efforts and cross-party alliances that were common among Japan's political parties throughout the period of LDP domination. This history better explains the events of 1993, and it provides a basis for predicting the future trajectory of Japanese politics.

This analysis of the historical record, including the events of the 1990s, leads me to the conclusion that the opposition has succeeded in fundamentally changing the path of Japanese politics. The barriers to a variety of formal party coalitions have been eliminated as the need for such coalitions has increased with defections from the LDP. Japanese politics in the 1990s and perhaps well into the future was, and may continue to be, the politics of coalitions. Only Ronald Hrebenar (1986) has extensively examined these relationships. I build on his work, integrating the historical context with recent events into a more complete understanding of interparty relations in the Japanese setting. Such an understanding will be essential for interpreting the next decade of Japanese politics.

I argue for a different conception of the Japanese opposition parties. They have not denied the LDP its electoral dominance, but they have succeeded in challenging LDP rule and coordinating their response to LDP dominance. In analyzing the efforts of these parties, it is important to avoid the bias of looking for the mistakes of the opposition and the successes of the LDP. Instead, the efficacy of party actions should be judged against the goals that the party was pursuing. When the actual goals of the Japanese opposition, such as cooperating electorally and building alliances, are compared with their performance, the opposition has had some notable successes. Overall, the LDP has had more success than the opposition, but the record is more complicated than other analyses seem to suggest. The opposition failures that have occurred are primarily the result of the LDP's bargaining advantage. The opposition has made mistakes; it lacks the resources of the LDP; it has been more ideological than the LDP. However, the events of the 1990s show that these explanations are not the deciding factors for opposition failure. Chapter 2 explores the 1990s events in detail.

2

The LDP Fall from Power

ON 29 JANUARY 1994, the last day of an extended legislative session, both Houses of the Japanese Diet in a combined session approved political reform legislation. This legislation changed the Japanese electoral system, put greater restrictions on political fund-raising, and introduced government subsidies of political parties. These changes would be unremarkable if they had not been the fruition of a wide range of activities that had culminated in the breakup of the LDP and the downfall of the sitting LDP government six months earlier. The legislation also represented five years of debate and a history of failed attempts to change the electoral system dating back to the 1950s.

The story of Japanese politics in the 1990s begins with electoral reform, because this issue was the catalyst for the political changes that convulsed Japan in 1993. Political change in Japan cannot be understood without understanding the promise that electoral reform held for the various political actors. Because this story can be traced back to the late 1800s, what follows are only the most recent events in the saga.

The Japanese Election System

From 1947 until 1994, when the reform legislation passed, Japan used an electoral system in which voters could cast only one vote for a single candidate in multiseat districts. The number of districts varied from 124 to 130, and each district generally had three to five seats.[1] Typically, five or six candidates would run in a three-seat district, and the three with the highest number of votes would go on to serve in the House of Representatives.

This system had many interesting consequences. Because multiple

9

candidates were elected from the same district, large parties generally ran more than one candidate in every district. Voters were forced to choose between multiple candidates from the same party or alliance, meaning that in essence these candidates were running against each other. Thus, larger parties split into factions, and candidates strove to distinguish themselves from their party or alliance colleagues running in the same district. Conservative candidates distinguished themselves with their regional or occupational ties, or with their organizational acumen.[2] In the opposition parties, ideology or organizational ties separated the candidates.[3]

The ties and organizations that conservative candidates built created a strong, personal vote for that candidate. To create and maintain this vote, conservatives built personal support organizations *(kōenkai),* which required large sums of money to be sustained. Kabashima Ikuo and Yamada Masahiro (1994) estimate the direct *kōenkai* expenses at $200,000 a year, but when personnel and office expenses are included, the cost of maintaining a *kōenkai* rises to $1 million a year.[4] These yearly operating costs do not include the additional expenses of an election campaign. The monetary demands of setting up and maintaining a personal-support infrastructure encourage the intense fundraising that contributes to the recurring, endemic scandals in Japanese politics.

In addition, the multiseat districts of the electoral system produced what is commonly referred to as "semiproportional effects." Because districts elected as many as five representatives, a candidate needed to win only 15 percent—occasionally as little as 10 percent—of the vote to be elected. This feature opened the door to smaller parties, which would have been shut out under a less proportional system, such as single-seat districts.[5]

A desire to change some of the negative consequences of this electoral system drove the 1993–1994 push for electoral reform and party reformulation; however, this desire to change the electoral system was not new. Those who desired change fell into two camps, which had different motivations. The first camp wanted to make the electoral system less proportional, thereby increasing the LDP's parliamentary majority. In 1956, Prime Minister Hatoyama Ichirō of the newly formed LDP introduced such a proposal to change the electoral system to single-seat districts. The advantage of this proposal to the LDP was clear: With its consistent share of more than half the vote, the LDP could take a far larger share of seats under single-seat districts than under the existing, semiproportional electoral system. This proposal was rejected by the opposition parties and by many members of the LDP, who feared the consequences of changing district boundaries.

Similar proposals to introduce single-seat districts surfaced in 1965 and 1973; each proposal would have helped the LDP to win more seats without increasing its share of the vote. In 1973, Prime Minister Tanaka Kakuei suggested that some of the seats be assigned proportionally, safe-guarding the smaller parties against being frozen out. This compromise proposal retained advantages for the LDP, but it also allowed other parties some representation. Despite these compromises, opponents of the reform in the LDP and the opposition parties blocked serious con-sideration of the reform proposal in the Diet.

The second camp urging electoral reforms was motivated by a desire to end corrupt campaign practices, such as the flow of illegal campaign money. As early as 1956, Yanaga Chitoshi (1956, 300) stated, "Electoral reforms with a view to establishing clean elections have been the peren-nial issue and problem of Japanese politics. . . . Movements for clean elections have been carried on continuously since before World War II." In 1962, Prime Minister Ikeda Hayato asked the LDP politician Miki Takeo to lead a committee that would make recommendations for reform. The prime minister lamented that politics was becoming dirtier, specifically mentioning problems with money politics and factions. He warned that these problems could lead to the collapse of democratic politics (Kujiraoka et al. 1993, 6). Miki's reform proposals languished when Prime Minister Ikeda became ill, but were revived in the 1970s when a series of scandals rocked the LDP and brought down Prime Minister Tanaka. Party leaders chose Miki as Tanaka's successor, and Miki led the battle to reform money politics in Japan. The reforms that passed were an improvement, but key elements of the reform package were eliminated by the other members of the LDP, and the underlying incentives to continue raising campaign funds illegally remained untouched (Kujiraoka et al. 1993). The next major effort to clean up politics came in the early 1990s. Ironically, the movement's leader, Ozawa Ichirō, was a most unlikely reformer—a protégé of scandal-tainted Prime Minister Tanaka and the heir to a long line of corrupt, money-oriented LDP politicians.

Fall of the LDP Government in 1993

Ozawa Ichirō was the key actor in 1993 because he led the most signif-icant defection of politicians from the LDP, an act that brought down

the government. He also put together the non-LDP coalition government that took power after the 1993 election, and he led the effort to
change the election system and to reform Japanese politics. Analyzing
his motives for taking these bold actions is difficult. Certainly, his own
pursuit of power played a role in his efforts to reformulate the Japanese
party system; however, he also seems to have been an earnest proponent
of reform. Though he adopted the anticorruption banner, his main focus
was to eliminate the multipartism that was fostered by the semiproportional characteristics of the Japanese electoral system. Ozawa wanted to
begin a wave of party mergers and defections that would result in two
major parties that would compete under a new electoral system of single-
seat districts. Electoral reform was crucial to his plan; without single-seat
districts, there would be little incentive for groups to merge into two
major parties.

Ozawa wanted two major parties that alternated in power because he
and others had long since recognized the immobilism of the ruling
LDP's hegemony. These reformers argued that Japan needed two conservative or moderate parties alternating in power, rather than having
the monolithic LDP, which had an iron grasp on power. Two different
parties would allow the articulation of different policy positions, and the
winning party in the election would then have a mandate to implement
those policies.

Ozawa grafted his reform ideas onto a growing public ground swell
for anticorruption reform measures, which came in the wake of what
became known as the Recruit Scandal. This scandal resulted from the
efforts of the Japanese Recruit Corporation to buy influence with politicians by illegally giving large amounts of cash and stock contributions.
Prime Minister Takeshita Noboru resigned his position when he was
implicated in the scandal. At the peak of the scandal, a LDP committee
on the issue of electoral reform reported back to the party its suggestions for changing the electoral system. Ozawa linked the issue of anticorruption reforms to single-seat election districts. He and his allies
repeatedly argued that single-seat districts would reduce campaign
spending. This argument was not a new tactic; at its inception in 1925,
proponents of the existing electoral system had also argued that their
new system would help reduce corruption (Mitchell 1996, 45). Ozawa's
reform proposal strengthened political parties by allowing parties to run
media campaigns and give government funding to parties. These changes
were supposed to reduce the need of candidates to raise their own campaign funds. This linkage of anticorruption reforms with single-seat dis-

tricts allowed Ozawa to recast himself as the champion of political reform, despite his questionable credentials.

Ozawa first pushed this reform agenda during the 1989–1991 prime ministership of Kaifu Toshiki. The timing could not have been better. The Kaifu government was similar to the Miki government; it was a "clean" government that had been set up to restore public confidence after the fall, in rapid succession, of two scandal-tainted prime ministers. With Prime Minister Kaifu's support, Ozawa promoted electoral reform legislation, but his efforts were in vain. Internal LDP opposition to changing the status quo combined with opposition distrust of the legislation to kill it in the Diet. Shortly thereafter, Ozawa's career took a nosedive when he resigned from his cabinet position to take the blame for a party loss in the Tokyo governorship election. As time passed, the clamor for reform ebbed, as it had after previous LDP scandals. Ozawa suffered a further setback when he failed to take over as the new leader of the Takeshita faction. After this defeat, Ozawa and his allies left this faction to create one of the smallest factions of the LDP—a move that drastically reduced Ozawa's influence.

Fortunately for Ozawa, renewed campaign funding scandals, this time the 1992 Sagawa Express Scandal, refocused public and legislative attention on the issue of reform. Ozawa again pushed for these changes from within the LDP, and he made significant progress in recruiting opposition party leaders to the cause. Ozawa's influence with some opposition leaders had risen because he had sided with them against local LDP leaders in the Tokyo gubernatorial race.

The new prime minister, Miyazawa Kiichi, finally relented and publicly pledged to pass reform legislation that focused on electoral reform, though it did contain some anticorruption measures. When internal LDP opposition blocked this legislation, Ozawa and his friends joined the opposition parties in a vote of no confidence against the Miyazawa government. An election was called, and Ozawa left the LDP with a group of legislators to form a new political party, the Renewal Party. Other proreform LDP legislators also left the LDP and formed a second new party, the New Party Harbinger. These LDP renegades had been preceded several years before by Hosokawa Morihiro, a former LDP governor and member of the House of Councillors who had formed the Japan New Party. This party had already successfully run candidates in the 1992 House of Councillors election.

The 1993 election represented a radical change in the lineup of political parties and the choice of candidates. Besides the traditional array of

Table 2.1 1993 Election Results

Political Party	Seats Before the 1993 Election	1993 Election Results
Liberal Democrats (LDP)	222	223
Renewal Party	36	55
New Party Harbinger	10	13
Japan New Party	0	35
Socialist Party	136	70
Clean Government Party	45	51
Democratic Socialist Party	14	15
Communist	16	15
Independent and Minor	26	34

LDP candidates and those from the four main opposition parties, there were former LDP or new candidates in many districts who were moderate or conservative but who opposed the status quo politics of the LDP. These candidates were members of the three new, conservative/reformist parties: the Japan New Party, the Renewal Party, and the New Party Harbinger. The voters supported these conservative, anti-LDP, proreform candidates. Two of these three new parties won significant numbers of new seats in the Japanese Diet; the Socialist Party lost the most seats.

In the coalition negotiations that followed the election, Ozawa bested the LDP in negotiating strategy. The LDP could count on the support of some conservative independents; it needed to entice only one or two parties to become its coalition partner in order to have a parliamentary majority. The most likely candidates were the Japan New Party or the New Party Harbinger. Both were close to the LDP, and both had reasons to be reluctant about an alliance with Ozawa's Renewal Party. Ozawa, however, proposed that Hosokawa of the Japan New Party be the coalition's candidate for prime minister, thus securing the support of these parties in an anti-LDP coalition government.

The new coalition government spanned the ideological spectrum, from former LDP members to the Socialist Party. The coalition had six major party members: three conservative/reformist parties, the Socialists (on the left wing), and the centrist Democratic Socialist and Clean Government Parties. Though the parties had divergent ideologies, they agreed to make electoral and political reform their legislative priority.

The Hosokawa government pursued this agenda in negotiations with the new LDP president, Kōno Yōhei, but the two sides failed to agree on the actual details of the electoral reform proposal. Hosokawa then pushed for passage of the reform proposal based on the governing coalition's parliamentary majority, but in a crucial House of Councillors vote, significant defections from the Socialist Party led to the defeat of the reform package. In a flurry of last-minute negotiations with the LDP, Hosokawa conceded some of the details of the reform proposal, and the modified proposal passed with the overwhelming support of both the LDP and the members of the coalition government.

With the passage of reform legislation, the coalition began to fall apart. Tensions heightened between Ozawa and the leader of the New Party Harbinger, Takemura Masayoshi. The coalition's one unifying goal —the passage of reform legislation—had been accomplished, and dissatisfaction with that legislation was rising in the largest member of the coalition, the Socialist Party. Some Socialists were also becoming disillusioned that the leadership of the anti-LDP block had been taken by someone with the notoriety of Ozawa Ichirō.

Ozawa, meanwhile, was maneuvering to exclude the Socialists from the coalition. Phase two of Ozawa's political reform was to unify the disparate anti-LDP opposition into one new party that could fight the LDP in the new single-seat districts. As Ozawa discussed this goal with party leaders, it became clear that the Socialists, as a party, would not be included. The Socialists responded by distancing themselves from the increasingly Ozawa-led coalition, and they were joined by the New Party Harbinger. When Hata Tsutomu replaced Hosokawa as prime minister, these two parties formally began dissociating themselves from the coalition. Prime Minister Hata served only two months, leading a minority government in the summer of 1994.

The LDP now out-negotiated Ozawa in its bid to return to power. As Ozawa had proposed giving the prime ministership to the wavering Hosokawa of the Japan New Party in negotiations eight months earlier, the LDP now offered to support Murayama Tomiichi of the disenchanted and wavering Socialist Party as the next prime minister. The Socialists and the New Party Harbinger joined the LDP in a new, three-party coalition government, which ruled Japan until the 1996 elections. The LDP dominated the coalition in size, but the prime ministership and some other prominent cabinet posts were given to the Socialists and the

New Party Harbinger. Murayama ruled until January 1996, when the prime ministership slot passed to the LDP and its new president, Hashimoto Ryūtarō.

In the summer of 1996, in preparation for the upcoming election, an additional, significant event occurred that grew out of the hopes and aspirations of the 1993 party realignment. With the defection of the Socialists and New Party Harbinger from the anti-LDP coalition in 1994, the anti-LDP coalition came under increasing domination by Ozawa Ichirō and his allies. Ozawa's new party officially formed in December 1994 as the New Frontier Party. This merger left those reformers who were both anti-Ozawa and anti-LDP with no political home. Some of them were part of the coalition government, but they were unhappy with the LDP control of the government. Others were part of Ozawa's New Frontier Party, but they were unhappy with Ozawa's leadership, even mounting an unsuccessful challenge to Ozawa's bid for leadership of the new party.

Some of these people came together to form a third political party that could compete with the LDP and the New Frontier Party in the single-seat districts. They named this party the Democratic Party. Prominent members of the New Party Harbinger became its leaders, and it recruited heavily, though on an individual basis, from the ranks of the Socialist Party. Past leaders of both parties remained in those parties, running under these identities in the 1996 elections. For example, Murayama Tomiichi was reelected in a new single-seat district under the Socialist Party name. Takemura Masayoshi was also reelected under the New Party Harbinger name. Despite rumors of defections from the New Frontier Party, only one Democratic Party incumbent running in 1996 had switched from the New Frontier Party. Of the fifty-four founding members of the Democratic Party, twenty-eight were former Socialist incumbents, and fourteen were incumbents from the New Party Harbinger. Four other incumbents running in 1996 came from minor parties.

The 1996 election results were inconclusive, despite press reports of an LDP victory. As in the 1993 election, the biggest reallocation of seats was from the former Socialist Party to the other parties. In 1993, these seats went largely to the Renewal Party and the Japan New Party. In 1996, twenty-eight of the sixty-nine sitting Socialist incumbents joined the Democratic Party before the election; though fourteen of the twenty-eight were defeated, victories in other districts allowed the Democratic Party to maintain its preelection level of strength. In

Table 2.2 1996 Election Results

Political Party	Seats Before the 1996 Election	1996 Election Results
Liberal Democrats (LDP)	211	239
New Frontier Party	160	156
Democratic Party	52	52
Communist Party	15	26
Socialist Party	30	15
Clean Government Party	45	51
New Party Harbinger	9	2
Independent and Minor	16	10

the election itself, the greatest net flow of seats was from the Socialist Party and New Party Harbinger to the LDP and the Communists.

The year 1996 was a victory for the LDP in that it bested its main rival, the New Frontier Party, in 123 of 213 head-to-head contests, but the LDP share of the vote was still weak. In Japan's eleven regions, the LDP's share of the proportional representation vote ranged from a low of 27 percent to a high of 43 percent. In three of these regions, either the New Frontier Party or the Democrats won more votes than the LDP. In addition, though closer to the magic number of 251 needed for a parliamentary majority, the LDP still came up short.

Since that election the LDP has worked steadily to improve its position. After the 1996 elections, it continued to rule Japan in what should properly be called a minority government. Its two former allies, the Socialists and the New Party Harbinger, shrank to a combined total of only seventeen seats as the bulk of their incumbents shifted to the newly formed Democratic Party. The seventeen remaining in these two parties agreed to support the LDP minority government, though they no longer accepted cabinet positions nor were they formally part of a coalition government with the LDP.

The LDP's position improved even further with the disintegration of its main competitor, the New Frontier Party. This party disbanded in December 1997, but in the year before this breakup, twelve of the fifteen representatives who joined the LDP came from the New Frontier Party. This flow of representatives to the LDP actually gave the party a parliamentary majority of 251 seats in September 1997. Immediately before the breakup of the New Frontier Party, the LDP had already increased to 254 seats; after the breakup, the LDP rose to 265 seats. The New Frontier Party disbanding had an even greater effect on Democratic Party numbers. While the LDP gained twenty-six seats in 1997 and 1998, the Democrats increased from fifty-two seats to ninety-four, consolidating its position as the largest opposition party. The demise of the New Frontier Party also created the Liberal and the New Peace Parties, which were formed out of Ozawa supporters and former Clean Government Party supporters, respectively. The Liberal Party emerged with thirty-eight members; the New Peace Party attracted fifty-two members.

Though these events gave the LDP a slim majority in the House of Representatives, its control of the government was still incomplete. In 1998 elections, it again failed to win a majority in the House of Councillors, whose approval is needed for all legislation except treaties, budgets, and the selection of prime ministers. The LDP negotiated with the two most likely candidates for a House of Councillors legislative coalition, the Liberal Party and the New Peace Party. Ozawa's Liberal Party reached an agreement that was very close to an eventual merger of the Liberals back into the LDP. In exchange for support of LDP legislation in the House of Councillors, the LDP agreed not to run candidates in districts already occupied by Liberal Party incumbents.

It took five years, but the LDP recovered from the downfall of 1993, regaining its parliamentary majority and no longer ruling as a coalition or minority government. It cobbled together a legislative coalition to facilitate the passage of bills through the House of Councillors. The LDP even entered into an exclusive electoral alliance with the architect of its own 1993 demise, an alliance that could easily lead to the reabsorption of those party members into the LDP.

The events of the 1990s may appear to have come full circle, with the LDP gradually regaining from 1994 to 1998 all the power it had lost from 1989 to 1994. During this period, however, the Japanese political system was transformed in ways that make it unlikely for policies to revert to the same pattern of LDP domination that existed for the thirty-eight years from 1955 to 1993. For example, all types of coalitions are now possible. The opposition parties are viable alternatives to the voters. The new electoral system increases volatility in party fortunes, making it easier to deprive the LDP of its parliamentary majority in times of LDP unpopularity. In addition, the mix of seats in the new electoral system makes it difficult for the LDP to win parliamentary majorities at its present support levels. How did these momentous changes come to pass?

Explanations for the LDP's Fall from Power

The LDP fell from power in 1993 because of defections over the issue of political reform, specifically the issue of electoral reform. Why did this issue split the LDP, ending thirty-eight years of unquestioned LDP rule? The issue was not new; it had divided the LDP as far back as the Hatoyama reform proposal of 1956. What distinguished the plotting and maneuvering in 1993 from the many past unsuccessful efforts to change the electoral system?

Some of the explanations prove inadequate upon close inspection. For example, the recent string of campaign financing scandals, beginning with the Recruit Scandal, could explain the public outcry for reform and the legislative response. Scandals are endemic in Japanese politics, however, occurring with frightening regularity in the postwar period; much of what is considered fodder for scandals now was the accepted norm of political behavior in the prewar period. The timing of scandals does not explain why past reform efforts failed or why successful reforms passed in 1994, rather than two, three, or four years earlier.

Another interpretation treats the 1994 reforms and the 1993 political earthquake in Japan as discrete events. Reform occurred in 1994 because the LDP was no longer in power. Yet the Hosokawa coalition government was led and run primarily by former LDP politicians. In addition, the reforms passed only after the government struck a compromise with the LDP. Hosokawa's government did not have any numerical advantages in passing legislation that previous LDP governments did not also share.

A third analysis might point to Prime Minister Hosokawa's commitment to political reform. His coalition government took shape around the issue of political reform, and he staked his career on a promise to enact political reform legislation. Prime Ministers Kaifu and Miyazawa also made similar commitments to enact reforms (in 1991 and 1993, respectively); however, their commitments were insufficient. Indeed, when the passage of the reforms appeared doubtful, Hosokawa began to back away from his threat to resign the prime ministership if the reforms did not pass.[6] A committed leader does not appear to be the crucial explanatory factor in understanding the recent success of reform efforts.

A fourth explanation is the LDP's 1989 loss of control of the House of Councillors. This loss forced the LDP to work with the centrist opposition parties to pass legislation. After the 1990 elections for the House of Representatives, the LDP faced the pressing task of reducing malapportionment in that House. The passage of such redistricting legislation required the cooperation of at least some opposition members in the House of Councillors. In previous reapportionments, the LDP had simply reallocated the minimal number of seats necessary to bring the level of malapportionment under the levels ruled as unconstitutional by the Japanese Supreme Court, though the opposition parties had long demanded that a more comprehensive reapportionment be enacted. With the LDP's loss of its House of Councillors majority, the opposition could have forced a more comprehensive reapportionment. If the boundaries of many electoral districts were to be jumbled by such a broad reapportionment, then, by comparison, it would not seem as disruptive to install a completely new electoral system. In fact, opposition parties did cooperate with the LDP in passing a limited reapportionment in late 1992, but they were unable or unwilling to force a more significant reapportionment.

A fifth explanation highlights the importance of changes in the international arena and the end of the Cold War (Johnson 1997). LDP dominance was buttressed by the American desire for Japan as a stable, reliable ally. In the atmosphere of the Cold War, any alternative to the pro-American policies of the LDP was not acceptable. With the fall of the Berlin Wall, different issues arose, and unthinkable possibilities became possible. In Japan, as in Italy, the international rationale for conservative dominance of politics disappeared, cutting out the last remaining supports of a tottering political regime.

International changes certainly provide part of the explanation, but why was change in Japan delayed until 1993? What prevented reform efforts from succeeding in 1991? Conversely, what characteristic of the 1993 events would have been objectionable under the conservative domination framework dictated by the Cold War? Because the New Frontier Party was as conservative as the LDP, there should have been no objection to its advance under a Cold War scenario. International events coincided and supported domestic changes, but in and of themselves, they do not provide a complete, or even a primary, explanation of events.

Another possible explanation focuses on the personal ambition of Ozawa Ichirō and his frustration at losing the battle for control of the Takeshita faction. In this explanation, the electoral reform issue alone was not significant; it was merely an issue that could be used to divide the LDP, bringing in the parties of the former opposition as Ozawa's allies. Ozawa saw that his career in the LDP had been dealt a staggering blow when he lost the battle for faction leader. He could continue to fight for political power as a leader in the smaller Hata faction, gradually expanding his factional power base and influence, or he could strike out on a bold new course as the leader of a new political movement. Presumably, he chose the latter course because if successful, it would be a quicker route to the power and influence he desired.

This explanation holds much merit; politicians respond to incentives, and personal power is a strong incentive. The factional battle explanation by itself is insufficient, however; the LDP has had countless battles for factional leadership. Occasionally, they have led to threats of defection from the LDP, but only in this instance were the threats carried out. The incentive structures that influenced Ozawa and others to leave the party were much more complex than simply a desire for greater power and influence.[7]

Each of these explanations aids in understanding the events of 1993. All of them emphasize a break with the past, but in doing so, they ignore the historical continuity inherent in the events of 1993. This alliance of LDP defectors with the opposition serves as a perfect window to begin an inquiry into the postwar history of Japanese interparty relations.

The LDP broke apart in 1993, and political reform succeeded in 1994, because of the convergence of three motives that had a long history in Japanese politics. First was the LDP's desire to implement single-seat districts—an idea that began as a means for the LDP to win more seats, but was later transformed into a vehicle to produce a two-party system. Second was the desire of reformists in each of the parties to reduce the role of money in Japanese politics, or at least to go through the motions of reform in order to address the public clamor to do something about the scandals. These two motives were related to the structure of the electoral system discussed earlier. Additionally, the opposition parties had long desired to participate in the governmental power structure. One of the most common scenarios for these parties to obtain a seat at the table was for them to entice defectors from the LDP to join a coalition government.

Each of these ideas existed and had been seriously discussed for many years before 1993. That year was different from previous "dry runs" because of changes in the preferences of political actors and support groups. Ideas that, in a previous iteration, had been a minority view had gained more acceptance and power, either within the LDP or within the opposition. Many more politicians favored either some kind of anticorruption reform or a reform of the entire political system by using single-seat districts to force a party reformulation. Proreform politicians skillfully linked reform supporters in the LDP with those in the opposition who viewed reform not only as a way to clean up politics but also as a path to political power. In doing so, they cobbled together a majority that favored change.

The events of 1993 could not have been accurately predicted; they might have failed, as similar efforts did in 1991. However, seeds that explain the events do exist in the historical record. These seeds sprouted and grew in 1993 because there was greater support for each of these initiatives than had existed in times past, and because the disparate agendas of the three initiatives now were successfully linked in one electoral reform proposal. Thus, the year 1993 represents both the culmination of decades of effort and a break with the past, in that these efforts were finally successful.

Decision Making in Japan

What is the relevance of politicians in the decision-making process in Japan? My analysis claims that it is politicians who are the primary decision makers in these areas of dispute, but there are many competing models. One of the most famous is Chalmers Johnson's (1982) model of bureaucratic control over economic policy. J. Mark Ramseyer and Frances McCall Rosenbluth (1993) posit an opposite claim; they maintain that the influence exercised by bureaucrats in Japan simply manifests a delegation of tasks to them by politicians. Richard Samuels (1987) lies in between; he asserts that companies (at least in the energy sector) have much more autonomy than the bureaucracy and politicians. Muramatsu Michio and Ellis Krauss (1987) also disagree with Johnson's claim that the bureaucracy is all-powerful; they see a form of pluralism made up of rigid alliances, which they call "patterned pluralism." Kent Calder (1988) finds that, in the realm of public spending, LDP politicians respond directly to perceived electoral threats.

Despite their diverse approaches and conclusions, these authors agree that the dominant political actor varies with the issue. Politicians, they agree, have greater influence in "political" areas, such as cabinet selection or pork-barrel projects for local districts. Politicians do not have a completely free hand in these areas; their decisions can still be constrained by other factors. For example, the LDP's choice of a new prime minister was twice constrained by public opinion after prominent scandals, and "clean" politicians were chosen for the job. Party bosses hoped to use the relatively pristine reputations of these men to recast the scandal-tainted LDP. Similarly, institutions can also constrain these purely political decisions. Satō Sezaburō and Matsuzaki Tetsuhisa (1984) illustrate and explain how the LDP made routine the selection procedures for cabinet posts.

Electoral reform in Japan is primarily a political issue. Narita Norihiko (1996, 408–410), a bureaucratic insider in the Hosokawa government, agrees that the major reform decisions were all political rather than bureaucratic. Though the public, big business, and the relevant bureaucracy all supported reform, their support cannot explain the 1994 passage, the previous five-year debate, or the failure of past reform efforts.[8] In Japan, as in any country, the fate of electoral reform legislation clearly lies in the hands of the politicians who must enact the legislation. Unlike economic, budgetary, or welfare policy making in Japan, in electoral reform, the preferences of politicians, rather than the bureaucrats or executives, are paramount. The most important of these preferences is the politicians' known desire for reelection (Duverger 1972; Mayhew 1975).

Electoral Reform and Incentives to Maintain the Status Quo

Institutions are not easily changed. By definition, an institution is more stable than a fleeting, transitory preference. Electoral systems present a subset of institutions that are exceptionally difficult to change; most sitting politicians would not volunteer to revamp their own electoral system. Unless there has been a radical change in the electorate's preferences, most sitting politicians will be reelected under the existing electoral system. They are therefore loath to change the system, perhaps ending up as victims of redistricting or new electoral practices.

This aversion to electoral reform is particularly strong in Japan, for several reasons. Parties, not individual politicians, have the strongest incentives to change an electoral system. A party might be willing to sacrifice a few of its incumbents in an electoral change that was overall advantageous to the party, but individual politicians would be likely to block such a change. In Japan, however, parties are generally weak. Though politicians vote along party lines in the Japanese Diet, the LDP and the Socialists become immobile when they are divided internally.

The facade is one of party unity, but in practice, groups of politicians within parties regularly block their parties from taking stances on controversial issues. This problem is precisely what Ozawa hoped to change through electoral reform. The desires of individual politicians cannot be ignored in Japan, and individual politicians have few incentives to change an electoral system or district boundaries under which they have been successful.

Conservative politicians have an additional aversion to electoral change: They are elected on the basis of a strong personal vote. Their support organizations are an extremely valuable electoral asset; these organizations likely account for the high number of second- or third-generation politicians in Japan.[9] With few exceptions, these hereditary politicians are elected by their father's personal support organization. Sasaki Takeshi (1991) quips that these networks are the only asset a politician can pass on to his heirs without paying an inheritance tax.

LDP incumbents have the strongest personal support networks, and they rely on them most heavily for reelection. It is unlikely that these incumbents would willingly abandon their organizational advantage over potential opponents by drawing new district boundaries or changing the electoral rules to make such personal support networks less crucial to electoral victory.

The difficulty of electoral reform in Japan also stems from the strength of individual politicians in Japan. Each of the reform proposals put forth in the 1990s strengthened political parties at the expense of individual politicians or party factions (Christensen 1994, 593–594). Individual politicians would likely oppose reforms that take away any of their power. Proportional representation, single-seat plurality districts, or any combination of the two all strengthen political parties, rather than individuals, by making party nominations for office a more important factor in a successful campaign. Though parties have always controlled nominations, in the past, any strong candidate who failed to be nominated could run and win without any formal party affiliation. If a conservative, the winner was then admitted into the LDP and nominated at the next election. Given the barriers to unaffiliated candidacies that exist in both single-seat districts and proportional representation systems, all the reform proposals made the party's power to decide candidate nominations much more significant.

The reform proposals also reduced the fund-raising abilities of individual politicians, replacing those activities with government financing of political parties and the channeling of large, private contributions through party organizations. All proposals called for government funding of elections with funds the parties could distribute and control. Large contributions to individuals either were banned or restricted under each of the reform proposals. These changes give parties, instead of individual politicians, greater control over campaign funds.

Institutional and Preference Changes That Made Reform Possible

Given these disincentives to electoral reform, it is not surprising that individual politicians scuttled previous reform attempts. These disincentives did not magically disappear in 1994; they were overcome by the linkage of the three long-standing reform urges discussed earlier: single-seat districts that would bring about a two-party system, anti-corruption legislation, and party reformulation linking the opposition parties with LDP defectors. These three reform proposals were linked to create a proreform majority, but this majority was made possible by changes in the 1980s and 1990s that increased support for each of the three specific reform proposals.

The first of these changes was that reform of the LDP became a policy position advocated by the LDP's most powerful politicians. This reformist urge had a long pedigree in the LDP, but rarely had it been promoted by the party's most powerful faction leaders. In the 1990s, the most vocal advocates of such reform were those heirs to the Tanaka-Takeshita line of powerful king makers. The most notable proponents were Kanemaru Shin and Ozawa Ichirō, but they were joined by Gotoda Masaharu, who also came from the Tanaka faction. Tanabe Makoto (1997), a reformist leader in the Socialist Party, stresses the importance of this change, that the most powerful LDP politicians were supporting reform. He notes that the Socialists would have preferred to link up with what traditionally were the progressive elements of the LDP, men like Kōno Yōhei, Miyazawa Kiichi, or Kaifu Toshiki. However, these leaders lacked the resources and courage to undertake such an audacious and dangerous move as bringing down an LDP government and leaving the party. Action of this type became possible only when the more powerful line of LDP leaders became proponents of reform.

Another change was the increased support for the anticorruption reform agenda in the 1990s, during the unrelenting string of scandals that plagued the LDP. If there had been a hiatus in the scandals, the reform movement might have met the fate of its predecessors. Indeed, the whole issue of reform disappeared temporarily after the brouhaha over the Recruit Scandal died down. The second Kaifu cabinet even reinstated many of the scandal-tainted party bosses. The 1992 Sagawa Express Scandal once again breathed a sense of urgency into political reform, however. These continuing scandals made it impossible for opponents to permanently kill reform legislation.

The public pressure was intense for some kind of political reform, though it is difficult to show the actual efficacy of the public clamor. In the 1993 elections, most LDP incumbents were reelected; it did not appear that the electorate was severely punishing the LDP for dragging its feet on reform legislation. Nevertheless, LDP legislators did seem to respond to public opinion polls; they believed that some action must be taken to at least preserve the appearance of meeting public demands.

This desire to appear responsive to public demands is illustrated by the names of the proreform and antireform groups in the LDP, the League of Representatives in Support of Political Reform (Seiji kaikaku suishin giin renmei) and the Liaison Conference of Representatives in Support of Political Reform (Seiji kaikaku suishin giin renraku kyōgikai), respectively. Both sides accepted the political necessity of some political reform, though they disagreed about the need for a new electoral system. A similar phenomenon existed in the Socialist Party: Nineteen of the twenty Socialist defectors who helped defeat the government reform bill in a House of Councillors vote met the next day, forming the Representatives Roundtable to Stop Corruption (Fuhai bōshi giin kondankai) and asking other legislators to help them write a new anticorruption bill.[10] Even those who opposed reform legislation took a public stance in support of political reform.

The need for a public proreform stance is also illustrated in the January 1994 negotiations between the government and the LDP about a compromise reform bill. Antireform members of the LDP still objected to reform when the government accepted nearly all of the LDP reform proposal, which had been introduced into the Diet as an alternative to the government proposal. These legislators were then in the difficult position of trying to explain why they continued to oppose electoral reform, even after the government had deferred on every major difference between the two competing proposals. The antireform legislators were not interested in any reform that promoted realignment; coalition leaders outmaneuvered them by accepting, in large part, the LDP reform proposal, leaving these opponents no reasonable explanation for their continued opposition to reform.

A third change in preferences was Ozawa Ichirō's revival and sponsorship of political realignment between the opposition parties and the LDP. Political realignment has been a perennial topic of Japanese politics since the late 1960s. It has been discussed and proposed by politicians in every political party except the Communists. These realignment proponents hoped to link the non-Communist opposition parties and form a coalition government. From the outset, however, it was understood that this goal would be difficult to attain without the addition of defectors from the LDP to the coalition government. In this realignment, it was also expected that the Socialist Party would be forced to split between radical and moderate factions, since only the moderates would be able to accept the compromises necessary to make them part of a coalition government.

The non-Communist opposition parties seriously pursued this option in the 1970s. When Eda Saburō, the main proponent of realignment within the Socialist Party, left the party with only a handful of allies, the movement lost credibility within the Socialist camp. The centrist Clean Government and Democratic Socialist Parties continued to advocate realignment by encouraging the Socialist Party to move toward the center while simultaneously pursuing every potential coalition opportunity with the LDP. In the 1990s, the movement was revived within the Socialist Party when one of its main proponents, Tanabe Makoto, assumed the party's chair position. Tanabe had clear ties not only with the other opposition parties but also with the most powerful person in the LDP, Kanemaru Shin.

Ozawa Ichirō inherited the mantle of Kanemaru when both Tanabe and Kanemaru faded from the political scene. Ozawa had been one of Kanemaru's lieutenants and had many personal ties with all of the opposition parties. His connections included a leader in the Clean Government Party, Ichikawa Yūichi, and the secretary general of the Socialist Party, Akamatsu Hirotaka. When Ozawa began to vigorously promote and discuss the option of political realignment, a new generation of leaders in the Clean Government, Democratic Socialist, and Socialist Parties began once again to consider this option seriously.

Opposition politicians shared many of the concerns of the LDP. By 1993, most strongly favored allying with potential LDP defectors. Moderates led the proreform camp in each of the opposition parties. Their policy positions were not radically different from those of the progressives in the LDP. The opposition moderates were also willing to compromise on some positions to gain a position in the government. Not only did they desire the benefits that came from being in power, they genuinely believed they could accomplish more of their agenda by compromising and taking a place in government. They saw little value in maintaining a principled stance that permanently excluded them from political power and influence.

Opposition moderates also agreed with each of the reform agendas, believing that politics in Japan would improve if two relatively moderate parties alternated in power. They believed this alternating in power would decrease corruption in the ruling party by making the possibility of losing power a reality, and that two political parties would be better positioned to debate policies, gain mandates from voters to implement those policies, and create a more active, vibrant political arena in Japan. Some opposition party members differed from conservatives in their expectations regarding the second moderate party; many were uncomfortable with Ozawa Ichirō, rather than one of the leaders of the former opposition parties, assuming leadership of this party. This difference did not become an issue until after the Hosokawa coalition government was formed, however.

The attitudes and strength of the moderate camp within the opposition were also affected by the moderation and unification of Japan's labor union movement. Historically, the labor movement has been divided between the labor federations Dōmei and Sōhyō, with one labor federation supporting the Democratic Socialists and the other supporting the Socialists. These two movements merged in the late 1980s to form the organization Rengō; at that time, Communist sympathizers left the former Sōhyō unions and formed a smaller, Communist-affiliated labor federation. The merger left Rengō in the commanding position as the dominant labor federation.[11]

Rengō and its predecessors were important in Socialist and Democratic Socialist politics because they provided the primary source of organizational and monetary support of these parties' candidates. They also provided a core block of voters, which was crucial to these parties' success at the polls. Though constituent unions may have held dissenting views, the Rengō leadership strongly supported political realignment. Because the unions had purged Communist-affiliated radicals out of their organizations in the late 1980s, they viewed purging radicals from the Socialist Party as a natural progression. These unions no longer cared that a political reformulation would lead to a splitting of the Socialist Party; they had already encouraged a similar ideological split in their union organizations. As evidence of this attitude, in 1993, Rengō raised the ante by declaring it would not support any candidate who did not favor political reform.[12]

Rengō's prorealignment stance affected the calculations of self-interest by Democratic Socialist and Socialist politicians. Without Rengō's pressure, some of these politicians would likely have opposed drastic electoral reform. However, when an antireform stance endangered their financial and organizational support in the next election, more of these politicians concluded they should support realignment.

Union support of moderation and reconciliation was important, but the opposition parties themselves also had moderated their positions on many of the issues that distinguished them from the LDP and from each other. For example, in the 1970s, both the Socialist Party and the Clean Government Party called for the abrogation of the United States–Japan Security Treaty. Later in that decade, the Clean Government Party began supporting the treaty, and in the 1980s, the Socialists stopped insisting on abrogation. A further example of moderation by the Socialist Party is the successful election of the moderate Tanabe Makoto as party chairman in the 1990s, after moderate Eda Saburō's several failed bids for leadership posts in the 1970s. This moderation can be explained by several factors: the collapse of Communism, the decline of United States–Soviet Union hostilities, the success of Japan's postwar economy, and the decline of radical public-sector unions.

Opposition motivations can also be explained in purely strategic terms. Some politicians believed they could use this issue to their own personal advantage. Politicians in the Socialist Party, in particular, could use reform to drive radicals out of the party, thereby giving themselves undisputed party control. These politicians also hoped to become important factional leaders within a reformulated coalition party.

Despite the increased support in both the LDP and the opposition camp of all three agendas (i.e., creating two parties that could alternate in power, reducing corruption, and party realignment), the road to reform was not well paved. Tension existed between the supporters of the three reform initiatives. Anticorruption advocates were uncomfortable allying with party realignment proponents, such as Ozawa and Tanabe. They distrusted these leaders because both Ozawa and Tanabe allegedly were involved in the same corrupt practices that the reform bill was supposed to eliminate. Further, they distrusted the motives of these leaders, correctly perceiving that Ozawa and Tanabe's real agenda was realignment, not the reduction of the influence of money on politics. Distrust and dislike of Ozawa were often cited as reasons for opposing the reform bill. Indeed, the most vehement opposition to the reform bill in the LDP was led by three politicians who were given the acronym "YKK" (Yamasaki Taku, Katō Kōichi, and Koizumi Junichirō). Their opposition to the bill was grounded in their distrust and dislike of Ozawa.[13]

In the Socialist Party, some proreform politicians set up a second proreform organization. They wanted to distance themselves from the dominant proreform organization, which was perceived to be run by Tanabe and tainted by his close ties with corrupt LDP politicians. These feelings are illustrated by an exchange that occurred at a crucial Socialist Party convention held two weeks before the bill passed. Hecklers repeatedly interrupted a speech by the proreform leader of the Rengō confederation, Yamagishi Akira. They taunted him with "Did Ozawa Ichirō tell you that?" (Ozawa Ichirō ni iwareta ka?), to which he responded, "Shut up and listen" (Damatte kike).[14] This tension between advocates of different reform agendas is further illustrated by the strategies used in achieving electoral reform.

Tactics in the Electoral Reform Struggle

The most important tactic of the politicians battling for electoral reform was linking electoral reform with anticorruption measures. The debate about reform shows how important this linkage was. It was clear from the outset that the most important feature of the reform legislation was the alteration of the electoral system, not the relatively weak anticorruption measures. Opponents of the legislation in both the LDP and the opposition worked together to stop the legislation, despite their widely divergent agendas. Some opposed the legislation because they wanted more strict anticorruption measures; others opposed it because they wanted to maintain the status quo. The strange bedfellows of this alliance worked together to block reform legislation under the Hosokawa government, and they came together again in 1994 when the left wing of the Socialist Party teamed up with the LDP to take power from the Ozawa-dominated coalition government. Their differing desires for stricter anticorruption measures rarely came out in the open, because in public statements, all sides supported anticorruption legislation. The anti-Ozawa members of the LDP manipulated the debate over reform in general, and over anticorruption legislation in particular, to disguise their opposition to the electoral system provisions of the reform bill.

The anticorruption measures of the bill, the supposed reason for the reform legislation, were never seriously debated. Commentators and politicians stated that the reform measures would not make money less important in elections but merely force the money to take different routes.[15] The anticorruption measures were, at worst, mere window dressing; at best, they were only a preliminary step toward significant reform. LDP legislators who called for a real anticorruption bill were told by a veteran LDP leader that "such strict measures will get us all arrested" (sonna kibishii koto o yattara, minna tsukamatchau yo).[16]

The second main tactic of the proreform forces was the threat of defecting from a party to a new coalition. This threat is always present in Japanese politics, but in the early period of reform (1989–1992), it lacked credibility. In this period, prorealignment forces in the opposition maintained their public stance against the LDP's reform proposals, though they were preparing for a possible realignment. Similarly, though powerful LDP leaders were discussing realignment, none of them were openly threatening to leave the LDP.

As the conflict over reform culminated with the introduction and debate of the reform bills in the spring of 1993, proreform forces in the LDP made explicit threats to leave the LDP. The events of the summer of 1993 were not a complete surprise; they had been predicted in the spring as the likely result if antireform forces in the LDP killed the bill.[17] When the bill was killed, Ozawa and his allies in the LDP made good on their threat.

The threat of defection from the LDP was more credible in 1993 than in times past, for several reasons. By 1993, the Socialist Party had moderated many of its positions, and more of its members were receptive to political realignment involving the LDP. In addition, the prospect of electoral reform meant that after defection, a new electoral system could create an incentive structure that would maintain the realigned party system created by the defection. With these changes, Ozawa could take the first step, making it easier for opposition politicians to support realignment without irrevocably jeopardizing their political careers.

Ozawa's threat to defect also had greater credibility in 1993 because of the recent emergence of the Japan New Party, a party made up of conservatives and moderates who had become disaffected with the LDP. In the 1992 House of Councillors election, this party surged in popularity, winning 10 percent of the vote. It blazed the trail to realignment by becoming a proreform, conservative alternative to the LDP. Ozawa and his friends would not be alone in the wilderness if they left the LDP;

they could count on prospective allies both in the Japan New Party and in the non-Communist opposition parties.

Threats to defect, in order to bolster prorealignment forces within the LDP, did not end with Ozawa's defection from the LDP. The later use of such threats is the crucial, proximate factor in explaining the passage of reform legislation in January 1994. If the LDP leaders did not agree to compromise, Hosokawa threatened to amend the reform bill to make it more appealing to potential LDP defectors. He would then send the bill back down to the House of Representatives for a two-thirds vote, which would override the House of Councillors. If such a vote were to occur, LDP leaders were convinced that many more proreform LDP legislators would leave the party, and the party would become even more crippled and divided.[18] It was this fear that gave the upper hand to the proreform forces of the LDP and forced LDP leadership to accept the compromise proposal, thereby preserving party unity.[19]

Ozawa's defection also gave a tremendous boost to the proreform forces in the Socialist Party. The threat of defection from the Socialist Party had always been weak and noncredible. The defection of the Democratic Socialists in 1960 and of Eda Saburō in the late 1970s had been disastrous for the defectors. This history, coupled with the importance of union support, had been important in holding the Socialist Party together despite the deep divisions within it. LDP defections changed these calculations. With LDP defectors ready to align in a coalition government, leaving the Socialist Party suddenly became a more attractive prospect. With unions in a prorealignment stance, there was little danger of losing organizational support. These changes put proreform forces in a more powerful position to coerce left-wing elements of the party to go along with compromises to preserve party unity. Because proreform forces had less to lose than the left wing if the party split, they could threaten defection quite credibly. Left-wing forces were now making concessions to preserve party unity because they had much more to lose in a party split.[20]

Though the use and threat of defections did not become crucial tactics until 1993, prorealignment forces had already discussed the inevitability of defections. After the LDP lost control of the House of Councillors in 1989, it was understood that reform legislation could not pass without the support of at least part of the opposition. With this in mind, the advisory council that convened to draft an electoral reform proposal differed from past councils. It was composed of neutral members who did not directly represent party interests. In contrast to the seven previous electoral advisory councils, this eighth council produced a unified compromise recommendation that was strikingly similar to the reform bill that was ultimately enacted. Previous councils had always submitted either multiple reports or no report, reflecting the conflicts between the party politicians who made up the council membership. To avoid this result, the 1989 advisory council was composed entirely of nonpoliticians. Even at the advisory council stage, realignment proponents made sure they issued a recommendation that had the greatest chance of being accepted by the LDP and by the prorealignment forces of the opposition parties.

Horie Fukashi (1997) explains the consideration given to the pro-reform forces both of the LDP and Socialist Party during the council's drafting of the reform proposal. Besides being a member of the general advisory council, Professor Horie also sat on the committee that drew the proposed new election district boundaries. He cited the division of the former Ibaragi second district as an example of consideration given the Socialist Party in these deliberations. The former second district was to be divided into two new districts. If the old district were divided keeping its coastal cities together, the Socialists might win that new district. If, however, the district were divided so that the coastal cities were split and combined with more rural, conservative inland areas, then the LDP would easily win both new districts. Horie says that no one made explicit arguments in the discussions, but it was understood that the committee had to create some districts advantageous to the Socialists if their reform proposal was to pass. The committee kept the coastal cities together in the new district. In the 1996 elections in this district, the former Socialist incumbent garnered 53,000 votes to the LDP candidate's 69,000 votes.

The tactics of the antireform forces were largely the mirror image of the proreform forces' tactics. Because they could not actually oppose political reform, they decoupled, derailed, and delayed reform legislation.

The primary opposition tactic was to decouple party realignment and its catalyst, electoral reform, from anticorruption measures. Opponents insisted, with some accuracy, that the electoral reform aspects of the reform bill would not reduce the influence of money in elections and could easily exacerbate corruption problems. They insisted that anti-corruption measures be fast-tracked and that the electoral system be discussed afterward at a more leisurely pace. This maneuver was extremely popular because it allowed politicians to kill electoral reform while appearing to be adamantly proreform. For example, in the January 1994 Socialist Party convention, the antirealignment group proposed a resolution urging priority passage of the anticorruption measures of the government reform bill.[21]

This tactic put each side in a curious position. Opponents of realignment and electoral reform insisted that they were adamantly proreform, and they called for immediate passage of anticorruption legislation. Prorealignment forces defended their position that both anticorruption legislation and a new electoral system were needed to change Japanese politics. The opposition parties had also used the decoupling tactic, before their leaders had been persuaded to support reform legislation. From 1989 to 1992 the opposition responded to LDP proposals for a new electoral system by insisting that the malapportionment of the present system be corrected before considering any other reform proposals. This tactic was also a way to oppose reform while publicly favoring it.

A second antireform maneuver was to derail the legislative process by insisting that other legislation or political events take priority over electoral reform. This tactic often was successful; the political reform debate was sidetracked by leadership struggles within the LDP and debate on Japan's role in United Nations–sponsored activities. In the last month before the reform proposal's passage, some argued that the recession should be a higher legislative priority than reform; an antireform LDP group calling itself the Association to Give Priority to Economic Policy and Enact Political Reform (Keiki taisaku saiyūsen seiji kaikaku jitsugen no kai) organized at this time.[22] As with decoupling, derailing was a popular tactic because it allowed opponents to stall reform legislation without actually opposing reform legislation publicly. Ultimately, however, such delaying tactics were unsuccessful. An issue could derail the reform bill from consideration for a time, but when the other issue was resolved or faded off the political radar screen, another scandal resuscitated the issue of political reform.

A third antireform strategy was to delay legislation. The Japanese legislative process is cumbersome and is severely constrained by time limits on legislative sessions. At the end of each session, all pending legislation is effectively killed. A tried-and-true tactic in Japanese parliamentary maneuvering is to delay all the bills under consideration in a legislative session, forcing the government to prioritize its bills. The government must then choose which part of its legislative agenda to pass and which part to sacrifice to the delaying tactics of the opposition.

This strategy explains why Socialists and minor party legislators in the House of Councillors joined with antireform forces to defeat the government bill. The result of their actions was a compromise bill that was more hostile to the interests of the Socialists and minor parties than the government bill they had helped defeat. Their actions were even more curious, given the possibility that the government would compromise with the LDP if the government bill was defeated in the House of Councillors.[23] These legislators speculated on the parameters of the probable compromise bill before the actual government bill was defeated in the House of Councillors. Why, then, did these legislators act in a way that was likely to turn a bad bill (from their perspective) into something worse?[24] The answer lies in their reliance on delaying tactics to block undesirable legislation in the Japanese Diet. These legislators were well aware of the risks of a compromise bill with the LDP when they voted against the government bill, but they were hoping that such a compromise could not be worked out before the end of the legislative session. They would then fight the reintroduction of the bill in the next legislative session, possibly preventing the passage of reform legislation that included a new electoral system.[25] Unfortunately for them, they miscalculated.

Conclusion

The transformative political events of 1993 resulted from several factors. Ozawa's personal ambition, the changing international environment, and other factors contributed to the changed preferences of the important political actors. More important, Ozawa and his allies skillfully linked desires for different varieties of reform and then managed to hold together this unstable coalition long enough to see reform legislation passed.

The next chapter describes and examines the strong incentives for party cooperation, as well as the barriers to such cooperation. This discussion sets the stage for analyzing electoral cooperation and past efforts to do exactly what was accomplished in 1993: wrest power from the ruling LDP.

3

Strategic Dilemmas and Options of the Opposition

THE TWISTS AND TURNS of Japanese politics in the 1990s seem to support the conclusion that the opposition parties failed in their attempt to wrest power from the LDP. The few who have paid attention to this ignominious record have blamed the incompetence of opposition leaders, the rigid ideology and inflexibility of the opposition camp, and the lack of political resources in this camp. Though each of these explanations has some validity, they do not clearly distinguish realms in which the opposition has been successful from those in which they have failed. Furthermore, these explanations leave unexplored the coordination dilemma that the opposition faced. The opposition's failure to take power in the past thirty years is best explained by this dilemma rather than the incompetence of its leaders, its rigid ideology, or its lack of political resources.

An opposition party may follow any of three possible paths to power: it can grow, trying to become a majority party; it can try to become a coalition partner of a ruling party; or it can cooperate with other opposition parties to deprive the ruling party of its majority status. In Japan, no opposition party has grown significantly, so coalitions have become the path to power with the greatest prospects of success. The prospects of an opposition coalition government are especially appealing to opposition parties, but to succeed, this path requires that the parties cooperate with each other.

Incentives to Cooperate in Parliament and in Election Districts

There are strong incentives for opposition cooperation both in the Diet and in the elections. When the LDP has not had a majority in the House of Councillors (after 1989) or in the House of Representatives (1993 to 1997), opposition cooperation could block LDP legislation or even block the formation of LDP governments. In other periods, a unified opposition could significantly delay LDP legislation through parliamentary procedures that value consensus in agenda setting, and through cultural norms that restrain a simple majority from running roughshod over the desires of a sizable minority.

The incentives for opposition cooperation in elections are also obvious. In the 1996 elections, for example, the LDP's two main opponents, the New Frontier Party and the Democratic Party, cooperated in twenty districts, winning seven of those districts. In fifty-seven districts, the LDP candidate won against the two candidates sponsored by the New Frontier Party and Democratic Party, respectively. In forty-six of those districts, the combined vote of the two opposition candidates was greater than the vote of the LDP victor. If these two parties had cooperated to win these seats, together they might have won as many as thirty-six more seats than the LDP in Japan's single-seat districts. Similar, though less dramatic, cooperative opportunities in elections have been present since the mid-1960s, and opposition efforts to reap the benefits of such cooperation have been a part of Japanese elections since 1971.

The incentives to cooperate electorally vary according to the type of electoral system and the number and size of political parties in the system. These incentives are based on the existence of what political scientists call "wasted votes." A wasted vote is either a vote cast for a losing candidate or a vote cast for a winning candidate that is not necessary for that candidate's victory. The 1996 House of Representatives race in the Mie fifth district illustrates how wasted votes are calculated.

Candidate	Party	Votes Received	Wasted Votes
Fujinami	LDP	115,959	72,614
Kurogi	Communist	43,344	43,344

All of Kurogi's votes are wasted votes because Kurogi lost. In addition, more than half the votes cast for Fujinami are also wasted votes because Fujinami only needed 43,345 votes to win. All of Fujinami's excess votes are also counted as wasted votes. In this election, 72 percent of the votes cast became wasted votes.

Different electoral systems yield different numbers of wasted votes, and the number of wasted votes produced is important because it is a major incentive for electoral cooperation. The electoral system that creates the greatest number of wasted votes—hence, the strongest incentives for electoral cooperation—is that of single-seat districts in which one, nontransferable vote is cast for a candidate, as in the example just presented. Such districts always produce more than 50 percent wasted votes. In an extremely close race in such a district, the loser will have nearly 50 percent of the vote, and all of his votes will be counted as wasted votes. In addition, all of the victor's votes that exceed the loser's vote total will also become wasted votes. In a lopsided victory such as Fujinami's in Mie 5, not only do all of the loser's votes become wasted votes, but many, sometimes even more than half, of the victor's votes are wasted votes.

In contrast, the incentives to cooperate and the number of wasted votes are less important in more proportional electoral systems, such as the system used in the Japanese House of Representatives from 1947 to 1993. Because the Japanese system typically elected from three to five representatives from each district, smaller parties found it easier to elect at least one representative. Thus, a greater proportion of the votes were allocated to winning candidates, producing fewer wasted votes and weakening the incentives to cooperate electorally. Two examples illustrate the high and low ends of wasted votes it produced (victors are in bold).

Party	Niigata 1, 1990 Election Vote (%)	Wasted Vote (%)
Socialist	**32.2**	4.2
LDP	**29.2**	1.2
LDP	**28.0**	0
Democratic Socialist	6.1	6.1
Communist	4.5	4.5
Total		16.0

Party	Niigata 2, 1990 Election Vote (%)	Wasted Vote (%)
Socialist	**23.2**	7.4
Ind/LDP	**16.6**	0.8
LDP	**15.8**	0
LDP	14.6	14.6

Continued on next page

Continued from previous page

Party	Vote (%)	Wasted Vote (%)
LDP	13.6	13.6
IND/LDP	13.3	13.3
Communist	3.0	3.0
Total		52.7

This Japanese electoral system typically produced wasted vote totals of less than 50 percent, unlike the system of single-seat districts.

A third example shows how increasing proportionality reduces the number of wasted votes even further. The 1996 returns for the Hokkaido proportional representation district in Japan show how apportioning seats proportionally, according to the votes received, drastically reduces the number of wasted votes, even when a relatively disproportional system of seat allocation (the d'Hondt system) is used.[1] In this district, nine seats are awarded, and six parties ran in this election. Voters cast 2,626,326 valid ballots.

Party	Votes Won	Seats Won	Wasted Votes
Democrat	835,072	3	94,394
LDP	740,677	3	0
New Frontier	552,847	2	59,061
Communist	396,923	1	150,030
New Socialist	100,807	0	100,807
Total			404,292

Fifteen percent of the votes cast in this district became wasted votes. The number of wasted votes declines even further in proportional representation districts of larger magnitude. In the same election, the thirty-three-seat Kinki region district had only 8 percent of its votes cast as wasted votes.

These three examples show how the electoral reform of 1994 both increased incentives to cooperate electorally in the new single-seat districts and decreased incentives to cooperate in the new proportional representation districts. The discussion thus far, however, has ignored the second necessary incentive to cooperate electorally. Besides large numbers of wasted votes, there must also be sufficient numbers of parties contesting for votes, such that allied parties could have benefited from a different allocation of votes. For example, in the Mie fifth district, there was not sufficient party competition to warrant electoral cooperation, despite the large numbers of wasted votes. If there had been two losers in that race, they could have coordinated their efforts and presented a united front against Fujinami, but when there is only one loser, there is no potential for electoral cooperation.

In contrast, the other examples all illustrate incentives to cooperate electorally. The weakest incentives to cooperate exist in Niigata 1, where the losing Democratic Socialists could have combined their votes with the losing Communists. Their joint candidate would still have lost, but would have done better in the district. In Niigata 2, the LDP and LDP-affiliated independents had the votes to win all three seats, but because they ran too many candidates and divided the vote unequally between those candidates, they lost one seat to the Socialists. Similarly, if the Socialists and Communists had joined forces in this district, they could have assured themselves of one seat, regardless of any further coordination that the LDP and its affiliated independents may have attempted. In the Hokkaido proportional representation district, if the New Socialists had combined forces with the Communists, together they would have won two seats, depriving the LDP of a third seat.

These districts show the existence of wasted votes and the potential for electoral cooperation in a variety of settings. The importance of wasted votes in creating electoral incentives to cooperate supports Maurice Duverger's (1965, 325–336) assertion that electoral coalitions will not form in integrated proportional representation systems or in plurality systems that have only two parties. Duverger's integrated proportional representation system is a system that reduces wasted votes to their absolute minimum by aggregating at the national level votes that are left over in districts. In contrast, electoral coalitions should be common in electoral systems that produce more wasted votes and that have multiple parties positioned to take advantage of a reallocation of those votes.

The Strategic Dilemma of Parliamentary Cooperation

Incentives for the Japanese opposition to cooperate, both in the Diet and in elections, have always existed, though they have varied in strength. Nevertheless, the record of successful cooperation is spotty in both of these arenas. Why have the opposition parties in Japan so often failed to unite in taking power away from the LDP? Why have their electoral coalitions been the exception rather than the rule? The answers to these questions lie in the disincentives to cooperate. Often the costs or difficulties of cooperation outweigh the potential benefits.

In the parliamentary realm, opposition cooperative efforts have been hampered by the LDP's long-standing size advantage. Because the LDP is a large party, historically with either a parliamentary majority or a near majority, it is difficult for the opposition parties to create or maintain an opposing coalition. All three options for the opposition—going it alone, building a unified opposition coalition, or defecting from the opposition and joining an LDP coalition—are negatively affected by the size advantage of the LDP. Opposition parties in other countries face the same array of possibilities, but in Japan, the difficulty of unifying is exacerbated by the size of the LDP and by the strategic advantage that size gives the LDP in its efforts to disrupt opposition unity.

This advantage of the LDP can be illustrated by modeling the bargaining process as a game, with the following assumptions: (1) bargaining is costless, (2) political parties act as units, (3) each party is equally happy to be a coalition partner with any other party, (4) the payoff for not being part of the ruling coalition is zero, and (5) the total payoff for a ruling coalition is 100. In a game with only two political parties, there will not be a coalition, as the majority party will form a government, taking the entire payoff for itself. If there are three political parties, none having a majority, yet any two of them capable of forming a majority, then two of the parties will form a coalition, dividing the payoff equally. The payoff will be divided equally because the excluded party will counter with a higher offer to any party that receives less than 50. Imagine that the three parties are the Conservatives, the Liberals, and the Nationalists. If the Conservatives demand more than 50 as their share of the payoff, their potential partners, the Liberals, will have to receive less than 50. The excluded party, the Nationalists, will then counter with an offer of 50 to the Liberals, and the Liberals will accept the Nationalists' offer and reject the Conservatives' demands.

This principle of equal payoffs, however, is affected by the existence of possible alternative coalitions. The equal payoffs that a party can receive in one coalition can be used by that party to receive more than its equal share in an alternative coalition. For example, consider the following scenario:

Party	Party Strength
Conservative	30
Liberal	30
Small party A	10
Small party B	10
Small party C	10
Small party D	10

Because 51 is a majority, there are many coalition alternatives. The Conservatives could join with the Liberals, or either one of these two major parties could join with any three of the smaller parties to form a coalition. The payoffs for the different coalitions are as follows:

Coalition 1	Payoff	Coalition 2	Payoff
Conservatives	50	Conservatives	50.0
Liberals	50	Small party A	16.7
		Small party B	16.7
		Small party C	16.7

The participants in coalition 2 are interchangeable. The Liberals could replace the Conservatives as the major party in this coalition; likewise, the four small parties can be interchanged. The payoffs outlined above occur because the Conservative-Liberal coalition is governed by the principle of equal payoffs; each party would receive 50. Because coalition 1 always remains an alternative, either of the larger parties can demand 50 if it joins with three of the smaller parties to form coalition 2. The three smaller parties then split the remaining 50 evenly among themselves. If the three small parties refuse to give the larger party 50, that party will just join with the other larger party in a two-party coalition.

The bargaining situation of the Japanese political parties can be modeled similarly. If the LDP were to lose its Diet majority, the division of power would resemble the following:

Party	Party Strength
LDP	45
Opposition party A	11
Opposition party B	11
Opposition party C	11
Opposition party D	11
Opposition party E	11

Though many coalitions are possible, all possible coalitions can be grouped into two categories: the LDP allied with a smaller party or an all-opposition coalition. The payoffs for these two alternatives are as follows:

Coalition 1	Payoff	Coalition 2	Payoff
LDP	80	Opposition party A	20
Opposition party A	20	Opposition party B	20
		Opposition party C	20
		Opposition party D	20
		Opposition party E	20

These five opposition parties can only split the payoffs equally, giving each party 20. The LDP can woo just one of the smaller parties to its coalition and offer that party a payoff of 21. The five-party coalition cannot match that offer without reducing the payoff to one of it members. In that case, the LDP would then be able to offer the party that got the reduced payoff a higher payoff of 20. Thus, the LDP can always outbid the five-party coalition for one of its members.

This game, of course, is based on a series of assumptions that render its results questionable in the real world of Japanese politics. Parties are not unitary actors, and it is possible to make offers to factions or groups within parties, as Ozawa Ichirō's defection from the LDP illustrated. Bargaining is not costless, and certain kinds of coalitions have greater costs and fewer benefits than others. It is less costly for the Socialists in France to ally with the Communists than to ally with the National Front. Similarly, the payoff for not being in the ruling coalition is never zero, because parties gain advantages from being in the opposition; they are not responsible for the policies of the government.

This simple game model is also complicated by the fact that, in reality, the various games of making and breaking governments and running campaigns are all interconnected. A party is most likely to at least begin coalition negotiations with a party with which it was allied during the previous election. A party that has just fought a hard election battle by attacking another party will find it more difficult to join that party in a coalition government. Parties may also employ different strategies at different stages in the process. For example, a party might pursue a coalition strategy with its opposition allies during an election and then position itself to join the former ruling party in a coalition government after the election. Similarly, a party might reject all alliances during an election and then pursue coalition strategies during postelection negotiations.

Despite these complications, the game described earlier does illustrate the essence of the bargaining advantage the LDP has in coalition negotiations. The LDP used this advantage when it lured the Socialists and the New Party Harbinger into a coalition in 1994 by giving the prime ministership to the Socialists. The LDP paid dearly for this coalition. To use the payoff numbers of the game described above, the Socialists could have expected a payoff of 20 for their participation in the opposition party coalition. The LDP countered with a payoff that gave the Socialists 40. The Socialists would not have joined with the LDP for a payoff of 21, but with a higher payoff their leaders were willing to join the LDP in an unprecedented coalition.

Even with its ability to pay a high price, the LDP does not always win. The Hosokawa coalition of 1993 shows how real-world factors can cause the LDP to lose in such a bargaining situation, despite its advantage of being the largest party and within a few votes of a parliamentary majority. The opposition coalition gave a higher payoff to the two parties (the Japan New Party and the New Party Harbinger) that were most likely to defect to an LDP coalition. This higher payoff (the prime ministership) enticed these parties to join the opposition coalition. The LDP could not entice any other party out of the coalition because bargaining time had run out; moreover, these parties had just run a campaign against the LDP and were unwilling to consider an LDP coalition.

The three power-winning strategies available to the opposition each have pitfalls that can work to the advantage of a large, ruling party, such as the LDP. The "anxious suitor" scenario plays right into the LDP hand.

If opposition parties are willing to be partners with the LDP, then conditions resemble closely the bargaining game described earlier, in which the LDP has an undisputed advantage. The LDP can play the opposition parties off each other by trying to get the best deal from a potential junior coalition partner.

The opposition strategy of going it alone can also work to the advantage of the LDP. Japan's multiseat districts forced parties to compete against those who were their allies or were most similarly situated. If the Socialists were to increase in size, for instance, they would draw most of their increase from the Communists or from the centrist parties. This is what happened in the 1990 elections, when the Socialists won fifty-one additional seats and the other opposition parties lost a combined total of thirty-three seats. The Socialist victory took more seats away from the other opposition parties than it took away from the LDP.

This second strategy would work if a party were able to expand significantly and to maintain that expansion in consecutive elections. The French Socialist Party followed such a strategy to power, with much of its growth coming at the expense of the French Communist Party. The option is less viable in Japan, because the organizational nature of voting and the lack of an efficient means to appeal directly to unaffiliated voters makes it difficult for any party to grow by a direct appeal to the voters. Sustained, substantial growth is obviously an attractive option for each of Japan's opposition parties; no party has been successful in pursuing this option, however, and their attempts have produced only temporary fluctuations that disrupted opposition cooperative efforts.

The third strategy—building a unified opposition coalition—is the option that most threatens the LDP. However, this option is fraught with problems of defection and of the inability of the parties to make credible, binding commitments to the coalition strategy. If the opposition parties can agree on an agenda and an electoral strategy, they can run a unified campaign targeting the LDP as the opponent. This is the scenario under which they are most likely to deprive the LDP of its parliamentary majority. In that instance, they can keep the coalition together and take over the reins of government. Given the likely size of the LDP, however, they have to ensure no party defections from their coalition; even just one defection will ruin their plan and allow the LDP to stay in power, as the Socialist defection from the opposition coalition in 1994 allowed the LDP to come back into power.

The likelihood of defection, and hence the LDP's ability to maximize its position of advantage, turns on whether party relations are fluid—

similar to the assumptions of the game theoretic model—or are sticky, with certain alliances set in stone and other alliances regarded as impossible. If parties are equally willing to ally with each other, then the LDP has something closer to the bargaining advantage described in the game. If, on the other hand, the costs of an alliance with the LDP are so high that no party would join them in a coalition government, then the LDP has no bargaining advantage.[2] This is an empirical question that changes with each election, party leader, and policy dispute, but the historical evidence suggests that, in Japan, the game model is closer to reality. Three relevant aspects of Japanese fluidity are the strong ties between the LDP and each of the opposition parties, the LDP's efforts to divide the opposition, and significant divisions within the opposition camp. All these issues will be taken up in chapter 5.

Strategies of Electoral Cooperation

A party that is disadvantaged by an electoral system—that is, many of its votes are wasted and it could benefit from a different allocation of votes—also has three options. It can advocate changing the electoral system; it can try to restructure the party system; or it can enter into electoral coalitions. Thus far I have focused on wasted votes as an incentive to create electoral coalitions, but in many cases, parties opt to merge or to change the electoral system rather than to create electoral coalitions. The opposition parties in Japan, which have seen many of their votes wasted in elections, have tried all three strategies at different times. In the 1990s, they pursued all three, with varying degrees of success.

A party's choice of electoral strategy is influenced by its parliamentary strategy. For example, a party with a go-it-alone strategy probably would not agitate to change the electoral system away from one that favored large parties, because that party would expect to soon be in a position to benefit from the electoral system. A party that was working for opposition unification most likely would support electoral cooperation as a precursor to parliamentary cooperation, or might support a restructuring of the party system along the lines of its plans for opposition alliance and unification.

In the short term, however, the divergent electoral strategies of opposition parties all boil down to one consistent strategy, that of depriving the ruling party of seats. Even a party that hopes to become a junior coalition partner of the ruling party will still struggle to maximize its seats, minimizing its potential partner's seats to force the ruling party to consider coalition partners. A party that is going it alone will also be interested in maximizing its seats in the next election. Thus, electoral coalitions, as a vehicle of seat maximization, will be the preferred strategy in the short run, regardless of a party's long-term strategy in the arenas of electoral and parliamentary politics.

Defining Electoral Coalitions

The short-term incentive to maximize seats by using electoral coalitions is affected by the perceived costs and benefits of such coalitions. Electoral cooperation can take different forms, each requiring different actions by political parties and politicians, and each having different costs and benefits. Several different forms of cooperation are possible.

Electoral coalitions can be defined simply as an arrangement or agreement by two or more parties to elect a single candidate. There are, however, several different kinds of payoffs for participation in an electoral coalition. The form that an electoral coalition takes can vary with the type of payoff between barter, side-payment, and joint-backing coalition agreements.

Barter arrangements are the most common type of electoral coalitions. They are simply arrangements in which a party supports its coalition partner in one district, in exchange for that party's support in another district. In barter arrangements, the coalition candidates remain affiliated with their respective parties, with rarely any explicit restrictions on the selection of the barter candidates, their subsequent voting records, or their affiliations in the national legislature. The support a party gives to another party's candidate in a barter arrangement also can vary from mutual, formal endorsements of candidates from the other party to tacit agreements not to run candidates in districts that are designated for the allied party.

Side-payment coalitions are characterized by a party's seemingly unilateral support of another party in certain districts. Many types of side payments are possible. For instance, the party could receive electoral support in exchange for changing one of its policy stances. Side payments can also be intangible. For example, a fringe or extremist party might benefit from merely being associated with a more dominant party; its participation in an electoral coalition might be a first step in creating a new, more responsible image with the electorate.

Joint-backing coalitions occur when the coalition candidate is not formally affiliated with any of the existing political parties. This type of electoral coalition is often a halfway point between electoral cooperation and the formal merger of the cooperating parties.

These three types of electoral coalitions are not as discrete as the above categorization seems to suggest. Many barter coalitions also include side payments as part of the overall agreement. Similarly, a joint agreement to back certain unaffiliated candidates is often preceded by detailed negotiations over which party each of the "unaffiliated" candidates will come from. In this situation, a joint-backing coalition can closely resemble a barter coalition.

Besides the different kinds of payoffs, electoral coalitions can also be either public or secret. Public electoral coalitions tend to be universal; the supporting party instructs all of its supporters in a certain district to vote for the coalition candidate. Secret electoral coalitions can be either universal or particularistic. Duverger (1965, 331) describes a secret universal coalition:

> In the French system with a free second ballot the simple withdrawal of a candidate without his officially asking his voters to transfer their vote to a neighboring candidate is often the result of a tacit alliance: each of the two parties avoids being compromised by its neighbor and none the less benefits from the advantages of union; an open alliance would be more effective but more embarrassing.

Secret particularistic coalitions are similar, in that the agreement to cooperate is never made public. However, in particularistic coalitions, votes are also shifted to the coalition candidate through the party apparatus or through support organizations that are closely affiliated to the party. By using such organizational links, coalition support is obtained without having to resort to public announcements or exhortations. Though this kind of electoral cooperation is never truly secret, it does allow party officials to deny the existence of any cooperative arrangement. The party leaders remain free, however, to encourage or tacitly approve electoral cooperation through the means of secret vote exchanges between affiliated support organizations.

Electoral Coalitions: Uncommon and Largely Unstudied

The incentives for parties to cooperate electorally are generally strong. Most electoral systems create wasted votes, and there is sufficient party competition in most countries to create beneficiaries from electoral cooperation. In addition, maximizing seats through electoral cooperation is a first step for all the strategic alternatives that opposition parties face. Nevertheless, electoral coalitions are not a common occurrence in most countries. Though they regularly occur in Japan, Ireland, France, and Finland, and in Italy under its new electoral system, they are rare in other countries. In Germany and Sweden, for example, a larger party has occasionally lent support to an ally that was in danger of not reaching the threshold to win seats, but in such countries, electoral coalitions are a minor footnote in a specific election. Despite the existence of incentives to cooperate electorally in many countries, coalitions occur with regularity in only a few countries.

This infrequency of occurrence may explain the relative lack of focus on electoral coalitions by political scientists and other analysts. Analysts of coalitions focus almost exclusively on governing coalitions. The conditions from which governing coalitions arise are so different from the scenarios of electoral coalitions, however, that only some of the more general insights from the vast coalition-governments literature can be applied to electoral coalitions.

For example, the initial argument among analysts of governing coalitions was the debate between those who argued that size and numbers (Riker, 1962) best predict the makeup of a coalition and those who argued that policies and party ideology (Swaan, 1973; Axelrod, 1970) best explained who became members of a coalition government. This debate mirrors previous, contrasting descriptions of coalition bargaining as a game in which coalition partners are interchangeable (the size explanation) and of real-world conditions that hinder the interchangeability of coalition partners (the policy and ideology explanations). Other useful work in the coalition literature relaxes the assumption that parties act as unitary actors (Luebbert 1986, 45–65), models coalition negotiations as a noncooperative game (Laver and Shepsle, 1990), and puts electoral coalition negotiations in the larger context of multiple or simultaneous games or bargaining situations (Tsebelis 1990, 187–234).

None of this work addresses the cooperation dilemmas that are specific to electoral coalitions, and what little analysis of electoral coalitions exists is country-specific. Only Duverger (1965, 324–351), and more recently Cox (1997), have analyzed electoral coalitions from a cross-national perspective. Duverger looks at the characteristics of electoral coalitions as a subset of his more general discussion of party alliances; Cox analyzes electoral coalitions in the context of strategic voting.

Duverger's study of electoral coalitions is comprehensive and discusses with clarity the incentive structures of electoral coalitions. He notes that electoral alliances are influenced by the number of parties, by tradition, and most important, by the type of electoral system.[3] Duverger also explores the factors that influence both the type and the frequency of electoral coalitions within a country. His explanation includes the ideology or policy positions of a party, a party's organizational power, and the degree of centralized control within a party.

Some of Duverger's ideas are examined in other country-specific studies of electoral alliances. These works employ differing explanations for why cooperation does not work, but none of them recognizes the existence of basic disincentives to cooperate. For example, Thomas Rochon and Roy Pierce (1985, 438) use a social-psychological theory of interpersonal comparisons to explain instances in which the electoral alliance of the Left broke down in France. Allies become jealous of their partners when they are in competitive districts, and they work to undercut their partners rather than to support them. Tsebelis (1990, 213) also postulates a competitiveness between similarly situated allies that is overcome only in districts with "visible" politics (i.e., where undercutting an ally could clearly be blamed on the supporting party). Stefano Bartolini (1984, 103–127) stresses policy proximity in understanding alliances in France. Michael Laver and Norman Schofield (1990, 206) conclude that electoral alliances in Ireland depend entirely on the success or failure of parties in forming governing coalitions.

Cox (1997) discusses electoral coalitions within the larger context of strategic voting. Strategic voting occurs when voters desert their preferred candidate who is heading for defeat and vote "strategically" for a less preferred candidate who has a chance of victory. Cox is therefore less concerned with the empirical question of where electoral coalitions will actually occur, focusing instead on showing the theoretical possibilities of strategic voting in all electoral systems. Nevertheless, his observations about the factors that affect strategic voting coincide with an analysis of the incentives and disincentives that affect the formation of electoral coalitions. Cox points out four conditions under which strategic voting will not occur: (1) when voters are not short-term instrumentally rational, for instance, when a voter supports an acknowledged loser for reasons such as "building for the future" or "sending a message"; (2) when there is insufficient information to determine who the sure losers are; (3) when a clear winner exists (there is no reason to desert a preferred candidate if this action cannot affect the ultimate outcome); and (4) when voters only care about their first preference.

Of Cox's four factors, numbers one and three are common to both electoral and governing coalitions; their influence is indirectly acknowledged in the discussion of incentives earlier in this chapter. For example, all parties prefer more seats or cabinet posts in the short term, but a party might forego these opportunities for ideological reasons or other goals that take priority (factor one). In addition, parties usually do not form losing governing coalitions, and electoral coalitions are rare in districts where the winner is a foregone conclusion (factor three).

Factor four, indifference to the fate of other candidates or parties, actually facilitates the formation of governing and electoral coalitions, despite its deleterious effects on incentives to vote strategically. Such indifference makes a party a flexible partner in coalition negotiations. Though the party may not care about the fortunes of other parties, it will cooperate with those parties to reap the benefits of cooperation.

Cox's second factor, the lack of information, is one of the crucial barriers to electoral cooperation. This and other barriers make it significantly more difficult to form and maintain electoral coalitions, in contrast to the relative ease of forming governing coalitions.

Barriers to Electoral Cooperation

Electoral coalitions do not form in all the countries that have incentives to cooperate because there are significant barriers to the creation and maintenance of such coalitions. Electoral coalitions are fundamentally different from governing coalitions, and most of these differences work against forming electoral coalitions. Party leaders therefore discount the potential benefits of electoral cooperation by a large factor that represents the difficulties inherent in negotiating and implementing an agreement to cooperate electorally. The differences between governing coalitions and electoral coalitions can be grouped into four categories, and it is the degree to which these differences operate in the electoral and party systems of different countries that best explains cross-national and internal variations in electoral coalitions.

First, the formation of electoral coalitions is plagued by a deficit of accurate information, a problem that Cox identifies in his study of strategic voting and underlies Tsebelis' (1990) observations that parties give better support when they know they will be blamed if the coalition candidate loses. The lack of information exists on both sides of the bargaining process; both a party's contribution to an electoral coalition and the benefits it receives from electoral cooperation are unclear. For example, in most electoral systems there is no way to observe, monitor, and verify the actual transferal of votes to a coalition candidate. A party leader can claim that his party gave full support to another party's candidate, but his claim can be neither proved nor disproved. Polling data and a close reading of election results can approximate levels of support, but in many countries such district level polling data do not exist, and divining trends from aggregate election returns can be difficult. As a result, the contribution of a party to an electoral coalition is subject to a gray area of interpretation, which often becomes a source of contention between parties after the election. If the cooperative efforts of the elections are unsuccessful, the postelection analysis can easily degenerate into mutual recriminations as to which party failed to deliver the votes that were promised.

Informational uncertainty also exists with regard to the benefits of electoral cooperation. In some electoral systems, electoral cooperation is needed only in certain districts. If there are significant costs to electoral cooperation efforts, parties and candidates in marginal districts face the vexing choice of deciding whether they should go it alone and try to win without coalition support, or whether they should play it safe and seek the support of another party. If party support is volatile, this problem of accurately calculating the need for electoral cooperation is present in a larger number of districts. The problem is exacerbated by the organizational imperative that party leaders face to be optimistic about their party's prospects in an upcoming election. A conservative stance of seeking cooperation in all possible districts telegraphs to supporters and potential candidates that the party expects to do poorly in the election.

Another informational uncertainty is the anticipated growth or decline of cooperating parties. The attitude of parties about electoral cooperation is affected by the size of the party and by whether party leaders anticipate further growth or decline. Electoral cooperation will be less likely if a small party faces decline or if a large party is experiencing or expecting growth.

Small parties in decline often oppose electoral cooperation because such cooperation threatens their very existence. In most cooperative arrangements, the dominant member of the arrangement has an advantage, not only in terms of its ability to mold compromise decisions in its favor but also in the threat of absorption that it poses to the smaller participant. In the context of electoral coalitions, the closer the parties move together, the more indistinguishable they will become. The larger party has an advantage because voters will switch their allegiance to the larger party if both parties resemble each other too closely. This problem occurs in many coalition settings. For example, the Free Democrats in Germany are constantly threatened with losing their identity in governing coalitions. The party therefore faces the imperative of creating and maintaining relevant policy and functional differences from its coalition partners (Broughton and Kirchner 1986, 78–80).

In contrast, larger parties in decline see cooperation, except for alliances with predatory extremist parties, as a safe way to shore up their electoral position. The incentives to cooperate diminish, however, when a large party is growing because party leaders see evidence that theirs can become a dominant party. Therefore, even if the party could still benefit from cooperation in a few districts, its leaders might nevertheless refuse to enter cooperation negotiations. Given the small potential advantage, they might view such negotiations as not worth the bother. They refuse to cooperate, because they are looking toward a future in which they expect to no longer need the cooperative support of other parties.

Bargaining over governing coalitions shares some of the informational uncertainties described above. For example, a large, growing political party may be unenthusiastic about coalition options because its leaders are hoping to continue party growth and become a solo, majority government. Similarly, a small, declining party may opt to strengthen its own identity by refusing to participate in a coalition government.

In other areas, a governing coalition has better access to accurate information. Party leaders usually observe, monitor, and verify the votes cast in a parliament to form a government. There is also very little disagreement during negotiations over the number of votes a party can contribute to a coalition government. Party discipline is typically very strong on investiture votes. Furthermore, the benefits derived from the coalition are clear and assured. A government that reneged on a promised portfolio assignment or policy would be subject to defections and to the disintegration of the coalition in a vote of no confidence. There are some informational uncertainties, of course, even in the bargaining for governing coalitions and other types of coalitions. William Riker (1962, 78), recognizing these in his early work, allowed that minimum winning coalitions would form, given perfect information; larger coalitions will form because parties have "imperfect" information (they do not know either the other parties' preferences or the other, competing offers that have been made in the bargaining process) and "incomplete" information, where the rules of the game are unclear (e.g., in the context of governing coalitions, a party may not have absolute control over the votes of its members in the national legislature). These serious problems hinder the formation of governing coalitions, but they pale in comparison with the information difficulties that plague electoral coalitions.

A second problem of electoral coalitions is that they require the agreement of many more participants than in governing coalitions. At first blush, electoral and governing coalitions seem to have similar bargaining processes, because party leaders meet and hammer out an agreement. In actuality, the processes require quite different numbers of participants whose views must be taken into account. To be successful, electoral coalitions require, at minimum, the consensus or obedience of local party functionaries and often the consensus of those voters who ordinarily support the party. The necessary level of agreement depends on the type of coalition and on the organizational strength of the party. For example, an agreement to shift only those votes controlled by a certain support organization can often be made simply with the agreement of the party leader and the organization's leader.

In contrast, a general agreement for all of a party's supporters to support another party in a certain area requires the acceptance of the agreement by local party officials, local leaders of support organizations, and voters who ordinarily support the party. The greater the extent of the coalition, the more people whose opinions must be considered when deciding to cooperate.

The organizational strength of participating parties is much less crucial for the successful negotiation of governing coalitions than for electoral coalitions. Party leaders take into account the reactions of voters, local party leaders, and activists to the compromises that accompany party participation in a coalition government, but neither the voters nor the party rank and file can block the coalition negotiations. They cannot act on their dissatisfaction until the next election or party convention. In electoral coalitions, these same people are integral to the successful implementation of an electoral cooperation agreement, so their views cannot be ignored or discounted. Indeed, each of the parties to an electoral coalition agreement has the incentive to force its coalition partners to be realistic in assessing how the cooperation agreement will be received by their own rank and file.

The difficulty of reaching an agreement among the many potential participants in an electoral coalition leads to the observation that parties with greater organizational strength will be more likely to participate in electoral coalitions, all other factors held constant. Organizationally strong parties can transfer potential wasted votes effectively to coalition candidates. In contrast, loosely organized, catchall parties or protest parties are very ineffective in shifting votes. Such parties are not worthless coalition partners—the withdrawal of their candidate from a district should help the coalition candidate—but it is also possible that their withdrawal could benefit other candidates more than the coalition candidate. Their fluid or unorganized support base makes coalition agreements difficult to implement successfully. The votes may transfer from such parties, or they may not.

Party leaders discount the benefit of a potential electoral coalition by their assessment of a party's ability to actually deliver votes to the coalition candidate. Parties with strong organizations will be able to deliver most of their supporters to a coalition candidate; therefore, these parties will be more highly valued (all other conditions equal) as coalition partners than weakly organized parties. Thus, even in districts with strong incentives to cooperate, cooperation will not occur if these numerical incentives are significantly discounted by the low probability of a party actually being able to transfer its votes to the coalition candidate.

The organizational strength of a party also affects the ease with which coalition agreements are negotiated. Parties that have strong central organizations are much more able to conclude an election agreement centrally and afterward instruct local party functionaries and the rank and file to implement the agreement. Parties that lack such central organization are bound more tightly by the attitudes of the local party leaders, support group leaders, and individual voters. Thus, parties with strong, hierarchical organizations will make final decisions about electoral cooperation at the national level. In decentralized parties or in parties with weak organizations, national-level decisions either will have to be renegotiated with each relevant local decision-making body, or national party leaders will have to take into account the viewpoints of local party leaders as well as the party rank and file in their national-level negotiations.

Parties typically are organizationally strong if they have a unifying ideology, a common characteristic such as religious beliefs or ethnicity, or an extensive party organization (or parallel support organization) that creates meaningful organizational links to every party supporter. In some situations, these same characteristics can make parties undesirable as a potential electoral coalition partner. Parties that are distinct from the rest of the electorate often have a stronger organization and stronger supporter attachment, but this strength and distinctiveness may provoke a negative reaction among other voters. Such parties may be able to effectively deliver blocks of votes to their coalition partners, but their partners often suffer from associating with them.[4]

Furthermore, such highly organized parties can sometimes become predators of their less-organized coalition partners. A strong party can recruit new members from the supporters of its coalition partners, and it can dominate campaign activities with its ability to muster large numbers of election workers. The coalition partner often reaches a point at which it is forced to increase its organizational strength in response to this threat or to break off relations with its partner. Duverger (1965, 348) observes that though communist and fascist parties often oppose compromising with other parties,

> electoral, parliamentary, and governmental coalitions can prove a very effective means of action for such parties; all the more so because their very complicated and very sound organization safeguards them from contamination and disintegration, to which their allies are consequently vulnerable.

Though this competition and threat to the organizational vitality of a party in an electoral coalition are also a core assumption of Tsebelis (1990) in his study, he does not differentiate between the levels of threat that different parties can pose to their coalition partners. Though Tsebelis is correct that some level of competition exists between any two cooperating parties, he fails to recognize that a party's organizational strength can drastically change the level of competition between cooperating parties.

A third characteristic that vexes the formation of electoral coalitions is the time lag that exists between the conclusion of a cooperative agreement and its implementation. To be most effective, agreements to cooperate electorally are usually concluded before election campaigns, but the actual delivery of votes and distribution of benefits occur on election day. It is precisely during the election campaign that parties have the opportunity to defect from an agreement. The incentive to defect is created most often by the changing circumstances characteristic of an election campaign.

For example, a party may receive polling data that indicate it is doing better or worse than expected. Party leaders may receive indications that their coalition partner is having difficulties fulfilling its part of the agreement. A local party leader could announce her opposition to a national cooperation agreement. A party official could make statements that are highly critical of a policy that is near and dear to his party's coalition partner. By comparison, governing coalitions do not face such a time lag. Once an agreement to form a government is reached, it is usually implemented immediately.

A fourth problem with electoral coalitions is that they have no realistic mechanism to enforce electoral cooperation agreements or to punish those who renege on agreements. Even if it were possible to observe and verify compliance with a cooperation agreement, enforcing the agreement would still be impossible because of the lack of an appropriate enforcement mechanism. If a party defects from a cooperation agreement, its erstwhile allies have no recourse; they cannot rescind the election results nor can they sue the defecting party for breach of contract.

Because there is no enforcement mechanism, electoral cooperation would never occur if the agreements had to be negotiated outside the context of ongoing political relations. Outside the relevant political context, an electoral cooperation agreement would present the classic prisoner's dilemma. Both parties would be better off cooperating, but they would also have stronger incentives to defect from the cooperation agreement, regardless of the other party's actions. This dilemma is overcome only by the ongoing relations between party leaders and the repetitive nature of elections. Because party leaders know they will not be trusted in the future if they completely renege on an electoral agreement, they have some incentive to maintain a good reputation.

Robert Axelrod (1984) is associated with this theory that repetition often solves the dilemma of noncooperation by creating incentives for the "evolution of cooperation." Thus, cooperation should beget cooperation. If an electoral coalition was successful, and if at the next election the political situation and leaders remain relatively unchanged, the electoral cooperation arrangement should repeat itself. Indeed, repetition may actually create an inertia that preserves electoral cooperation in a district, even when the numerical incentives to cooperate have disappeared. Similarly, if two parties already cooperate significantly on a whole range of other important policy, legislative, and governmental matters, electoral cooperation between them should also develop easily.

Governing coalitions, in contrast, do not have to rely so heavily on reputation or repetition to provide indirect enforcement of cooperation agreements. These coalitions have very explicit enforcement devices,

such as the no-confidence vote or the assignment of ministerial portfolios.[5] The cost of using the no-confidence vote may take away from its
usefulness and even make the threat to use it noncredible in certain
instances. Yet it is a much surer enforcement mechanism than reputation, the only method of enforcing electoral cooperation agreements.

The Ameliorating Effects of Some Electoral Systems

These four problems highlight the additional difficulties parties face
when trying to conclude agreements to cooperate electorally. The impli-
cation of these findings is that electoral coalitions should be quite rare,
or, alternatively, that they should exist in countries where these difficulties have been eliminated or compensated by some other means. An
analysis of these four difficulties explains variance in the frequency of
electoral coalitions, both between countries and within a country. Elements of certain electoral and party systems have compensated for some
of these difficulties, however, allowing electoral coalitions to flourish in
some countries.

FRANCE

In France, the two-ballot system ameliorates two of the problems of
electoral coalitions. The initial ballot gives party leaders and candidates
a clear estimation of actual party strength in the subsequent second
ballot; there is no room for unsubstantiated optimism. The first ballot
also provides a neutral judging mechanism for deciding which party's
candidate should be the coalition candidate for each district, creating
what Thomas Schelling (1980, 111) has called a "focal point," an obvious
point of agreement that facilitates the actual conclusion of a cooperation
agreement.

Relying on the first ballot to decide the contours of the cooperation
agreement does have its own problems. For example, the Communists
ceded thirteen districts to the Socialists in 1967, even though they outpolled the Socialists in all thirteen on the first ballot. They did this to
ensure enthusiastic Socialist participation in the cooperation agreement,
by correcting a perceived imbalance in the ratio of Communist to
Socialist second-ballot candidates. Similarly, in 1978, the Socialists had
surged ahead of the Communists, so the Communists did not agree to
cooperate until after they had seen the results of the first ballot. They
did not want to be obligated to cooperate when there was still a possi-

bility that the benefits from cooperation would flow disproportionately to the Socialists. These problems exist, but they do not detract from the usefulness of the first ballot as a focal point or neutral arbitrator in the bargaining process.

The time lag problem also is ameliorated in France, because the time between the cooperation agreement and the election itself is much shorter. Even though parties usually commit before the first ballot to cooperate in the second ballot, the actual details of the cooperation arrangement do not become clear until after the first ballot. Then the agreement need only weather a one-week election campaign, in which the tone of the campaign has shifted from intracoalition competition to intercoalition competition.[6]

France also provides an interesting test of the organizational strength hypothesis. It appears that Communist voters follow cooperation instructions in greater numbers than their partners, Socialist voters. This observation supports the idea that parties with strong organizations are better able to transfer their votes to a coalition partner. Bartolini (1984, 103–127), however, explains this phenomenon with a spatial model. Because the Socialists are located between the Communists and the parties of the Right on a policy continuum, in districts where the Socialists are supporting a Communist coalition candidate, some Socialists will support the coalition candidate of the Right instead. The Communists, on the other hand, give total support to the Socialist coalition candidate in Socialist-led districts because the Socialists are clearly the party closest to the Communists in policy.

Tsebelis posits another explanation. He shows that variations in party support of coalitions depend entirely on how equivalent the allied parties are in size. Because neither explanation is supported with compelling evidence, there is room to suggest that in Japan, and perhaps in France, Communists are more effective participants in electoral coalitions because of their superior organization.[7]

The importance of organizational power is also supported by historical evidence that communist parties have used their organizational superiority to infiltrate and colonize unwary allies. Trond Gilberg (1989, 69) notes that communist parties in Western Europe historically have been predators of their coalition partners. From 1921 to 1928, the Western European communist parties pursued two simultaneous coalition agendas—a "united front" of the political parties of the Left in a broad political coalition and a "united front from below," which he describes as their efforts to undermine the mass base of the very parties with whom they negotiated and cooperated at the leadership level. Small wonder that subsequent communist coalition efforts were spurned or seen with a great deal of skepticism among social democrats and socialists.

Though this predatory nature of communist parties was most pronounced earlier in this century, Gilberg (1989, 103) observes that communist parties in Western Europe still face the dilemma of "whether or not they represent a fundamentally different political organization, which is indeed stressed in the ideological tenets of Marxism-Leninism, or just another party, another political line."

The French example also supports the observation that numerical incentives are the driving force behind electoral coalitions. French parties adjust to first-ballot results to create an appropriate balance between the cooperating parties. The Communists deferred to Socialist candidates in some districts to raise the incentives for the Socialist Party to cooperate electorally. In other districts, the parties did not cooperate, because of the strength of the right-wing candidate. Decisions about French electoral cooperation are colored at every level by estimations of party support based on first-ballot results.

IRELAND

The incentives to cooperate in Ireland are much weaker than in France. Ireland's multiseat districts produce fewer wasted votes; hence, parties have less to gain from cooperation than in the single-seat districts of France. However, the Irish electoral system facilitates cooperation in several ways. The Irish electoral system, like that of France, increases the amount of information available. Ireland is one of the few nations to employ a single, transferable vote system. Because members of Parliament are selected from multiseat constituencies, each voter is presented with a rather long list of candidates, including several from each of the political parties. The voter has the option of ranking any or all of the candidates in a preference ordering. If her highest priority vote is beyond the quota of votes a candidate needed for victory, or if it was cast for one of the candidates who was eliminated in one of the first rounds of vote counting, her vote is reassigned to other candidates according to her preference ordering.

This system gives better information about past levels of interparty cooperation. Voters record preferences on their ballot, making it possible to estimate the general levels of support voters are giving to candidates from other parties (Laver and Higgins 1986, 178). Parties may use this information to withhold support for a governing coalition if promises of electoral cooperation are not kept. It is possible for electoral cooperation agreements to piggyback on the enforcement mechanisms inherent in governing coalitions. Disgruntled coalition partners can credibly threaten to refuse to participate in a coalition government if their concerns about electoral cooperation are not adequately addressed.

The transferable ballot also eliminates a party's difficult task of estimating the need for electoral cooperation in each district. Electoral cooperation in Ireland is not a zero-sum proposition; voters can transfer their votes to another party after their votes have done all they can for their own party's candidates. There is no need to negotiate the particulars of a cooperation agreement; the system clearly creates the incentive to enter into nationwide, universal agreements—agreements that exhort all of the parties' supporters to give subordinate preferences to their coalition ally.

The only cost of such cooperation is a party becoming too closely associated with its coalition partner, especially if the electoral coalition becomes a governing coalition. These special features of the Irish electoral system underlie Laver and Schofield's (1990) conclusion that electoral coalitions in Ireland are merely governing coalitions that are formed before, rather than after, the election. In Ireland, then, it is easier to use participation in a governing coalition as an indirect enforcement mechanism of electoral coalition agreements.

The Irish case also provides evidence supporting the hypothesis that both small parties in decline and larger, growing parties will refuse to cooperate electorally. During the 1970s and 1980s, the Irish Labour Party occasionally found it necessary to pull out of its coalition with Fine Gael to rebuild party support back to respectable levels. The largest party, Fianna Fail, also refused to consider electoral coalitions during this period.

Other hypotheses, based either on the organizational strength of parties or on the importance of numerical incentives to district-level decisions about electoral coalition participation, do not apply to the Irish example. The major Irish parties have similar levels of organizational strength, and the costless form of electoral cooperation possible under a single, transferable vote system removes the need to consider district-by-district distributions of party support. The hypothesis about the repetition of coalitions on the district level is also untestable in Ireland, because electoral coalition agreements are not differentiated on the district level. On the national level, repetition seems to occur: Fine Gael and Labour consistently entered into electoral coalitions over a span of many elections. In the 1990s, however, as Fine Gael and Fianna Fail have both declined in strength, doors have opened for other coalitions.

ITALY

Italy has a mixed electoral system with single-seat districts and proportional representation districts. Small- or moderate-sized parties can do well in the proportional representation races, but they suffer an enormous disadvantage in the single-seat districts because the Italian electoral system does not consider how many seats a party has already won before it awards proportional representation seats. Thus, there are strong incentives for parties to cooperate electorally in the single-seat districts. Italian electoral law facilitates this cooperation by allowing parties to jointly sponsor candidates in the single-seat districts without diluting party labels (Cox and Schoppa 1998). Other elements of Italian electoral law do not ameliorate the barriers to electoral cooperation, but the strong incentives of certain electoral annihilation in the single-seat districts push Italian parties to solve their coordination dilemmas and cooperate electorally.

FINLAND

Electoral coalitions are common in Finland, though not universal. The Finnish system creates fewer wasted votes, resulting in weaker incentives to cooperate. Seats in Finland are allocated proportionally among party lists in multiseat districts. Similar to Italy, Finnish electoral law allows for party alliances among parties that maintain their identity and separate lists. Still, large parties are more reluctant to enter such alliances; Voitto Helander (1997, 68) explains this reluctance by noting that the alliances tend to benefit small parties more than large parties. This occurs because the actual winners on a party or alliance's list are determined by the number of votes a specific candidate receives. (Unlike most proportional representative systems, parties put up lists in Finland, but voters vote for a specific candidate on the list, rather than voting for the party that put up the list.) Thus, the most popular candidate on a small party's list often will win one of the alliance's seats, beating out a fourth- or fifth-place candidate from the larger party's list.

The Finnish example also supports two other theoretical observations. Cooperation is not universal in Finland, because the incentives to cooperate are much weaker. Large parties can, at best, hope to gain an additional seat in a few districts through cooperation. If the personal vote for specific candidates means that these marginal gains will probably be won by smaller parties, the larger parties have lost even this small benefit of cooperation. In contrast, smaller parties likely face the prospect either of winning no seats without cooperation or the chance of garnering one seat by cooperating. Helander (1997, 68) also describes how alliances with some extreme parties can drive away more voters than are initially brought in through the alliance.

SINGLE-SEAT DISTRICT SYSTEMS

The electoral and party systems of other countries can also explain why electoral coalitions are rare in most other single-seat plurality systems, despite the presence of more than two parties. In a single-seat plurality system, the four main difficulties of electoral coalition formation and enforcement are heightened rather than ameliorated. These systems have the greatest disparity between the number of seats won and the votes won by a party. Therefore, small swings in vote totals can drastically change the number of seats won. This greater variation produces a corresponding greater level of informational uncertainty. A third party in such a system hopes that even though it won very few seats in the last election, say with only 20 percent of the vote, it could win a parliamentary majority in the next election if it increases its share of the vote to only 30 percent. These extreme variations create greater barriers for parties or candidates to enter into a cooperation agreement.

Single-seat plurality systems also create a strong contradictory incentive for parties to merge or to dissolve. It is difficult for a small third or fourth party to occupy a stable electoral position. Small parties require the possibility of victory in some districts to continue attracting supporters and viable candidates. This imperative, of course, affects all parties in all electoral systems, but the high threshold for successful participation in single-seat plurality systems makes it extremely difficult for small parties to resist a merger or dissolution. Such parties continue only when their leaders can make a plausible case for their party's resurgence in the next election. If a string of defeats makes such claims implausible, the party either merges with another party, disbands, or sinks into obscurity as the bulk of its supporters transfer allegiances to other parties or become nonvoters.

Some electoral provisions can ameliorate this harsh set of outcomes, as rules allowing fusion tickets helped the Populist Party remain a viable competitor for several decades in the United States. In many Midwest states, the Populists competed against Republicans and Democrats in single-seat districts; fusion ballots allowed two of the parties to cooperate in elections, to minimize their wasted votes and maximize their seats. Similar to Italian and Finnish electoral practice, the fusion ballot allowed each party to maintain its separate identity while avoiding the harsh consequences of single-seat districts on the second- or third-place party. However, the third party ultimately disappeared as a relevant entity in the United States, and this disappearance was hastened by the elimination of the fusion option in many states (Argersinger 1991).

In a system with these incentives, electoral coalitions are useful only between unstable parties as an interim step to a merger or dissolution, or between stable, small parties as a recurring strategy. Stable, small parties in a single-seat plurality system typically have regional support bases. A regional support base allows a small party to continue to elect its members to the national legislature from its stronghold districts. Two regional parties conceivably could enter into electoral coalitions with each other. For example, a party with a strong urban support base would be well situated to cooperate with an agrarian party that was strong in the country's farm belt. However, the incentives to cooperate would not be strong; parties that have mutually exclusive support bases generally have few supporters in one another's areas who can be encouraged to back a coalition candidate. The two parties could cooperate easily, but they would benefit little from their cooperation. An extreme example is potential cooperation between the nationalist parties in Scotland and Wales. Neither party has supporters outside of its own stronghold, so there is no incentive for these two parties to cooperate electorally.

In sum, single-seat plurality systems are quite volatile, and they accordingly create strong disincentives and incentives. Parties under such systems take correspondingly radical actions. Electoral coalitions, therefore, are usually only useful as a way station to a more permanent restructuring of the party system.

JAPAN

In incentives to cooperate, the Japanese electoral system of 1947 to 1994 is most similar to Ireland. District magnitudes in both countries are low, creating fewer wasted votes than the single-seat districts of France or Italy and more wasted votes than the larger districts of Finland, which elected from seven to thirty-one representatives. As could be expected, electoral cooperation under this Japanese system was common but not widespread. Cooperation was less common in Japan than in other countries, because Japan lacked both the electoral mechanisms to facilitate cooperation that exist in France and Ireland, and the provisions facilitating joint ballots that exist in Finland and Italy.

Some conditions did encourage electoral cooperation, however. Japan's electoral system created a stable environment for smaller parties. The large magnitude of some of Japan's electoral districts lowered the threshold that a small party faced to as little as 10 or 15 percent of the vote in those districts. This low threshold allowed small parties to regularly elect a stable cohort of representatives, reducing incentives to merge or threats of party dissolution that such a party would have faced in a single-seat plurality system.

The relative stability of Japan's party system also facilitated calculating the costs and benefits of electoral cooperation. Parties in Japan generally did not see wide fluctuations in their share of the vote. Therefore, they could predict more easily the districts requiring their electoral cooperation, and those where they had safe seats without cooperation. For example, from 1969 to 1983, the Clean Government Party's share of the vote varied only between 8 and 10.9 percent. The vote for the Democratic Socialists declined substantially in the 1990s, but from 1963 to 1986, this party always received between 6.3 and 7.7 percent of the vote. Similarly, the Communists received between 7.7 and 10.5 percent of the vote from 1972 to 1993. Even the Socialist Party, which saw a steady decline in its share of the vote followed by extremely volatile support in the 1990s, polled between 19.3 and 21.9 percent of the vote in the six elections from 1969 to 1983. Minor parties in Japan were also remarkably stable. The Social Democratic League won between 0.7 and 0.9 percent of the popular vote in every House of Representatives election from its formation in 1979 to 1993. Similarly, the New Liberal Club took between 1.8 and 4.2 percent of the popular vote in the five elections it participated in from 1976 to 1986.

The party system in Japan also creates stronger incentives to cooperate electorally, because the smaller parties share secure, overlapping support bases. The centrist parties and the Communist Party are all strongest in urban areas, though each party has supporters and local organizations in every area of the nation. These parties are secure in their overlapping areas because the low-threshold vote necessary for victory allows each party to win seats in urban areas. In other districts, where their support begins to taper off, they still have a large block of supporters who can be marshaled to support a coalition candidate. This low distribution of supporters nationwide, combined with greater concentrations in certain districts, creates all kinds of opportunities for electoral cooperation. The small parties can cooperate with each other in their districts of moderate strength, and they can cooperate with the larger parties in rural districts where even small-party cooperation would not be sufficient to elect a candidate.

The new election system has changed both the incentives and the disincentives to cooperate. The creation of single-seat districts, as in Italy, has vastly increased the number of wasted votes and hence the incentives to cooperate in those districts. However, at least in the first elections, the incidence of cooperation has not drastically increased from past levels. Several possible explanations exist. Japan, unlike Italy, does not facilitate the creation of alliances between parties that allow each party to retain its own identity (Cox and Schoppa 1998). Party volatility in Japan has been extreme, increasing the informational uncertainty about the need for electoral coalitions. The personal vote for candidates is strong, making it possible for some minor party candidates or independents to win in single-seat districts even without an electoral coalition. Thus, despite the potential for extensive coordination, there have been large numbers of wasted votes and many districts where the potential benefits of cooperation remain untouched. This could easily change if the party system gains greater stability.

The evidence from both Japanese election systems supports additional theoretical observations. The Japanese example illustrates the importance of party ascendancy or decline on coalition decisions. The largest opposition party, the Socialists, was most enthusiastic about cooperation when it was declining. It was dismissive of cooperation when it was growing. The New Frontier Party in 1996 eschewed many cooperative opportunities as it saw itself rising to become the alternative to the LDP. In contrast, smaller parties were most reluctant to cooperate when they were in decline.

The Japanese historical evidence also verifies other theoretical observations. The strength of party organizations was a highly regarded variable in coalition negotiations. Party organizational strength affected the local party leaders' involvement in the coalition decision, as well as the ability of the agreements to create cooperation. The level of cooperation was also greatly influenced by numerical incentives (i.e., the distribution of party support in specific electoral districts). In addition, a significant number of the electoral coalitions that did occur replicated past cooperative arrangements. These coalitions in Japan are described in the following chapter.

Alternative Explanations of Cross-National Variation

This chapter focused on the cooperation incentives created by wasted votes and on the ways in which a particular country's electoral and party system overcomes some of the barriers inherent in electoral cooperation. Alternative explanations of variance in electoral cooperation also exist. Swaan's (1973) and Axelrod's (1970) critiques of Riker's (1962) size principle concerning governing coalitions represent the most common alternative explanation. Despite the clear incentives that exist for parties to maximize benefits by forming minimum winning coalitions, parties fail to form these "most efficient" types of coalitions because they have competing concerns, such as policy or ideological differences. Both Swaan (1973) and Axelrod (1970) claim that a party will not form a minimum-winning coalition if significant policy distance exists between it and the most ideal (in terms of numerical strength) prospective coalition partner. If these and other concerns can prevent parties from extracting the maximum benefit from a governing coalition, then similar concerns should also be a factor in the formation of electoral coalitions.

How important is ideology as a barrier to some electoral coalitions? At the theoretical level, Duverger (1965, 333–334) asserts that electoral coalitions are easier for parties to form than governing coalitions because they do not require agreement on a positive program; they merely require a negative agreement to jointly oppose the opposition. Thus, ideology should be less of a barrier to electoral coalitions than governing coalitions.

In contrast, Laver and Schofield (1990, 206) note that in certain electoral systems, electoral coalitions can become synonymous with governing coalitions. In such situations, a vaguely worded cooperation agreement that fudges fundamental disagreements often increases the distrust between the activists and loyal supporters of the two cooperating parties.

Duverger (1965, 335) points out that elections are the time when parties are the most extreme. They highlight their differences with each other in an attempt to maximize their share of the vote. Parties often have certain key policy issues or ideologies upon which their electoral support is built. During election campaigns, parties must differentiate themselves from other parties, especially those that are contiguous to them on these key policy dimensions. In other words, in multiparty systems, the parties that are most likely to form a governing coalition because of their ideological proximity are precisely the parties that compete most fiercely in elections.

In addition, electoral coalitions that merely paper over major policy differences between parties will fail to attract unaffiliated voters, because they are seen as opportunistic, short-term arrangements. Unaffiliated voters, as opposed to party leaders and activists, often expect more from an electoral agreement than a mere swapping of votes.

These competing factors make it difficult to definitively assess the relevance of policy or ideological differences to the formation of electoral coalitions. Differences are clearly a factor, but their relevance diminishes as the distance between an electoral coalition and a governing coalition increases. In France, ideological patterns seem quite rigid in electoral coalitions. In Italy and Japan, electoral coalitions are more common between ideologically similar parties; however, ideological differences can be overcome, as shown by the 1994–1996 LDP-Socialist governing and electoral coalitions.

4

Electoral Cooperation
in Japan

NINETEEN SEVENTY-ONE was a watershed year for electoral cooperation in Japan. It marked the first time the political parties had formally cooperated in a national election. Their cooperation efforts have continued unabated since then. In the following three decades, four elections were crucial in the development of electoral cooperation: the 1971 House of Councillors election, the 1980 double election, the 1989 House of Councillors election, and the 1996 House of Representatives election.

The years 1971 and 1989 were smashing successes for Japanese opposition parties and for opposition electoral cooperation. The 1980 double election, though, was one of the worst opposition defeats in the entire postwar period. During 1996, parties showed how they might respond to the incentives of the new electoral system, in contrast to the three other elections that occurred under the former electoral system.

This chapter is an analytical narration of the events surrounding each of these elections. Though this format highlights the many unique features of each election, certain themes presented in the preceding chapter run through the descriptions.

First, contrary to the stereotype of opposition failure, opposition party leaders have made competent decisions regarding electoral cooperation in these elections. Parties have been willing to cooperate with a wide range of political actors. Their choices of political partners are guided more by the tangible benefits of cooperation than by ideological concerns. Though opposition cooperative efforts fell apart after the successes in 1971 and 1989, the difficulties inherent in electoral cooperation, as well as the siren call of the LDP to disrupt opposition cooperation, explain this acrimony better than assertions of poor leadership, fewer resources, or ideological rigidity within the opposition camp.

These elections demonstrate that the numerical incentives created by numbers of wasted votes and the position of parties to take advantage of these wasted votes were the two most important factors in determining party stands on electoral cooperation. When there were few numerical incentives to cooperate, the parties did not cooperate. When strong incentives to cooperate existed, parties cooperated.

The elections also illustrate the historical roots of the system of party relations. Cooperation between the conservatives and the Socialists did not begin in 1994. It had its beginnings in the immediate postwar period, and it has remained alive and well in Japan's gubernatorial elections. Cooperative efforts in one election spur cooperative efforts in other elections in the same locality; the best predictor of cooperation in a district was whether cooperation had occurred in that district in the previous election. Repetition is a crucial aspect of creating the necessary trust for successful cooperation, in the absence of formal measures of verification and compliance.

The description of events in this chapter does not force all explanations and effects into these themes; idiosyncratic factors unique to each election are also evaluated. The factors outlined above operated consistently in influencing the decision making of party leaders, however, and can therefore be separated out from the nonsystemic or idiosyncratic factors.

Electoral Coalitions from 1945 to 1971

Despite the fluid nature of party politics during the early postwar period, very little electoral cooperation took place except in local elections (i.e., gubernatorial or mayoral races). Socialist domination of the opposition camp is the main reason for this lack of cooperation. The other opposition parties were weak or nonexistent, and they generally refrained from running excessive numbers of candidates. Consequently, the Socialists had few incentives to cooperate electorally, since cooperation offered little in the way of expanded voter support. In the 1960s, however, the non-Socialist opposition parties gained political power, put up more candidates, and challenged the dominance of the Socialists. These changes created the numerical incentives that led to cooperation on the local level during the 1960s and on the national level during the 1970s.

The three most likely axes of electoral cooperation during this period were between the Communists and the Socialists, the two wings of the Socialist Party, and the Socialists and the Democrats—the most progressive party of the proto-LDP camp.

Socialist-Communist Cooperation

The Communists and the Socialists did not cooperate formally on the national level from 1945 to 1955.[1] Robert Scalapino (1967, 74) explains both parties' failure to cooperate by (1) general features of the Japanese political system that make cooperation difficult, (2) the tactics of the Communists, especially their strident attack on Socialist leaders from the very first postwar issue of their party newspaper *Akahata*, and (3) the weakness and unpopularity of the Communist Party. The Communists received very few votes in the 1950s (fig. 4.1); what few votes the Socialists might have gained through cooperation would have been offset by the negative reputational effects of associating with the Communists. The Socialists did not see the Communists as an attractive potential coalition partner.

Of Scalapino's three explanations, the third is most convincing because it also accounts for the rise in Socialist-Communist cooperation in

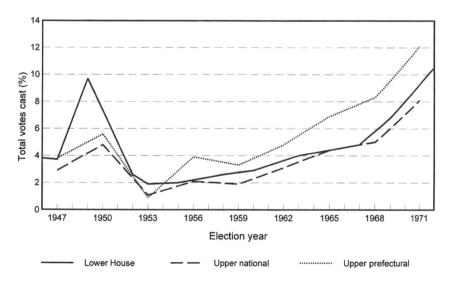

Figure 4.1 Japan Communist Party share of the vote in national elections, 1946–1972

the 1960s. From 1945 to 1960, when the Communist Party was weak and had nothing to offer the Socialists, there was no cooperation. In the 1960s, the Communists increased their share of the vote, often at the expense of the Socialists; the Socialists then began cooperating with the Communists, even though the other factors that Scalapino cites remained relatively unchanged.

In addition, the Socialists did not need to cooperate with the Communists in the 1950s because the Communists rarely put up candidates who siphoned away the votes of strong Socialist candidates. For example, in many of the twenty-five one-seat districts of the House of Councillors, the Communist Party did not run candidates in the 1950s (fig. 4.2).

The failure of the Communists to challenge the Socialists in the 1950s is anomalous. In Japanese elections since 1960, the Communists put up a candidate in every district, regardless of that candidate's chance of victory or the candidacy's splintering effect on the leftist vote. The anomalous behavior of Japan's Communists in the 1950s can be explained by the party's disarray at the time; perhaps the party lacked the resources

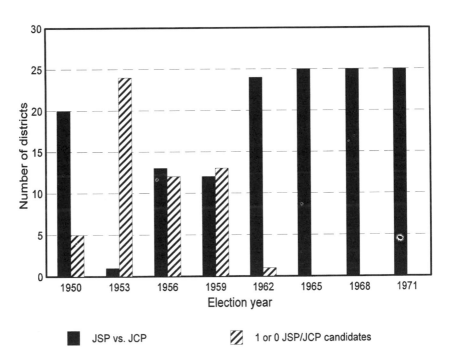

Figure 4.2 Socialist (JSP) and Communist (JCP) competition in the one-seat districts of the House of Councillors

and organizational strength to consistently put up a broad spectrum of candidates. They concentrated their resources on races they could win. Moreover, tacit agreements may have existed between local Socialist and Communist candidates in the same one-seat districts. Lastly, local Communist leaders could have unilaterally decided to further the cause of the Left by sitting out races in one-seat districts. The first explanation is the most consistent with the extremist policies of the Communist Party in the 1950s. Given the party's factionalism during that time, however, the other factors could have influenced races in some prefectures.

The Communists began to abandon some of their more radical policies in the late 1950s. The 1951 Thesis, a radical party platform, was finally replaced during the July 1961 party congress, in which Miyamoto Kenji consolidated his control over the party. The Communist Party also resumed its practice of running candidates in every district in national elections, regardless of the candidate's chance of victory (fig. 4.2). To date, the Communists have never won a seat in a one-seat district of the House of Councillors. Nevertheless, they have regularly run candidates even in these hopeless districts to raise public consciousness, educate the people, and build the party base for other elections.[2]

Gubernatorial races, the other major elections in Japan that are held in one-seat districts, showed a similar pattern. In the 1950s, the Communists rarely put up candidates in gubernatorial races already showing a Socialist candidate (fig. 4.3). Most Communist gubernatorial candidates were in districts having a conservative incumbent whose sole opposition was the Communist candidate. After 1960, the Communists put up more gubernatorial candidates, thereby increasing the number of races where Communists competed suboptimally against Socialist candidates. This suboptimal competition became the first target of Socialist-Communist electoral cooperation efforts, especially in those prefectures where the Communists commanded a large block of votes. For example, in the 1959 race for the governor of Miyagi prefecture, the Socialist and Communist candidates split the vote, allowing the conservative independent to win with only a plurality of votes. Four years later, the Communists agreed to back the Socialist candidate, who ran this time as an independent. The two parties entered into a formal cooperation agreement on the prefectural level. Though their cooperation negotiations were successful, they failed to wrest the governorship from conservative control.

Socialist-Communist cooperation became increasingly common as the Communist Party's strength increased in the 1960s and its candi-

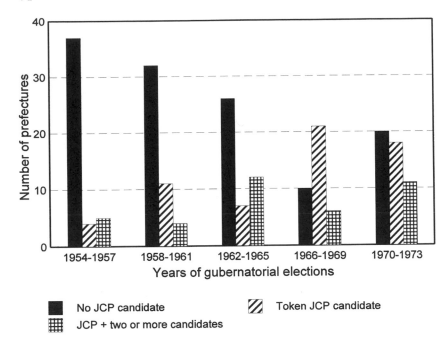

Note: "Token JCP candidate" refers to races in which there was only one serious candidate in the race. The category "No JCP candidate" can refer to races in which the communists declined to run candidates (common in the 1950s) and races in which the communists agreed to back a coalition candidate (common in the 1960s and 1970s).

Figure 4.3 Japan Communist Party (JCP) participation in gubernatorial races

dates challenged Socialists in more and more districts. Socialist candidates could no longer afford to ignore their potential Communist allies. Failure to link up with the Communists usually guaranteed the defeat of the Socialist candidate in the one-seat districts of gubernatorial and mayoral races.

The increasing numerical incentives to cooperate were further strengthened by a change in Socialist Party leadership. Socialist-Communist relations had worsened after the 1960 United States–Japan Security Treaty demonstrations. The parties also took opposing stances in response to the Soviet Union's 1962 announcement that it had detonated a hydrogen bomb. The split widened until late 1964, when Sasaki Kōzō consolidated his control over the Socialist Party, working closely with Narita Tomomi.[3] In January 1965, the two urged revival of the local Socialist-Communist cooperation organizations, which had originally been formed in 1960. Their new policy provoked a dispute in both the Socialist Party and the Sōhyō unions. Moderate elements in each opposed a resumption of close, cooperative relations with the Communists. Both sides reached a compromise that emasculated the Sasaki/Narita initiative. Though their initiative was defeated, Sasaki and Narita did succeed in restoring a procooperation atmosphere within the Socialist Party (Naitō 1965; Takeuchi 1965; Watanabe 1965).

Socialist-Communist cooperative efforts took off in the 1967 unified local elections. The two parties surprised the nation when their coalition candidate won the Tokyo governorship. This trend continued in 1971, when coalition candidates won the Osaka governorship and a second term in Tokyo. These new coalition governors joined an incumbent, leftist administration in Kyoto, giving control of Japan's three most prominent prefectures to the Socialist-Communist coalition.[4] The stage was set to expand Socialist-Communist cooperation to the national level in the 1971 House of Councillors elections.

Despite the advances in local cooperation, the Socialists and Communists never even attempted cooperation in national races until the 1971 election. The different incentives and barriers to cooperation in a national—as opposed to a local—election, and the differences in Communist and Socialist electoral strength in the two sets of election districts, account for this disparity.

National elections often focus on foreign policy or ideological issues that sharply divide the Communist and Socialist parties. Cooperation in gubernatorial races can be insulated from national-level party conflicts by focusing the campaign on issues of local interest. Cooperation is also easier in local elections because a national agreement to cooperate, with all the attendant policy compromises, is unnecessary. Local party leaders have strong incentives to be on the winning side in a gubernatorial race. Party members in the prefectural assembly can provide better constituent service if they are part of a winning gubernatorial coalition. Such access is important because prefectural politicians are expected to provide small favors to constituents, such as road improvements or interventions with local bureaucrats. Opposition members of the Diet, however, rely primarily on their party's stance on salient national issues to justify their existence.

Governors, who have more tenuous links to the interests of a particular party, have a greater incentive to expand their ruling coalition to ensure their reelection. In contrast, a prime minister cannot expand a national governing coalition, despite similar incentives, without the approval of all the relevant parties. The problem of party affiliation of the coalition's gubernatorial candidate is also easily solved; most guber- natorial candidates prefer to run as independents, to attract the widest voter support possible.

All these factors make electoral cooperation in Japan easier on the local level than on the national level. National-level cooperation is also affected by the distribution of the one-seat districts in national elec- tions. One-seat districts in the House of Councillors are obvious targets for electoral cooperation in national elections, but these districts are usually Japan's most rural prefectures, where the Communist Party is weak and Socialists have little to gain from cooperation (fig. 4.4).[5] Coop- eration with the Communists in such rural areas often has a net negative effect. The number of conservative independents driven away by the association with the Communists is greater than the Communist votes added to the coalition. Moreover, the LDP is strongest in the rural pre- fectures, so cooperation with the Communists is unlikely to help the

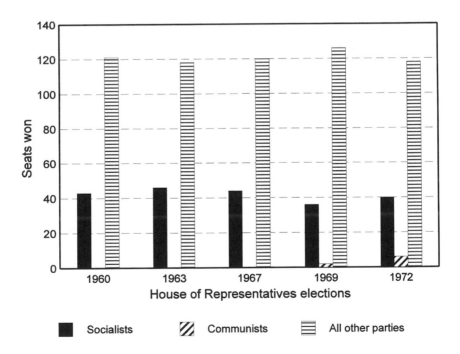

Figure 4.4 Comparison of Socialist and Communist strength in the House of Representatives districts of 25 prefectures that have one-seat House of Councillors districts

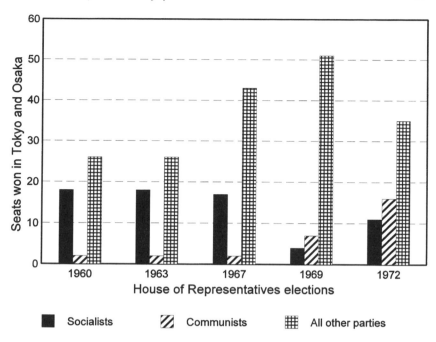

Figure 4.5 Comparison of Socialist and Communist strength in House of Representatives elections in Tokyo and Osaka

opposition wrest any seats away from the LDP. Such high odds against success remove the incentive to cooperate. The Communists are strong in urban areas, and the Socialist-Communist coalition had many impressive victories in urban gubernatorial races in the 1970s. In these prefectures, the LDP was more vulnerable to a Socialist-Communist coalition, and the Communist bloc was too large to be ignored (fig. 4.5). Urban prefectures are not, however, amenable to cooperation in Diet elections, because they have multiseat districts in House of Representatives and House of Councillors elections. Such districts discourage cooperation because the Communists and the other opposition parties can each elect candidates from these districts without cooperating.

Cooperation between Socialist Parties

Another potential cooperative alliance was between the two wings of the Socialist Party. The party split into the Left Socialists and the Right Socialists from 1951 to 1955, and the Labor-Farmer Party (Rōdōsha

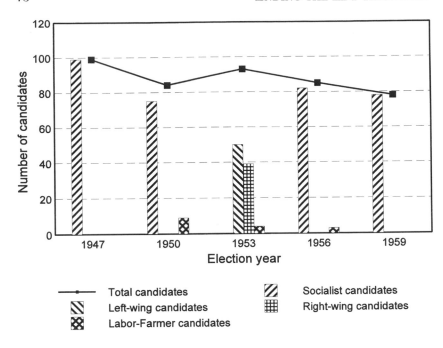

Figure 4.6 Candidates from Socialist parties in House of Councillors elections

Nōmintō) split off from 1948 to 1955. Formal cooperation was unnecessary despite these divisions, however, since the various factions generally did not undercut each other without reason. For example, in 1953,
the three socialist parties competed suboptimally (i.e., by putting up
more than one candidate) in only four of the twenty-five one-seat House
of Councillors districts. Of the twenty-one multiseat districts in that
election, the three ran against each other in thirteen of them, but they
lost a seat because they split the vote in only three of the districts. The
socialist parties also avoided undercutting each other's candidates in the
gubernatorial races of this period.

   These competing socialist parties occasionally challenged each other
in the multiseat districts of the House of Representatives and the House
of Councillors, but in many districts, the splintering of the Socialist Party
did not increase the total number of Socialist candidates running
for office. Rather, new party names were merely added to the existing
Socialist candidates (figs. 4.6 and 4.7).[6] Because these several socialist
parties held down the number of candidates and avoided unnecessarily
splintering the leftist vote, there was little need or incentive for further

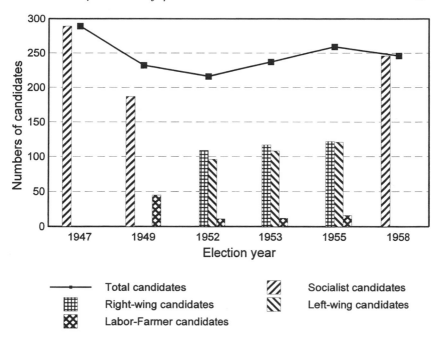

Figure 4.7 Candidates from Socialist parties in House of Representatives elections

cooperative efforts. Necessary cooperation was achieved by coordinating the districts in which each of the parties ran candidates. This is not to imply that these parties negotiated formal, reciprocal stand-down agreements. Rather, the existence of strong incumbents filing off to either party provided the focal coordinating mechanism to minimize inefficient competition between the two parties.

A second splintering of the Socialist Party occurred when Nishio Suehiro left the party in 1959. Nishio's Democratic Socialist Party challenged the Socialists in most of the House of Representatives districts, putting up 101 candidates in the 1960 election. Despite its efforts, the new party won only seventeen seats. In subsequent elections, the party has never expanded much beyond its core of union supporters; to date, it has never elected as many members of the Diet as it did at its founding.

The Democratic Socialists acted quite rationally to field many candidates in the 1960 election. Party leaders encouraged candidates to run in as many districts as possible. Candidates even ran in several one-seat districts in the House of Councillors. Though the party's efforts proved largely futile, they were rational, given the untested electoral support of the Democratic Socialists. A new party that hopes to attract voters from other existing parties cannot accurately gauge the support at the outset of its first election campaign (Cox 1997, 151–152). This creates a strong incentive to run as many candidates as possible, not only to give voters in every district an opportunity to vote for the party but also to support its aspirations to become a major, national party. To do otherwise would be to concede defeat from the outset.[7] When the Democratic Socialists failed to attract the support they had hoped for, they quickly scaled back their number of candidates.

This realistic assessment of electoral fortunes by the Democratic Socialists played an important role in opposition electoral cooperation. When the party scaled back the number of its candidates, it created "open districts"—districts where the Democratic Socialists were not fielding a candidate and were free to support another party. These open districts, and the core of Democratic Socialist voters in them, created tempting cooperative opportunities for other opposition parties. In the 1960s, however, the Democratic Socialists eschewed any formal cooperative arrangements in national elections, even in open districts, though it is possible that informal cooperative arrangements existed on the prefectural level. In local elections, the party quickly took a stance in many of the gubernatorial races. The Democratic Socialists, like the Socialists, often supported strong incumbent governors, but in hotly contested races, their central position between the Socialists and the LDP gave them greater freedom of choice. They could choose between joining the conservative coalition or joining the Socialist coalition.

Socialist-Conservative Cooperation

The third type of cooperation in this period was between the Socialists and the more progressive elements of the proto-LDP. The only formal cooperation on the national level between these two groups was the Socialist-Democrat coalition governments in 1947 and 1948. However, Socialist-conservative cooperation is one constant feature of gubernatorial and mayoral races throughout the postwar period. This local cooperation is significant because it illustrates the existence of ties between the Socialists and the LDP on the local level.

An early example of this cooperation was the 1951 unified local elections, in which the Socialists and the Democrats jointly backed independent candidates in twelve of the thirty-one gubernatorial races. Even after 1955, the Socialists continue to work with either the LDP or with

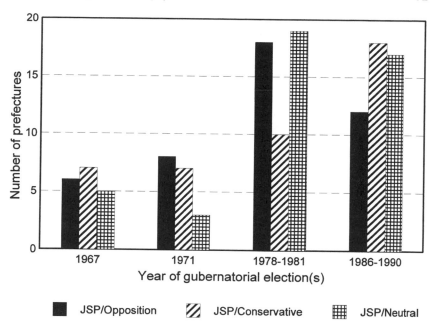

Note: "JCP/Conservative" includes all races in which the Socialists were reported to have formally or informally joined with the LDP or part of the LDP in backing a candidate. "JSP/Neutral" are those races in which the Socialists backed no candidate. Data for 1967 and 1971 cover only the gubernatorial races held as part of the unified local elections in those years. Sources are Miyakawa (1990); Miyakawa (1982); and *Mainichi Shimbun* (Tokyo), 3, 13, 17 April 1967.

Figure 4.8 Position of the Socialist Party (JSP) in selected gubernatorial races

factions of the LDP in these races. Socialist support of a conservative candidate is most common when the LDP splits into two competing factions or when the conservative candidate is strong enough to attract the support of most or all of the opposition parties.

When the conservatives have competing candidates in a gubernatorial race, often one of the conservative candidates obtains the official or unofficial backing of the Socialists. Such endorsements are delicate matters within the Socialist Party, because the decision not to field a Socialist candidate is often vigorously opposed by the more radical elements within the party. Nevertheless, such Socialist-conservative cooperation in gubernatorial races is much more common than is usually assumed (fig. 4.8).

The Socialist Party also supports conservative candidates for governor when the candidate is so popular that he or she becomes a bandwagon *(ainori)* candidate. These candidates often face either no opponent or only a token Communist candidate. Typically, a bandwagon candidate is a strong incumbent who was initially elected as either a conservative or a progressive. Through their administrations, however, these incumbents have built relations with all the political parties. They transform themselves from party politicians to politically neutral administrators who are acceptable to all the political parties from the LDP to the Socialists. Both the governor and the parties benefit from being on the bandwagon. The incumbents receive broad political support and an assured reelection; the parties receive the benefit of being part of the ruling prefectural coalition, thus being better able to distribute the benefits of government to their specific support groups.

Bandwagon candidates can even occur with nonincumbents, especially when a popular retiring incumbent selects a successor who is acceptable to all the political parties (usually a bureaucrat in the local administration who lacks any strong political affiliation). In addition, bandwagon candidates typically develop when a progressive governor is pulled to the right by the LDP in exchange for LDP support.[8] The Socialists rarely support governors who originally were partisan LDP politicians.

In a gubernatorial election, Socialist support of a conservative independent could be either a bandwagon situation or a coalition with an LDP faction. The two situations are quite different, however. A bandwagon candidate rarely has an opponent; an LDP split is usually a hotly contested election. Regardless of this difference, these ties are one constant of Socialist-LDP relations in the postwar era. Even though the relations are only on the local level, they provide a link between the parties and a model for such ties to be copied on the national level.

The 1971 Election

In the months before the 1971 House of Councillors election, the Communists and the centrists competed intensely to persuade the Socialists to be their cooperation partner. The Communists had long offered to cooperate in hopes of expanding Socialist-Communist cooperation to the national level. Democratic Socialist chairman Nishimura Eiichi initiated the competing centrist offer to cooperate in June 1970. Eda Saburō, a prominent Socialist Party politician, supported this centrist offer, making it difficult for Socialist chairman Narita to ignore the offer.

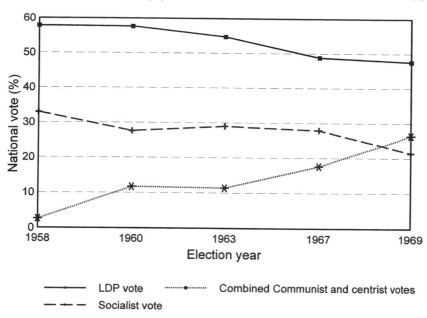

Figure 4.9 Comparison of popular vote totals in House of Representatives elections in the 1960s

Instead, Narita adopted a policy of "all-opposition cooperation," which served as the Socialist Party position from 1970 to 1980. The all-opposition cooperation platform was a compromise. It closed no doors. Moderates like Eda could continue to pursue cooperative relations with the centrists, and leftists within the party could continue to advocate Socialist-Communist cooperation.[9] It was a necessary neutral stance by the party leadership, given the deep divisions within the party that emerged when the centrists presented themselves as a cooperation alternative to the Communists.[10]

The key elements that explain this shift in policies have already been addressed. The first was the decline of the Socialists and the LDP, along with the corresponding rise of the centrists and the Communists in the 1960s (fig. 4.9). This realignment of electoral support encouraged cooperation in two ways: It decreased the Socialists' dominance within the opposition camp, and it increased the incentives for Socialist leaders to accept cooperation proposals. They recognized that cooperation would help them elect more Socialists, thereby shoring up their declining position. The realignment also made the LDP more vulnerable. Even in LDP strongholds, such as the rural one-seat districts of the House of Councillors, the LDP was winning by smaller and smaller margins. For example, in the 1968 House of Councillors election, the combined Socialist-Communist vote was greater than the vote for the LDP victors in two one-seat districts; in four others, the combined vote of the Left was between 90 and 100 percent of the vote for the LDP winner.

A second trend was the spate of victories by the Socialist-Communist coalition in several important mayoral and gubernatorial races. These victories not only were a manifestation of voter realignment, they also played an important exemplary role to the opposition parties. They constituted unmistakable evidence of the benefits that could be obtained by electoral cooperation. Further, these victories posed a threat to the centrist parties, who feared becoming politically isolated if Socialist-Communist cooperation became too successful.[11] This fear was greatest within the Democratic Socialist Party because anti-Communism was one of its fundamental policies; thus, it vehemently opposed Socialist-Communist cooperation and feared isolation by such cooperation.[12]

A third element in the policy shift was Nishimura Eiichi's assumption of Democratic Socialist leadership in 1966; he was more open to cooperative efforts than his predecessor had been. Additionally, the Clean Government Party promoted cooperation as a strategy to deal with a scandal faced in the late 1960s. The Clean Government Party wanted to build relations with the Democratic Socialists so the latter would ease their scandal-based attack on it. The Clean Government Party, like the Democratic Socialists, also wanted to use electoral cooperation as a first step toward a political realignment of moderate Socialists and centrists into a new political party. Critics of the Clean Government Party claim that its leaders were positive about cooperation because they were confident their superior organization would dominate any new political party that might result (Hirakawa 1971, 5–10).

Finally, cooperation was spurred by Japan's quadrennial unified local elections, which took place two months before the 1971 House of Councillors elections. The bulk of Japan's governors, mayors, prefectural representatives and city councillors are elected in the unified local elections. In 1971, Socialist-Communist coalition candidates posted several impressive victories in these elections. That the House of Councillors election followed these local elections so closely amplified the influence of local cooperation (as an example and as a threat) on discussions of national cooperation.[13]

In the hurried negotiations preceding the actual cooperation agreement, both the Communists and the centrists pursued the Socialists with vigor. The Communists offered to support the Socialists in all one-seat districts, in exchange for a promise from the Socialists to support Communist candidates in any future mayoral races having no Socialist candidate. In addition, the Communists required that the Socialists enter into an umbrella cooperation organization, which would be founded on three policy positions. It would function even after the election as an ongoing coordination mechanism between the two parties.

The Socialists rejected this proposal because it tied Socialist-Communist fortunes too closely together.[14] Most Socialists wanted greater flexibility than the Communists, for both tactical and ideological reasons. Tactically, the Socialists feared long-term organizational ties with the Communists because of the latter's superior organizational capabilities. Communist electoral advances already threatened the Socialist domination of the Left. Even though the Communists offered to support Socialist candidates, many Socialists feared that the cooperative arrangements would eventually work to the advantage of the Communists, giving them greater access to Socialist supporters. In the Sōhyō unions, leaders were even more fearful that extended relations with the Communists would allow Communist influence to grow within the union membership. This growth not only would challenge the existing, pro-Socialist Sōhyō leadership but also would weaken the rationale behind Sōhyō's policy of supporting only the Socialist Party. As a further tactical matter, some leaders within the Socialist Party saw the importance of maintaining a flexible Socialist position between the Communists and the centrists. Such a position would allow the Socialists to play both groups off each other, thus maximizing Socialist influence and control.[15] A good example of the fruits of this flexibility is the luxury that the Socialists enjoyed in 1971 of choosing between the competing cooperation proposals of the centrists and the Communists.

The Socialists rejected the Communist proposal for ideological reasons, too. A long-term arrangement with the Communists was anathema to the right wing of the Socialist Party. If the Socialist leadership had accepted the Communist proposal with its accompanying commitments to maintain and expand cooperative relations with the Communists, the Socialist Party would most likely have split along ideological lines. Ideological objections to cooperating with the Communists also served as a cover for tactical objections to the same cooperation. For example, right-wing Socialists did not object to all coop-

erative relations with the Communist Party; they accepted such cooperation as long as it was on Socialist terms, (i.e., occasional transfers of
votes to Socialist candidates with minimal policy coordination). They
rejected only the long-term relationship that the Communists required
for national electoral cooperation.

In contrast, the centrists offered the Socialists the same benefits of
cooperation without the distasteful baggage of long-term commitments.
They offered to support Socialist candidates unilaterally in several of the
one-seat districts. No formal strings were attached, no policy agreements were required, and no coordinating organization was necessary.
The centrists, however, implicitly expected the Socialists to modify their
policies in return. When it became apparent in early 1971 that the
Socialists would not change their policies, centrist (especially Clean
Government Party) enthusiasm for cooperation cooled. The centrists
also expected that their cooperative efforts would be only the first step
in their plan to unify the centrists with the right wing of the Socialist
Party. Not until the campaign did it become public knowledge that the
centrists were actually working with Eda to separate the moderate
Socialists from their more radical colleagues.[16]

Though the Socialist-centrist cooperation proposal was unilateral in
form, in actuality it was clearly a side-payment type of cooperative
arrangement. The centrists gave their support only to Socialist candidates that Eda recommended as supporting his efforts to moderate the
radicalism of the Socialist Party. Leftists within the Socialist Party
understood the real motivations behind the centrists' invitation to cooperate. It was, however, difficult for them to make a convincing case
against the centrist offer, because the offer required no formal commitments from the Socialist Party. Furthermore, their suspicions about the
centrists' plan to use Eda to split the Socialist Party were not verified
until after the campaign had begun. These doubts were trumped by the
priority Socialist leaders gave to electoral cooperation as a device to
shore up the Socialists' declining electoral position.

Faced with both cooperative options, the Socialist leadership played
their advantage to the limit and tried to force the Communists to back
off from some of their demands. They hoped to obtain the maximum
benefit for the party by entering into multiple cooperation agreements
with both the centrists and the Communists. This strategy backfired:
The Communists walked away from negotiations rather than making any
further concessions.[17] The centrists won their battle to make the
Socialists their cooperation partner not because they were more ideo-

logically acceptable to the Socialists or because the moderate wing was stronger within the Socialist party—Eda had just lost the battle to become party chairman. Rather, the centrist plan was accepted because no modification of the original centrist proposal was needed; it concealed reciprocal aspects of the cooperation arrangement that were disagreeable to elements within the Socialist Party. In contrast, the Communists refused to compromise or conceal their explicit demands that the Socialist Party publicly commit to a long-term, equitable exchange between the two parties.

The leaders of the centrist parties agreed to support three Socialist candidates—in Shimane, Oita, and Tochigi prefectures. This agreement, however, proved difficult to implement; many of the rank and file of the two centrist parties and of the Socialist Party objected to the cooperation agreement. The Socialists in Shimane prefecture, who had the task merely of graciously receiving centrist support, rebelled against the cooperation arrangement. During the campaign, a Democratic Socialist official made explicit the connection between his party's support of Socialist candidates and those candidates' support of "political reorganization." Many in the Socialist Party viewed "political reorganization" as a code word for splitting the Socialist Party and merging the moderate Socialists with the centrists into a new party. The Socialist candidate in Shimane promptly denounced cooperation as a "nuisance" and snubbed the acting Democratic Socialist leader, Sasaki Ryōsaku, when he made a campaign visit to Shimane in support of the Socialist candidate.[18]

The leaders of the centrist parties also underestimated the degree to which their rank and file opposed cooperation. The Democratic Socialists, with their weaker organization, were the worse offenders in this regard. For example, the local organization and its corresponding union organization in the first district of Tochigi prefecture passed resolutions stating that they would not cooperate. National party leaders lobbied them with great intensity, but these local party and union officials maintained their stance of noncooperation.[19]

Even the Clean Government Party, which had a strong organization, had problems with its local affiliates. A party official in Tochigi admitted that he was going along with the cooperation efforts only because of pressure from the national headquarters.[20] In Oita, the local party governing board did not endorse cooperation unanimously. This split vote in the usually monolithic Clean Government Party organization indicated the deep dissatisfaction at the prefectural level with the cooperation agreement.

Despite these difficulties, the leaders of the centrist parties, especially the Democratic Socialists, continued to work hard for the success
of cooperation. Sasaki Ryōsaku played down the snub he had received in
Shimane and arranged for the Democratic Socialists to formally support
Socialist candidates in two additional prefectures. Both centrist parties
called on their supporters in all open districts to support Socialist candidates, even those who were not included in the cooperation agreements.
By election day, both centrist parties were formally supporting the
Socialists in three districts, the Democratic Socialists had formally endorsed Socialist candidates in two additional districts, and the Democratic Socialists and Clean Government Party had urged their supporters to back Socialist candidates in an additional eighteen open districts.

The Socialists won eight of the twenty-five one-seat districts up for
election, their greatest victory in these LDP-dominated rural areas.
The Socialists won all three of the Socialist-centrist cooperation districts; they won one of the two Democratic Socialist–Socialist cooperation districts. They also won in five districts lacking formal cooperation
arrangements.[21]

The results would seem to indicate an impressive success for electoral cooperation, but they were not universally interpreted that way.
Newspapers credited the victory to the combination of a low turnout,
which generally favors the opposition parties because they rely more on
"hard" union or religious votes which vary less with turnout levels; rural
discontent with LDP agricultural policies; and electoral cooperation
efforts.[22]

Measuring the extent to which cooperation efforts actually contributed to the Socialist victories is difficult. This election is an excellent
example of the information uncertainties that plague electoral cooperation efforts. A comparison of cooperation districts with noncooperation
districts cannot show conclusively the influence of cooperation in the
1971 election, because the centrist parties urged all their open-district
supporters to support the Socialists. A comparison of the 1971 election
with the 1968 election shows how the Socialist vote increased, but other
factors, such as rural discontent and turnout levels, also influenced this
increase.

A reliable estimate of cooperation levels is possible. For example,
Mainichi Shimbun (Tokyo) compared election-day polling data of party
support and candidate support with the party vote in the national constituency portion of the House of Councillors election. They used these
numbers to estimate the percent of party voters who had switched their

votes to a coalition candidate. They found in Shimane that 73 percent of Democratic Socialist voters, 65 percent of Clean Government Party voters, and 7 percent of LDP voters had cast their votes for the Socialist coalition candidate.[23]

Yet even these polling data fail to prove conclusively the importance of electoral cooperation in Shimane. The Socialist incumbent, Nakamura Eidan, had won in 1965, with 204,000 votes. A different Socialist candidate lost in 1968, with 191,000 votes. Nakamura was reelected in 1971 with centrist support, yet he garnered only 164,000 votes in a turnout nearly identical to that of 1965. He won reelection in 1971 because there were two conservative candidates in the race. It is easy to claim that Nakamura won because of electoral cooperation; his margin of victory was less than 10,000 votes. It is also easy to discredit cooperation efforts, however, by simply pointing to the overall decline in Nakamura's vote, which occurred despite cooperation.[24]

Information uncertainty made it possible for anticooperation factions within the parties to make assertions that could be neither proved nor disproved. Because different politicians interpreted the election results differently, the reservoir of good feeling that the cooperation victories created quickly ran dry.

The breakdown in Socialist-centrist relations began as soon as the election results were in. The Socialist Party and Sōhyō gave due credit to the cooperative efforts of the centrists,[25] but individual Socialists, especially Nakamura in Shimane prefecture, made inflammatory statements to the effect that they would have won without the help of the centrists. Conversely, acting chairman Sasaki of the Democratic Socialists was equally adamant in his claim that all eight Socialist winners had won because of centrist support (Sasaki and Itō 1984, 234; Sasaki, 1991). Chairman Takeiri Yoshikatsu of the Clean Government Party also complained about the way the Socialists treated his party after the election. He blamed the Socialists for not adequately acknowledging the role of centrist cooperation and for not treating the centrists with greater respect after the election. He said that the Socialists refused to give the centrist parties a more prominent role either in the management committee of the House of Representatives or in the order of questioning during questioning sessions of cabinet ministers.[26]

The rebuff the Socialists directed toward their centrist allies after the election may seem irrational, and it is one alleged example of Socialist incompetence. The decision clearly reflects calculations of self- and party interest within the Socialist Party, however. The Socialist share of the vote increased in 1971 even in constituencies with no electoral cooperation, formal or informal. For example, in the national constituency of the House of Councillors, the Socialists polled 21.3 percent of the vote, compared to 19.8 percent in 1968. Many Socialists therefore felt that the party had finally reversed its long electoral decline. This increase in electoral support removed the incentives to cooperate; the Socialist Party was on the upswing and would soon regain its position of unquestioned dominance of the opposition. These assumptions proved wrong; Socialist victories in 1971 proved to be an anomaly rather than the beginning of a trend. Given the evidence available in 1971, however, a decision to downgrade the importance of cooperation was well supported by estimates of future Socialist strength.

The rebuff of the centrists also stemmed from the opposition of many Socialists to the Eda-sponsored, Socialist-centrist relations, because of rumors that Eda's ultimate goal was to split the party. Ishibashi Masashi (1991) claims that cooperation failed in 1971 because the centrists used Eda as their Socialist Party liaison rather than going through the elected party leadership. Socialist-centrist cooperation became associated with Eda, so it was naturally opposed by anti-Eda groups within the party. Ishibashi explains Nakamura's opposition to cooperation by citing his factional affiliation with the Sasaki faction, which opposed Eda. Ishibashi claims he warned his counterpart in the Clean Government Party, Yano Junya, to work through him rather than through Eda, since working through Eda would arouse antagonism within the party, but Yano ignored the warning. Ishibashi says the warnings were ignored because Eda and his centrist allies were not concerned about radical opposition to Socialist-centrist cooperation. They intended to exclude the radicals from their new political party anyway.

It would seem irrational for the Socialists to jettison the opportunity to cooperate simply because the cooperation proposals became fodder in the battle between party factions. From the standpoint of party leadership and of the rank and file, who preferred a unified party, rejecting cooperation was a calculated, strategic decision, however. They opposed cooperation in an effort to stop Eda before he could build support within the party sufficient to force a splintering of the party along ideological lines. In the long run, perhaps it was a tactical error to oppose centrist cooperation on the grounds of its association with Eda's ultimate objectives, but then it was also a tactical error (as Ishibashi points out) for Eda and his centrist allies to alienate large segments of the party by maneuvering around party leadership.

In the end, it was unfortunate for the Socialist Party that cooperation initiatives became so closely identified with its own factional struggles, but this particular struggle was an issue of grave importance to the party's future. Moreover, Eda and his centrist promoters of cooperation intended from the outset to use electoral cooperation as a lever to pry apart the Socialist Party. The intertwining of factional disputes with electoral cooperation should not be regarded as symptomatic of a Socialist tendency to embroil all decisions in factional disputes. Rather, it was a natural consequence of the objectives of the procooperation Eda faction.

Electoral Cooperation from 1971 to 1980

Electoral cooperation had its ups and downs through the several elections from 1971 to 1980, but four definite trends of this period directly affected electoral coalitions. First, in the early 1970s, there was a rise in leftist—especially Communist—electoral power. Cooperation with the Communists rose in prominence as a reflection of this shift in electoral power. Second, in the mid- to late 1970s, the centrist parties advanced electorally; not surprisingly, centrist-oriented cooperation rose in importance. Third, union-specific electoral cooperation began to replace the general cooperation agreements that were common in the early 1970s. Fourth, the centrist parties no longer viewed an opposition coalition government as the best path to political power. They switched back to their more pro-LDP stance of the 1960s and began to look for opportunities to join with the LDP in a coalition government.

A Shift to the Left

The aftermath of the 1971 election put Socialist-centrist cooperation in cold storage for a period. In contrast, Socialist-Communist cooperation revived as the alternative to the discredited Eda-centrist axis. Communist victories in the 1972 House of Representatives election further spurred this revival.[27] The focus of electoral cooperation shifted to the parties of the Left. An LDP strategist even went so far as to identify the Communist Party as the LDP's most threatening long-term rival. The centrist parties were eclipsed. A former leader of Sōhyō commented that Socialist-centrist cooperation had "blown up in mid-air" (Iwai and Shimizu 1973, 20).

However, Socialist-Communist cooperation never expanded significantly because the Socialists clearly limited their cooperation with the Communists. They were wary of Communist cooperation for reasons similar to those cited in 1971: (1) maintaining an all-opposition cooper-ation stance gave the Socialists greater influence and flexibility; (2) the sense of threat that Sōhyō unions felt from the Communists was only heightened by Communist electoral advances in 1972; (3) the Socialists continued to fear domination by the organizationally superior Commu-nists in any type of long-term or extensive cooperative arrangement; (4) the invective heaped on the Socialist Party by the Communists, as well as the latter's conspiratorial nature, alienated potential allies within the Socialist Party; and (5) the moderate wing of the Socialist Party main-tained ideological and tactical objections to sustained, long-term coop-erative relations with the Communists.

Some or all of these factors would have been overcome had the Communist electoral advance continued unabated. The increasing potential benefits of cooperation with the Communists would have created such strong incentives to cooperate that even these barriers would have fallen. Communist electoral power peaked in 1972, how-ever. In several mayoral races that followed the 1972 election, Socialist-Communist coalition candidates went down to defeat.

The Clean Government Party also responded to Communist elec-toral advances and moved toward the left in the early 1970s.[28] The party adopted policy platforms that resembled those of the Socialist and Communist Parties. In their 1973 proposals for a coalition government, all three parties called for rescinding the United States–Japan Security Treaty and the immediate reduction and eventual elimination of Japan's military (the Self-Defense Forces). Of the opposition parties, only the Democratic Socialists took a pro–Security Treaty and promilitary stance (*Ekonomisuto* 1973b). In some respects, the Clean Government Party was even to the left of the Socialists. For example, the party called for the "immediate" abrogation of the United States–Japan Security Treaty, while the Socialist platform called for a "negotiated withdrawal" from the Treaty. Yoshioka Yoshinori (1991), a former editor of the Communist newspaper *Akahata,* boasts that he often shows visitors the copy of the Clean Government Party coalition proposal from this period, with nine of ten people assuming that it was written by the Communist Party.

The Clean Government Party modified its anti-Communist stance and rhetoric. Party leaders agreed to join the Socialist-Communist coali-tion in the 1973 Nagoya mayoral race; however, local Clean Government opposition in Nagoya scuttled those plans. In a subsequent mayoral race in Hino, near Tokyo, the Clean Government Party joined with the Com-munists and the Socialists in an electoral coalition for the first time (*Sekai* 1973, 271). The party joined in electoral coalitions with the Communists and the Socialists in some subsequent local elections in 1973 and 1974, but this cooperation never expanded to the national elections.

During this same period, the Clean Government Party also developed a cooperative relationship with the Democratic Socialists. The two parties cooperated officially for the first time in the 1972 House of Representatives election, with thirteen coalition candidates. Their efforts were the first formal cooperation activities by any party in a House of Representatives election. The multiseat districts of the House of Representatives were (and continue to be) the best arena for cooperation between the centrists. These two parties do not have the votes to win a plurality in a single-seat district, but in many of the marginal multiseat districts of the House of Representatives, their combined vote totals are sufficient to win one of the three, four, or five seats available.

Centrist cooperation was the first example of a barter cooperation arrangement in a Japanese national election. The Democratic Socialists gave their support to Clean Government Party candidates in seven districts in exchange for Clean Government Party support of Democratic Socialist candidates in six districts.[29] This contrasts with the side-payment cooperative arrangements of 1971, in which the centrists supported Socialist candidates in exchange for nonelectoral benefits. One analyst interpreted the inauguration of centrist cooperation as an attempt to win more seats for both parties, and to prod Eda into quickly splitting the Socialist Party and joining the new centrist cooperative efforts (*Asahi Jānaru* 1972).

Revival of the Centrist Option

In the 1974 House of Councillors election, the emphasis of electoral cooperation began to shift once again to the centrist parties. This shift mirrored the opposition parties' change in electoral fortunes. Communist support had peaked and was about to begin its decline. The Socialists also resumed their electoral decline. Though the Socialist Party maintained its all-opposition cooperation stance, Socialist leaders began to shift their focus of cooperative efforts to the Clean Government Party.[30] This party became the key to Socialist-centrist cooperation because it controlled a large block of votes, was flexible about cooperative arrangements, and had some supporters in the rural and semi-rural districts in which the bulk of Socialist candidates ran.[31] Symbolic of this shift was the first-ever, national-level cooperation agreement between the Clean Government Party and the Socialists in the 1974 election.

Cracks in the Socialist-Communist relationship appeared at the same time. Emblematic of this troubled relationship was the 1974 Kyoto governor's race (Stockwin 1974). The incumbent, Ninagawa Torazō, had been in office since 1950, most of that time with the backing of the Socialists and the Communists. During this long period of cooperation, however, the Communists in Kyoto had built up their organization and electoral power at the expense of the Socialists. By 1974, the Communists clearly minimized the Socialists in Kyoto, both in power and organization. The Socialist leaders of Kyoto prefecture, hoping to reverse this decline, refused to cooperate with the Communists in Ninagawa's re-election campaign. The national Socialist headquarters rejected the local Socialist decision, expelling the prefectural leaders from the party. The expelled prefectural chairman of the party, Ohashi Kazutaka, entered the race against Ninagawa as an independent. He received centrist and tacit LDP backing, and he nearly defeated Ninagawa.

The Socialist leadership took a hard line on the Kyoto rebellion in order to maintain amicable Socialist-Communist relations for the upcoming 1975 unified local elections, in which the bulk of Socialist-Communist coalition candidates would stand for reelection. In national elections, however, the Socialist Party remained unenthusiastic about Socialist-Communist cooperation. Socialist leadership restricted such cooperation to one token district in each election of the 1970s.[32] For example, in 1977, the local Socialist organization in Shizuoka prefecture worked out a cooperation arrangement with their Communist counterparts and submitted it to the national headquarters for approval. Despite repeated pleas, the national headquarters refused to sanction the cooperative arrangement in Shizuoka, even though it had just approved a similar arrangement in Miyagi prefecture. Socialist leaders were unable or unwilling to approve anything beyond a token Socialist-Communist cooperation effort.

These trends continued in the unified local elections of 1975. Across the nation, Socialist-Communist coalition candidates for mayor and governor went down to defeat. In many areas, cooperation broke down because of disputes within a major leftist support group, the Buraku Liberation League.

Development of Union-Specific Electoral Cooperation

The revival of Socialist-centrist cooperation in the 1974 election failed to produce results similar to those of the 1971 election. Analysts cited two election-specific factors as an explanation of the failure of Socialist-centrist cooperation: (1) Because Clean Government Party activists were preoccupied with preparations for the next House of Representatives election, they gave Socialist coalition candidates only lukewarm support; and (2) Clean Government Party leaders and voters still harbored ill will toward the Socialists because of the parties' history of poor relations. Party members were especially incensed at the pro-Communist position that the national Socialist Party took in the 1974 Kyoto governor's election.

A broader explanation is that Socialist–Clean Government cooperation floundered because the Socialists were unable to actually deliver votes to Clean Government Party candidates. Unlike in 1971, the Clean Government Party insisted on a barter cooperation arrangement with the Socialists in 1974. The party supported Socialist candidates in three prefectures in exchange for Socialist support of a Clean Government Party candidate in Wakayama prefecture. However, the Socialist organization could not deliver the votes to the Clean Government Party coalition candidate nearly as well as the Clean Government Party could deliver votes to Socialist candidates. Clean Government leaders saw that general cooperation arrangements worked entirely to the advantage of the Socialists.

In the 1976 House of Representatives election, the Socialists were anxious to receive Clean Government Party support. However, learning from their experiences in 1974, the Clean Government Party refused to cooperate unless Socialist-affiliated unions promised to transfer specific numbers of votes to a Clean Government Party candidate. Procooperation Socialists suggested the first district of Gifu prefecture as one in which Socialist unions could divide their support between a Clean Government Party candidate and the Socialist incumbent. Socialist–Clean Government Party cooperation was possible in Gifu 1 because the Socialists had consistently run two candidates in the district until 1976. The party consolidated in 1976 to only one candidate, Yamamoto Kōichi, an ally of Eda. Because this consolidation created an excess of Socialist votes, the local party leadership, which was affiliated with Eda, agreed to shift excess union votes to the Clean Government Party candidate in the same district.

The cooperation negotiations in Gifu 1 focused not on whether the Socialists would agree to support the Clean Government Party candidate (they readily did that) but on which union would promise how many votes to the candidate. Clean Government Party leaders refused to accept general promises of Socialist support. They had learned their lesson that general appeals to support a coalition candidate were ignored by the vast majority of Socialist voters. The Clean Government Party's strength was also its weakness; the party provided most of the votes transferred in electoral coalitions, yet received none of the benefits. Clean Government Party leaders thus insisted on a union-specific agreement in Gifu 1. They knew that union leaders could actually deliver some votes to the Clean Government Party in accordance with a cooperation agreement. In addition, it was easier for party leaders to measure compliance with an agreement if vote totals were specified and if the Clean Government Party had direct relations with the source of the votes—the union organizations.

The Clean Government Party's demand for a specific vote transfer agreement created a new stumbling block in cooperation negotiations. There was still much rank-and-file Socialist opposition to participating in any cooperative arrangement with the Clean Government Party. Party and union leaders overcame this opposition only after long negotiations and through the explicit linkage of Clean Government Party support of specific union candidates in other districts to those same unions' support of the Clean Government Party candidate in Gifu 1.[33]

This election was one of the first in a wave of union-specific cooperation agreements that gradually replaced the general cooperation agreements first attempted in the early 1970s. Union-specific agreements and general agreements are not necessarily incompatible. In some instances, a union-specific agreement will form the core of a cooperative arrangement, and the agreement is also announced as a general cooperation agreement. The cooperation in Gifu 1 is an example of general cooperation based on a union-specific arrangement. Most centrist cooperation agreements are similar. They are based on specific linkages between certain unions in specific election districts, but they are also announced, and all party supporters are urged to join the cooperative effort.

In many districts, union-specific agreements are not announced. For various local reasons, the announcement of a cooperative arrangement could have negative consequences. Union-specific agreements also flourish in these informal-cooperation districts.

Centrist Disillusionment with the Socialists

Many Socialists were ambivalent about the Socialist-centrist cooperation promoted by party moderates like Eda or Yamamoto. In the 1976 election, party leaders were again reluctant to embrace the Socialist-centrist cooperation plan because of its close ties to Eda.[34] The divisions within the Socialist Party on this issue soon came to a head. In 1977, Eda lost another bid for party leadership, and thereafter he came under harsh attack from the radical left wing of the party (the Kyōkaiha). Eda and several other prominent moderates left the party in 1977, and the party entered a period of imbalance in which radical activists nearly took control of party leadership.

The events of 1977 did not resolve divisions within the Socialist Party. Despite the departure of five prominent representatives, the bulk of Socialist representatives remained divided on this issue of party cooperation. The radical Left made some advances, such as concluding the first national-level, Socialist-Communist cooperation agreement in the 1977 House of Councillors election. This breakthrough was largely symbolic, however; the same Socialist leadership continued to refuse to allow Socialist-Communist cooperation to spread beyond one election district in each election. These leaders maintained Socialist unity by retaining the policy of all-opposition party cooperation. They kept a balance in formal electoral cooperation by also pursuing Socialist–Clean Government Party cooperation in every election.

Eda's failure and the rise of the radical Left in the Socialist Party triggered a shift in the attitudes of the centrist parties, who had waited since 1971 for Eda either to transform the Socialist Party or to split it.[35] When Eda's departure and later death ended this possibility, the centrists reassessed their prospects of obtaining political power through a coalition with the Socialists, shifting their hopes instead to a coalition with the LDP. The Democratic Socialists began this shift before the Clean Government Party, but as Eda's failure became clear, Clean Government Party leaders turned their sights toward some type of coalitional arrangement with the LDP.

Though the changed goals of the centrist parties did not eliminate the usefulness of opposition electoral cooperation, the reasons for cooperating altered subtly. In the past, the centrists had used electoral cooperation as a carrot to encourage moderation within the Socialist Party. They hoped that the opposition parties could then be reformulated into a new and vigorous alternative to the LDP. By the late 1970s, electoral cooperation became only a tool by which the opposition parties could increase their share of seats and hasten the day when the LDP would lose its parliamentary majority. Then either or both of the centrist parties would join the LDP in a coalition government. Though different party leaders vacillated at times between these two rationales for electoral cooperation, the overall trend from the early 1970s to the early 1980s was one of increasing disillusionment with the prospects of a united opposition. This disillusionment increased with the factional battles and rumors of defections in the LDP that surrounded scandal-tainted Prime Minister Tanaka Kakuei's resignation.

By 1979, internal opposition to the leftist (Kyōkaiha) domination of the Socialist Party had crystallized and strengthened. In 1980, moderates in the party, with the support of Sōhyō unions, turned the tables on the Kyōkaiha and reestablished a more moderate line in the Socialist Party. Having finally resolved its internal divisions, the party now committed itself to Socialist-centrist cooperation. This momentous change led to the second prominent election in the development of opposition-party cooperation—the 1980 double election.

The 1980 Double Election

The 1980 double election represents the peak in the number of formal electoral cooperation agreements. The most important among several proximate causes for this increase was the signing of a joint policy statement and cooperation agreement between the Socialists and the Clean Government Party. With this agreement, the Socialists abandoned their ten-year-old policy of all-opposition cooperation, cutting off all cooperative ties with the Communists. This change suddenly revived the stagnant Socialist-centrist cooperation efforts; the 1980 election became the culmination of the formal cooperation efforts of the 1970s.

In a surprise double election, though, the LDP dealt the opposition parties a crushing blow. The extensive cooperative efforts produced contradictory results. Cooperation became more difficult, because of increasing reluctance by the Clean Government Party to carry an inordinate share of the costs of electoral cooperation efforts. The centrist parties abandoned the opposition agenda and became even more clearly oriented toward the LDP. Future attempts to cooperate, though, became easier because of the precedent, set in 1980, of independent coalition candidates.

Factors That Made Cooperation Possible

Two trends of the 1970s provide an initial explanation of the peak in electoral cooperation in 1980. One was the continuing decline of the LDP's share of the popular vote. The decline reversed in the 1979

House of Representatives election, but most analysts ignored this first indication of an LDP revival. Commentators focused instead on the number of seats that the LDP lost in 1979.[36] The LDP ran too many candidates in 1979, and the party lost seats even though it gained in its share of the total vote. Because of the LDP's poor showing in 1979, the opposition parties were emboldened in their electoral cooperation efforts. At the time, it seemed quite possible for the opposition to take control of the House of Councillors in the 1980 election.

The opposition parties successfully toppled the government in a vote of no confidence when a group of LDP legislators abstained from the vote. LDP leaders responded seriously to the cooperation efforts of the opposition, by using this opportunity to call a surprise House of Representatives election on the same day as the previously scheduled House of Councillors election. Their strategy was to make opposition cooperation efforts in the House of Councillors election more difficult, by forcing the opposition parties to compete in a House of Representatives election while simultaneously cooperating in a House of Councillors election.[37] The opposition parties met the challenge put forth by the LDP, and rather than scaling back their cooperation efforts, they expanded their efforts to include a record number of House of Representatives districts. The stage was set for a crucial test of opposition electoral cooperation.

A second trend that contributed to the 1980 peak in electoral cooperation was the improvement in relations between and among three important political actors: the Clean Government Party, the Sōhyō unions, and the Dōmei unions. Relations improved for several reasons. The Clean Government Party insisted on concrete vote-transfer agreements with these unions as a prerequisite for electoral cooperation. This union-specific electoral cooperation helped parties to cooperate at the district level, despite barriers to formal cooperation at the national level. It also led to increased relations and a growing interdependence between the Clean Government Party and these unions. Party votes elected increasing numbers of union candidates. As a result, many Sōhyō and Dōmei unions became enthusiastic advocates of cooperation with the Clean Government Party.

Socialist-centrist relations also improved because the Sōhyō unions were gradually moving toward the political center. Antagonism between Sōhyō and Dōmei unions, which had hindered cooperation in 1971, was quickly ebbing away. Increasingly, serious talk addressed the issue of merging the two competing labor federations.

As the Sōhyō unions moved to the right, they used their ample influence to oppose the Socialist Party's swing to the left in the late 1970s. In 1977, the Electrical Workers Federation (Denki Rōren) announced that it was reassessing its support of the Socialist Party.[38] Sōhyō weighed in with its own, slightly veiled threat. In the 21 May 1979 issue of the Sōhyō newspaper, a high Sōhyō official published an article titled "Suggestions for a New Cooperative Relationship with the Socialist Party." This article sent a shock wave through the Socialist Party (Takamune 1979, 108). Sōhyō's dramatic threat to reassess its exclusive support of the Socialist Party encouraged Socialist leaders to abandon their all-opposition platform and sign the 1980 cooperation agreement with the Clean Government Party.

As Japan became one of the richest nations in the world, Japanese unions in general were becoming more moderate; hence, the Sōhyō unions moved to the center.[39] The unions were also finding greater success in pursuing their agenda through conciliation and through developing nascent relations with the LDP, rather than through the confrontational tactics of the 1960s and 1970s. These factors, combined with the increasing importance of Clean Government Party votes for union candidates, gave unions the incentive to push the Socialist Party toward the centrists and away from the Communists.

The Socialist Party had its own incentives to move toward the center, independent of Sōhyō pressure.[40] The centrist parties were gaining seats at the expense of the Socialist Party. The Socialists' serious defeat in 1979 made them more enthusiastic about cooperation in 1980 (just as they were receptive to cooperation overtures in 1971, after their 1969 losses). There was also a natural response within the party to the excesses of the radical Leftists; indeed, the radicals were nearly driven from the party as the moderates reasserted control. At the same time, the Communist Party was in a slump that made it less appealing as a cooperation partner. Socialist-Communist coalition candidates for mayor and governor continued to go down to defeat across the nation. Communist support in national elections had stagnated or declined since 1972. With the benefits of Socialist-Communist cooperation decreasing, the problems of cooperating with the Communists were more evident. The decline of the Communists also reduced the tactical advantages of locating the Socialist Party between the centrists and the Communists in electoral cooperation negotiations. The unattractive nature of the Communist cooperation option was further accentuated by the Soviet Union's invasion of Afghanistan in late 1979.

The Extent of Electoral Cooperation

The lineup of coalition candidates in the 1980 election was extensive. In the one-seat districts of the House of Councillors, five independents ran as coalition candidates. One of the candidates was truly an independent, three others were clearly affiliated with the Socialist party, and one had close ties with the Democratic Socialists.[41] Their use of the label "independent" not only attracted the support of a wide spectrum of voters, it also made it possible for the Democratic Socialists to join in the cooperative efforts. Though the Democratic Socialists and the Socialists never formally agreed to cooperate in this election, the Democratic Socialists could support these five independents as independents, without formally acknowledging any relationship with the Socialist Party.

The centrists also cooperated in five of the twenty-one multiseat districts of the House of Councillors. Centrist cooperation in these districts was similar to their long-established cooperation in the multiseat districts of the House of Representatives.

In the House of Representatives, the centrists cooperated formally in a record thirty-three districts—most of the districts in which cooperation was possible. Figure 4.10 shows that in only two districts did the Clean Government Party and the Democratic Socialists compete against each other suboptimally. Suboptimal competition is defined as a party running a candidate who fails to receive at least 80 percent of the votes necessary to win a seat. The eighteen districts of Osaka and Tokyo are excluded; in Tokyo, the centrists cooperate only informally, and in Osaka, the two parties compete so fiercely that the prefectural party organizations have never cooperated in the open districts of the prefecture. The eight districts labeled "1 Candidate/no cooperation" also appear to be failures in formal cooperation, because the party without a candidate in those districts could have supported the other party's candidate. Given the extent of informal cooperation, though, it is possible that cooperation actually occurred in some of these districts also.

In addition, the Clean Government Party and the Socialists cooperated formally in four districts. This small number reflects the party's historically minimal cooperation with the Socialists in House of Representatives races; the Socialists typically run candidates in most districts, leaving little room for reciprocal agreements with the Clean Government Party. Besides the formal cooperation in these districts, significant informal cooperation also developed between the Sōhyō unions and the Dōmei unions, and between the unions and the Clean Government Party.

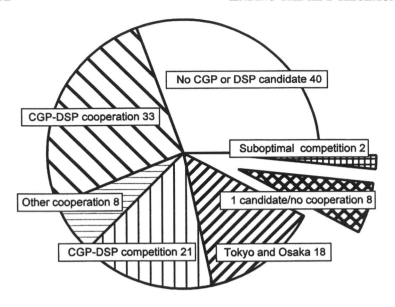

Note: Units are election districts. There were a total of 130 districts.

Figure 4.10 Clean Government Party (CGP)–Democratic Socialists (DSP) cooperation in the 1980 House of Representatives election

The LDP Victory and Its Aftermath

Despite the record number of coalition agreements, the LDP's double-election strategy was extremely successful in dividing the opposition. During the election campaign, the Socialist and Democratic Socialist leaders spent more time attacking each other than uniting in a common attack on the LDP. Democratic Socialist politicians attacked Socialist policies to shore up their positions with conservative-leaning voters.[42] Party chairman Sasaki Ryōsaku announced during the campaign that the Democratic Socialists would join the LDP in a coalition government if the LDP lost its parliamentary majority; Democratic Socialists would not participate in a coalition government dominated by the Socialist Party.[43] The Socialists quickly answered Sasaki's attack, and it became obvious to voters that the opposition parties were united only in their mutual dislike of each other.

When the votes were counted, the LDP scored a resounding victory —in terms of the popular vote, its greatest victory since 1967. The

Socialists had repeated their disastrous performance of 1979. The Communists lost one-fourth of their seats in the House of Representatives, and the Clean Government Party lost more than one-third of its seats. Four of the five independent coalition candidates in the House of Councillors, as well as most of the centrist coalition candidates in both houses, were defeated.

The twofold explanation for this defeat is opposition disunity and a high voter turnout that helped the LDP. The double election and a sympathy vote for the LDP because of the death of Prime Minister Ōhira Masayoshi during the election campaign helped raise the turnout of conservative voters. Clean Government Party leaders interpreted their party's defeat as a direct result of their overextending their party's resources in cooperation efforts. The experience of the 1980 election made party leaders much more careful about electoral cooperation. The Clean Government Party had enthusiastically embraced cooperative arrangements with both the Socialists and the Democratic Socialists, only to have its two allies undermine the cooperative agreements by viciously attacking each other during the campaign.[44]

This election reinforced two trends of the late 1970s: a movement toward union-based rather than party-based cooperation agreements, and a turning of the centrists away from the Socialists and toward the LDP. Clean Government Party disillusionment with electoral cooperation pushed that party more and more toward union-specific, often informal cooperative arrangements. These arrangements posed a lesser threat to, and had a more guaranteed return for, the party. It favored such arrangements because party leaders could limit their contribution to a set number of votes, with greater assurance that they would receive an equivalent number of votes from the unions in exchange. Informal cooperation arrangements were also less risky to the Clean Government Party because such arrangements were less subject to the election posturing of the parties.

The election also changed the ultimate cooperation goal of the centrist parties. The 1980 campaign destroyed even the facade of opposition unity. It was now publicly acknowledged that electoral cooperation was useful only as a tool to force the LDP into a coalition government. Nevertheless, the two centrist parties waited until 1985 to remove from their cooperation agreement a clause stating that the parties would "not enter into any coalition with the LDP."[45]

At the same time, the 1980 election had a positive effect on electoral cooperation. For the first time, the Socialists agreed to have coalition candidates run as independents rather than as party affiliates. Though four of these five independents lost in 1980, this breakthrough in opposition cooperation would come back to haunt the LDP in 1989. It was a significant development, because making a cooperation candidate an independent eliminates obstacles such as hostile relations at the party level, or animosity between supporters of different parties. Cooperation negotiations can take place informally; no formal agreement between the parties is needed.

Independent candidates also have an advantage in attracting unaffiliated voters, thus expanding the scope of electoral cooperation to include the entire electorate. Union-specific agreements and informal cooperative efforts are often limited to only the relevant sector of the electorate; the agreement to cooperate is often not publicized outside the cooperating organizations. In contrast, an independent candidacy can take advantage of its nonpartisan nature to make a broad appeal to supporters of any political parties.

Electoral Cooperation in the 1980s

From the 1980 double election until the 1989 House of Councillors election, the opposition parties were generally unenthusiastic about expanding formal electoral cooperation. The Socialists wanted to continue to receive one-sided support from the Clean Government Party, but the Clean Government Party was much more careful about entering cooperation agreements. Even the long-standing centrist cooperative arrangements began to decline in number. The era of unbridled optimism under the banner of electoral cooperation had come to a close. The number of formal cooperation districts declined. The increasing use of union-specific cooperation meant that cooperation helped only a few marginal candidates to victory. The idea of an opposition-led coalition government was ridiculed as a joke.

The Decline and Marginalization of Formal Electoral Cooperation

Electoral cooperation stagnated in the 1980s, but what did occur kept alive two important features of opposition party cooperation. Ties between the parties, especially between the Clean Government Party and the unions, became stronger as formal and informal cooperation arrangements were repeated in each election. Moreover, cooperative efforts in the 1980s provided the incentives for continued policy concessions from the Socialist Party. These policy concessions and improved relations preserved the potential to resume large-scale cooperative efforts, such as occurred in 1989.

Cooperation during the 1980s was more difficult because few elections presented good opportunities for cooperation. There was no cooperation in the 1983 House of Councillors election (with the exception of Okinawa) because the opposition parties were unsure of the effects of the brand-new, proportional representation system in the national constituency of the House of Councillors. Voters would now write a party's name, rather than a candidate's name, on the national constituency ballot. The Democratic Socialists tried to boost their proportional representation vote by running as many candidates as possible in the prefectural constituencies. Party leaders hoped that supporters attracted to the polling booth by the prefectural constituency race would then also cast their proportional representation ballots for the party.

Cooperation in the 1983 House of Councillors election was also discouraged by the threat of another double election.[46] The House of Representatives election was not held until six months later, but the rumors of a double election further diminished opposition enthusiasm for electoral cooperation. Cooperation in the 1986 House of Coun-

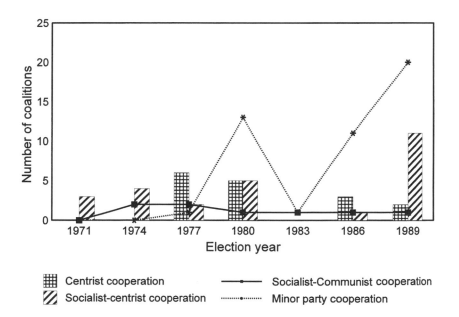

Figure 4.11 Formal electoral cooperation in the House of Councillors

cillors election was also hindered because it became Japan's second double election.

The stagnation or decline of electoral cooperation in the 1980s cannot be blamed entirely on double elections. Double elections increase competition in House of Councillors races, making electoral cooperation there more difficult, but in the House of Representatives, elections are already extremely competitive. The addition of a simultaneous House of Councillors race does not increase the level of competition in House of Representatives races.

Figure 4.11 shows how double elections and the new electoral system negatively affected levels of formal cooperation in the House of Councillors, but a more interesting trend is the decline in formal centrist cooperation in both houses in the 1980s (figs. 4.11 and 4.12). In figures 4.11 and 4.12, only the New Liberal Club and the Social Democratic League are counted as minor parties. Minor party cooperation includes agreements between the two minor parties or between the minor parties and only one of the major parties.

The decline in centrist party cooperation stems from the decrease in the number of districts having party support levels sufficient to create

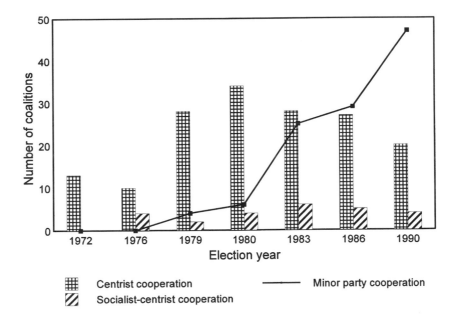

Figure 4.12 Formal electoral cooperation in the House of Representatives

incentives for coalition candidates. In particular, because the Democratic Socialist vote was shrinking, Clean Government Party operatives faced two barriers to maintaining high levels of centrist cooperation: (1) finding viable Democratic Socialist candidates whom the Clean Government Party could support, and (2) obtaining enough Democratic Socialist votes for Clean Government Party candidates to balance Clean Government Party support of Democratic Socialist candidates.

An additional difficulty arose from the geographic or union linkage mechanism of centrist cooperation. To have effective vote transfers, centrist leaders preferred to link cooperation districts that were contiguous or in the same prefecture, or to link districts by the union affiliations of the Democratic Socialist candidates. For example, a Democratic Socialist candidate hailing from the union Zensen Dōmei received Clean Government Party support in exchange for Democratic Socialist support of Clean Government candidates in two districts in which Zensen Dōmei was the dominant Democratic Socialist union.

These linkages facilitate vote transfers, but they also limit the number of cooperation districts to those that can be effectively paired with an equivalent district either geographically or organizationally. Thus, when one coalition candidate disappears because he retires, dies, or gives up, cooperation in that candidate's district is put on hold until a new candidate can be found. If a replacement cannot be found, cooperation in the formerly paired district also tends to fall apart, because local party activists and the union rank and file will cooperate enthusiastically only if their efforts are reciprocated in an appropriate companion district.[47]

Centrist cooperation also declined because in some districts the local Democratic Socialist organization refused to continue cooperative relations with the Clean Government Party. In at least one district, the Democratic Socialists switched to supporting the Socialist candidate because Socialist–Democratic Socialist relations improved with the creation of Rengō, the unified labor federation. In other districts, Democratic Socialist leaders were unhappy with the effects of continued cooperation on the political activity of their union supporters.

This decline in formal cooperation, coupled with the rise of union-specific agreements, led to the marginalization of electoral cooperation. Union-specific agreements helped the Clean Government Party by making it possible to better monitor the actual delivery of votes to the party, but one specific union can deliver only several thousand votes, at most, in one election district. Though an innovation in cooperation, the strategy significantly limited the scope of electoral cooperation. It was successful in dividing the votes equally between multiple candidates, but it was ineffective in creating broad, general support of a solitary opposition candidate.

A Shift toward the LDP

The marginalization of electoral cooperation was not totally inconsistent with each of the centrist parties' long-term strategies. Both the Democratic Socialists (since 1974) and the Clean Government Party (since 1980) desired to become a coalition partner of the LDP. The use of limited cooperation in marginal districts enabled them to reduce the LDP majority, possibly forcing it into a minority position, without accepting the leadership of the Socialist Party that more extensive forms of cooperation entailed. Informal cooperation allowed them to obtain the benefits of cooperation without significantly modifying their policies or constraining their independence.

The shift toward the LDP was exemplified in centrist support of the Nikaidō plot of 1984. Nikaidō Susumu sought and received promises that he could count on centrist support in his challenge of Prime Minister Nakasone's continued leadership of the LDP.

Centrist disillusionment with the Socialists also took the form of an increased emphasis on centrist cooperation. For example, the Democratic Socialists proposed in 1982 that the two centrist parties and two minor parties (the Clean Government Party, the Democratic Socialist Party, the Social Democratic League, and the New Liberal Club) form an election strategy committee. Democratic Socialist leaders wanted to cooperate in putting up centrist candidates in the many districts in which there were only Socialist, Communist, and LDP candidates. Clean Government Party leaders rejected the Democratic Socialists' proposal, citing their party's need to rebuild after its disastrous losses of 1980. The three remaining parties then continued to negotiate a possible merger within the Diet, but the Clean Government Party killed those plans when it announced in November 1982 that it "would not cooperate with a new political power formed by the joint efforts of the other three centrist parties."[48] Creating a significant centrist force would be doomed to failure if the Clean Government Party refused to cooperate.

Even the Socialists gave up on the possibility of an opposition coalition government. One commentator explained the Socialist reluctance to cooperate more extensively in House of Representatives elections. He said that many in the party believed that more effective electoral cooperation would only lead to an LDP-centrist coalition government. Greater Socialist efforts to cooperate would thus yield the ironic result of isolating the party and decreasing Socialist influence, if the cooperation efforts were successful and if the LDP then lost its parliamentary majority and formed a coalition government with the centrist parties (Semba 1986, 40).

Positive Features of Electoral Cooperation in the 1980s

The marginalization of electoral cooperation and the turning of the centrists toward the LDP enhanced the deep cynicism about electoral cooperation that developed in the 1980s; yet the cooperative efforts the opposition made during this period did bear fruit. The decline in formal cooperation was countered by a healthy level of informal cooperation and by the increasingly good relations between the Clean Government Party and the various unions. This party often bypassed other political parties to establish direct relations with each union's national headquarters. In the 1980s, these relations became quite stable and routinized.

The following is an example of how one such relationship developed between the Clean Government Party and a union affiliated with the Socialist Party.[49] Before the late 1970s, the Clean Government Party and this union cooperated informally on the local level. Union and party officials in a prefecture or election district would agree to a cooperative arrangement that did not involve the national headquarters of either group. In the late 1970s, this union formally announced that it would cooperate in some districts with the Clean Government Party. From that time forward, specific cooperation districts have been negotiated between the union and the party at the national level. In these cooperation agreements, both the party and the union promise to deliver specific numbers of votes in specified districts to a cooperation candidate. The union provides verification of this promise by turning over lists of union members who have agreed to support a specific party candidate. A union representative then accompanies a party activist to visit the listed union members. Though the union publicizes its cooperative agreements with the Clean Government Party, it never reveals specifics, such as the actual cooperation districts, because it does not want to be blamed if a Socialist candidate were to lose in a district in which the union was shifting some votes to a Clean Government Party candidate.

This cooperative arrangement operated smoothly in the 1980s in all the House of Representatives, House of Councillors, and unified local

elections. In the 1990 House of Representatives election, the union supported Clean Government Party candidates in four districts in exchange
for Clean Government Party support of union-affiliated candidates (all
Socialists) in five districts. In the 1990 election, the Clean Government
Party transferred 75,000 votes to the union, and the union transferred
23,000 votes to the party.

Informal cooperation between the Clean Government Party and
Socialist unions is quite extensive. In the 1983 House of Councillors election, the Socialists and the Clean Government Party formally cooperated in four districts, but cooperated informally in approximately six
others (Ishigami 1984, 138). Similarly, the union described above had
informal cooperative arrangements with the Clean Government Party
in nine districts in the 1990 election, whereas there was only one formal
Socialist–Clean Government Party cooperation district in the same
election.

In comparison, cooperation between the Clean Government Party
and the Democratic Socialist unions has been more formalized since its
inception. Union-specific cooperation agreements between the Clean
Government Party and the Democratic Socialists were always approved
at the party level because, unlike cooperation with the Socialist Party,
there are few party-level barriers to centrist cooperation. In some districts, however, the cooperation arrangements are kept secret. For
example, all cooperative arrangements in Tokyo are kept informal. This
happens because in Tokyo, the Democratic Socialists receive much
support from the Federation of New Religions—a rival of the Clean
Government Party's main support group Sōka gakkai. Estimates of the
extent of informal centrist cooperation are rare. One commentator indicates that the centrists cooperated informally in an additional eleven
districts in the 1979 House of Representatives election (Nagata Jirō
[pseud.] 1980, 86–87).

The extent of informal cooperative relations shows that a healthy
network of relations exists between the opposition parties and the various affiliated support organizations. These relations actually expanded in
the 1980s, despite the decrepit nature of formal party relations between
the Socialist and centrist parties. The affiliated unions put pressure on
their respective party organizations to improve relations, and they laid
the groundwork for improved future relations between the opposition
parties.

A second positive feature of electoral cooperation in the 1980s was
that the Socialists undertook policy modifications in exchange for Clean

Government Party electoral support.[50] Though members of the Clean Government Party expressed their frustration with the slow pace of change in the Socialist Party,[51] their pressure was crucial in bringing about changes in Socialist policies. Reformers within the Socialist Party have used the promise of Clean Government Party electoral support as a prod to promote changes in an otherwise reluctant party.

A New Era of Cooperation: The 1989 House of Councillors Election

In 1989, the opposition parties finally took control of the House of Councillors in a firm repudiation of the LDP. At the time, this victory was heralded as a turning point in Japanese politics. For the first time since its creation, the LDP had unequivocally lost control of a House of the Japanese Diet. Many expected that the opposition parties would also defeat the LDP in the House of Representatives election that had to be held within the year.

The LDP nevertheless went on to a resounding victory in the 1990 House of Representatives election. The 1989 victory of the opposition quickly came to be seen as a fluke, an unfortunate (for the LDP) coincidental occurrence of several factors that was unlikely ever to occur again. Though there is some truth in this analysis of events in 1989 and 1990, it misses some significant developments. Several barriers in opposition cooperation were overcome in the 1989 election that made a radical shake-up of the Japanese political system a much greater possibility in the future. The victory of the opposition in 1989, coupled with the creation of the unified labor federation Rengō, forced the centrist parties to reassess their strategic options. These events also helped pull the Socialists into a more moderate, procooperation position. The opposition parties were in a better position to cooperate (despite ill will over the subsequent 1990 election) than they had been in the past ten years.

Explanations of the 1989 Opposition Victory

From the outset, the 1989 House of Councillors election had prospects of being a banner year for electoral cooperation because of the recent progress in the labor federation unification movement. In November 1987, the private sector unions joined together to form the new national labor federation Rengō; the public sector unions had promised to disband their competing federation Sōhyō and join Rengō in the fall of 1989.[52] Despite the fact that union federation unification was not yet complete at the time of the 1989 election, the unified organization was functioning.

Rengō facilitated electoral cooperation because it provided an umbrella organization for the Socialist Party and the two centrist parties.[53] The main support unions for both the Socialists and the Democratic Socialists were Rengō affiliates; and the Clean Government Party not only had ongoing cooperative relations with many of the unions, but the party also had members in each of the unions. These links allowed Rengō to act as an important conduit for cooperation votes and resources. Whereas in the past, union votes may not have transferred effectively across competing union federation and party lines, the Rengō organization held out the promise of more effective vote transfers and a larger percent of union voters that could be effectively mobilized for an election.

The Rengō organization was important because of its relative impartiality, which could be used as a cover both for cooperation negotiations and coalition candidates, and its control of a large block of votes that could be mustered in support of electoral cooperation. The appearance of Rengō on the electoral cooperation scene meant across-the-board increased prospects for electoral cooperation success. Prefectural party leaders could now count on greater union support of coalition candidates for finances, personnel, and most important, votes. In addition, Rengō made it easier to recruit truly independent candidates. At least in the short term, Rengō promised to make many more districts winnable for coalition candidates than had ever been so in the past.

Besides heralding the new impetus to cooperate that Rengō provided, 1989 proved to be a year when the LDP appeared to be faltering. Enthusiasm for cooperation boomed as the prospects for an opposition victory increased. The list of LDP woes included the Recruit Scandal, which brought down the government of Prime Minister Takeshita Noboru. His replacement, Uno Sōsuke, was dogged by a scandal involving a former mistress. The public was also discontented with the newly enacted national sales tax; in rural areas, farmers were upset with LDP agricultural policies. The Socialist Party was being led by a woman, Doi Takako, who was popular and spearheaded Socialist efforts to field a large number of women candidates for the House of Councillors election; this also contributed to the LDP's decline.

As a result, coalition candidates were put up in ten of the twenty-six one-seat districts and in two of the two-seat districts. These candidates were listed as Rengō candidates, and party leaders agreed that the candidates would remain unaffiliated under the Rengō name after the election.

In the election, either the Socialist or the Rengō candidate won in twenty-three of the twenty-six one-seat districts.[54] In the simultaneous proportional representation voting, the Socialist Party actually outpolled the LDP, 35 percent to 27 percent. Many analysts were quick to credit opposition cooperation for the victory, but as is typical with electoral cooperation, it is difficult to prove that claim. For example, Miyakawa Takayoshi (Shinohara, Ishikawa, and Masamura 1979, 32–33) credits much of the boom to Rengō candidates. He claims that Rengō candidates did well because they were nonpartisan and therefore drew more unaffiliated or disaffected voters. Takagi Ikurō (1989, 72) is more conservative in his postelection analysis. He credits Rengō with pushing the opposition over the top in certain districts, but he also recognizes that all the Rengō candidates rode on the crest of a Socialist boom.

This dispute is difficult to resolve, just as it was difficult to show the exact extent to which electoral cooperation helped the eight Socialist victors in the 1971 House of Councillors election. In 1989, both Rengō and Socialist candidates did well. In their only head-to-head race in Okayama prefecture, the Socialist candidate defeated the Rengō candidate. Because of this ambiguity, both procooperation and anticooperation advocates could use the same election results to support their respective positions, even after the 1989 election.

Response of the Socialist Party

The success of Socialist candidates, especially in Okayama, encouraged many members of the Socialist Party to discount the effects of electoral cooperation in the 1989 election. Socialist leaders were circumspect in their expressions of gratitude to their centrist allies, but their honest opinions came out in postelection debates within the party over the best election strategy for the upcoming 1990 House of Representatives election. Cooperation veterans, such as former chairman Ishibashi, urged the party to enter into widespread cooperative arrangements with the centrists. He suggested that the Socialists help the weaker Clean Government Party by shifting excess union votes to threatened Clean Government Party candidates. He urged the Socialist Party to run only 150 candidates, shifting excess Socialist votes to centrist candidates in forty or fifty districts.[55]

The leaders of the Socialist Party, ignoring Ishibashi's suggestions, built on the Socialist boom in electoral support by running a larger number of candidates in the 1990 election. They agreed to cooperate with the centrists in only a few districts with special circumstances.[56] In other ways the Socialists showed their insensitivity to their centrist allies. Political commentator Tawara Kōtarō blamed the Socialist Party for alienating its centrist allies by getting the other parties to pay legislative investigation costs, to conserve party finances (Tawara, Masamura, and Inoguchi 1990, 130). Socialist-centrist cooperation was completely exhausted by the 1990 election. The centrist parties resented the fact that, even when cooperation was successful, as in 1989, all the benefits flowed exclusively to the Socialists. After the 1989 election, Clean Government Party chairman Ishida Kōshirō said, "When we rode the horse of opposition cooperation, we fell off and got trampled by it. We don't ever want to ride that horse again" (Nakamura, Uchida, and Matsuzaki 1990).

In the 1990 House of Representatives election, the Socialists and the LDP did well, winning additional seats from the Communists and the centrist parties. The Socialist boom died down by 1991, though, and in the unified local elections that year, the Socialists went down to a resounding defeat. The Socialist boom of 1989 and 1990 had become merely an aberration because of an unlikely coincidence of several events.

Effect of the 1989 Election on Electoral Cooperation

Despite the fact that the Socialist boom died out, the 1989 opposition victory does have long-term significance, which commentators often overlook. The opposition parties were very successful in fielding truly independent candidates as their coalition candidates. Of the twelve Rengō candidates, five were lawyers, two were educators, three were broadcast personalities, and only two were party politicians closely affiliated with the Socialist Party. This represents a significant increase in the independence of coalition candidates over the previous attempt in 1980. The agreement to have these candidates remain in the unaffiliated political group Rengō Sangiin after the election also ensured their continued independence. Though such single-seat districts were rare in Japan's electoral systems, they suddenly became much more common with the introduction of three hundred single-seat districts in the 1994 reforms. The 1989 election provided an opportunity for the opposition parties to develop their ability to run a single candidate.

The formation of Rengō, along with its political activities, also had long-term significance, becoming an important first step in the party reformulation that occurred in 1993. The actual reform scenario took a turn that was contrary to Rengō's interests: The Socialists and Democratic Socialists ended up in opposing camps from 1994 to 1997.[57] The Rengō connection was crucial, however, in gaining Socialist support for the initial Hosokawa coalition government, and Rengō's influence has increased again with the reunification of all of Rengō's unions under the banner of the Democratic Party.

The opposition victory in the House of Councillors cannot be entirely explained by the cumulative effect of a series of election-specific factors. The electoral system of the House of Councillors is not as favorable to the LDP as the electoral system of the House of Representatives. Voting can be much more volatile in the House of Councillors because the campaigns typically focus more on the party and on national issues than on local candidate identification. The proportional-representation vote is obviously influenced by party rather than by candidate identification. Even in the prefectural vote, the large size of election districts makes candidate-voter linkages more attenuated than in House of Representative elections. For example, in Japan's least-populated prefectures, House of Councillors candidates require twice as many votes as their counterparts in House of Representatives elections. In larger prefectures, the disparity is much greater. The top two House of Councillors candidates in Tokyo each won in 1989 with more than a million votes; the highest vote winner in a Tokyo House of Representatives race won 242,000 votes. This attenuation makes it more difficult for LDP candidates in the House of Councillors to use personal support groups as a buffer against national swings in LDP popularity.[58]

Besides the electoral system, strategic voting helps the opposition parties' efforts in the House of Councillors. Many Japanese voters favor continued LDP rule but vote for the opposition in House of Councillors elections to "send a message" to the LDP or to restrain excesses of the LDP. Determining conclusively the motivations behind such ticket splitting is difficult, but its existence is accepted as a given in the Japanese political landscape. Nevertheless, the stability of the gap between the LDP vote in House of Councillors and House of Representatives elections over time supports the contention that this gap stems, at least in part, from the different electoral systems, rather than solely from strategic voting (fig. 4.13).[59]

Given the distinct nature of House of Councillors elections, it is not

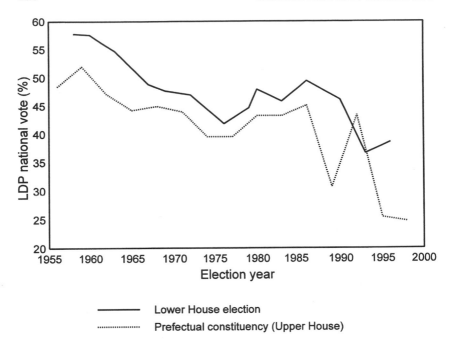

Figure 4.13 Comparison of LDP national vote percentages in House of Representatives elections and prefectural constituency races of House of Councillors elections

surprising that the LDP failed to win a majority in that House from 1989 to 1998.[60] Of course, the flip side of this argument is also true: LDP support is stronger in the House of Representatives than it is in the House of Councillors. Many of the same people who vote for a protest party or against the LDP in the House of Councillors election return to the fold to support their local LDP candidate in House of Representatives races. Opposition control of the House of Councillors also contributed marginally to the overall reformist impulse of Japanese politics. It forced the LDP to rely even more than it had in the past on at least partial opposition support for the passage of most legislation. It also increased the links between the opposition parties and the bureaucracy. Bureaucrats could no longer rely on the LDP alone to ensure the passage of important legislation. In the wake of the 1989 election, the ministries all expanded and enhanced their contacts with the opposition parties.

These increased contacts between the opposition and the LDP and between the opposition and the bureaucracy were significant not because they were new (they were only strengthened) and not because they gave the opposition greater power (indeed, these contacts made it more difficult for the opposition to remain united against the LDP). The contacts were significant because they laid the groundwork for a reformulation of the Japanese political system. These contacts made it easier for factional leaders of the LDP to envision themselves joining the opposition parties in a new political party. Through greater participation, the opposition parties gained more experience in governing, more information, and more contacts. These changes weakened the perception of the opposition as irresponsible and incapable of governing, thus opening the door to a shake-up of Japan's party system.

Electoral Cooperation in 1993 and 1996

It may seem incongruous to discuss electoral cooperation in 1993 and 1996 together, since these two elections were conducted under different electoral systems. The party reformulations that occurred before the 1993 election radically changed the pattern of electoral cooperation, however, making the cooperation patterns of these two elections more similar than all previous elections.

Both these elections show the importance of numerical incentives to cooperate. Cooperative alliances formed in 1993 and expanded in 1996 would have been unthinkable in previous elections, but they became a reality because of numerical incentives to cooperate in specific election districts. The numerical incentives were greater because many more parties were competing in the 1993 election. A greater number of national-level parties meant more districts in which one or more parties had no hope of electing a candidate. There were, therefore, more opportunities for parties to coordinate their support of each other's candidates.

The elections were also similar in that the door was opened to cooperation between the LDP and the opposition parties. This door opened slightly in 1993 when LDP renegades cooperated with the opposition parties. By 1996, the world of electoral alliances had turned upside down, every party cooperating with every other possible party with the sole exception of the Communist Party, which continued to run its own candidates in every district. The levels of electoral cooperation remained high in 1996 because, as in 1993, there were a large number of parties. Electoral cooperation was also spurred by the implementation of single-seat districts, which raised the threshold for election, making it imperative for small parties either to merge or join in electoral alliances.

Finally, the electoral cooperation of 1993 and 1996 show the candidate-centered nature of Japanese campaigns. Unlike more party-oriented campaigns in single-seat districts elsewhere, in Japan, many strong candidates won their districts regardless of their party affiliations. Though single-seat districts created strong pressure for party consolidation, some small parties survived the onslaught because of the popularity of some of their members in specific districts. For example, the New Party Harbinger and the Socialist Party won in some districts despite polling only 1 and 6 percent, respectively, of the proportional representation vote.

The 1993 election is most notable for the split in the LDP that produced the Renewal Party and the New Party Harbinger. These two parties joined the previously formed Japan New Party as non-LDP conservative parties. None of these new parties ran candidates in every district, so the door was open for cooperation between each other and between them and the other opposition parties. Table 4.1 shows how some parties had more open districts, districts where they were not running a candidate and therefore could have entered into a cooperation agreement with another party. The table also shows the wide variety of cooperation agreements reached between the different parties.

These patterns of cooperation show that no party completely exhausted its cooperation possibilities. However, two points should be kept in mind. First, this is a list only of formal cooperative agreements between parties at the national level. It excludes all cooperation agreements brokered locally, and it excludes cooperative arrangements with independents and minor party candidates.[61] It also excludes informal cooperation, such as agreements between unions and religious groups for vote exchanges. For example, the Clean Government Party and the Renewal Party informally cooperated extensively, despite the fact that they formally cooperated in only one district. Analysts at the newspaper *Asahi Shimbun* (Tokyo) observed that "without a doubt both parties had extensive and informal electoral cooperation with each other" (Asahi shimbun senkyo honbu 1993, 12). The Democratic Socialist Party and the Japan New Party also relied heavily on informal cooperation. The Japan New Party formally endorsed twelve Democratic Socialists, but there were no reciprocal endorsements from the Democratic Socialist Party. This was because the Japan New Party, wanting to preserve its image as a "new" party, asked that all Democratic Socialist support be conducted informally through union endorsements of its candidates. It is likely that if local and informal cooperation agreements are included, there was cooperation in most districts where cooperation meant there

Table 4.1 Formal Electoral Cooperation in the 1993 House of Representatives Election

Party	Number of Candidates	Number of Open Districts	Number of Districts with Formal Cooperation	Cooperative Partner and Number of Districts with That Partner
Liberal Democratic Party	285	1	2	Independent or minor party (2)
Socialist	142	7	12	Social Democratic League (3) Independent or minor party (9)
Communist	129	0	0	
Renewal	69	60	15	Democratic Socialist (5) Clean Government Party (1) Independent or minor party (9)
Japan New Party	55	74	36	Democratic Socialist (12) New Party Harbinger (9) Socialist (2) Independent or minor party (13)
Clean Government	54	75	7	Democratic Socialist (5) Independent or minor party (2)
Democratic Socialist	28	101	31	Socialist (8) Renewal (6) Clean Government Party (6) New Party Harbinger (1) Social Democratic League (1) Independent or minor party (9)
New Party Harbinger	15	114	46	Japan New Party (43) Independent or minor party (3)

Note: Party support of independent or minor party candidates often results in major party cooperation, as multiple parties often support the same independent or minor party candidate. In the multiseat districts of this election, larger parties can have more districts with cooperation than open districts because larger parties often run more than one candidate per district.

was something to be gained. I do not mean to claim that every party had a cooperation arrangement in every district. Rather, in districts where a party had a presence and a potential candidate to support, cooperation probably occurred.

In the climate of electoral cooperation in 1993 and 1996, barriers were broken down to all different forms of cooperation. The opposition parties were now supporting former members of the LDP. These conservative break-off parties were now supporting candidates of the opposition parties. The extent to which this occurred is more apparent in the evidence of informal cooperation. Despite only one instance of formal cooperation between the Clean Government Party and the Renewal Party, extensive informal cooperation existed between those two parties. Similarly, the Socialist Party did not formally endorse any of the LDP break-off party candidates, but affiliated unions in this election began endorsing such candidates and began withholding their support from Socialists who opposed their agenda to reform the party system. The Democratic Socialists also linked up informally with the Japan New Party. These links were perhaps less significant in 1993, but they paved the way for the growing cooperation among all parties in the 1996 elections.

In 1996, the possibilities for cooperation remained high because there were still many political parties. Though the Renewal Party, the Japan New Party, the Democratic Socialist Party, and the Clean Government Party had all merged into the New Frontier Party, one additional major new party—the Democratic Party—had been created. In the three hundred new single-seat districts, only the Communists ran candidates in nearly every district. The other parties expanded the varied patterns of cooperation that existed in 1993 (table 4.2).

These patterns of formal cooperation were repeated even more extensively at the informal level. Most of the major Socialist-affiliated unions endorsed the candidates of the Democratic Party, but in other districts, they often endorsed LDP or New Frontier Party candidates. The Clean Government Party retained its separate prefectural organizations even though its national organization had merged into the New Frontier Party. Though these local organizations formally endorsed all the candidates of the New Frontier Party, the support organization Sōka gakkai was more selective in its endorsements, and it continued its longstanding cooperative arrangements with unions at the local level. Similarly, the union federation Rengō identified twenty important districts for cooperation with candidates from both the Democratic and the New Frontier Parties, and its call for cooperation exceeded, both in number and influence, the eleven formal cooperation districts designated by the two parties themselves.

This wide-ranging pattern of new alliances was facilitated by the different alliances that had been created in the political realm over the pre-

Table 4.2 Formal Electoral Cooperation in the One-Seat Districts of the 1996 House of Representatives Election

Party	Number of Candidates	Number of Open Districts	Number of Districts with Formal Cooperation	Cooperative Partner and Number of Districts with That Partner
Communists	299	1	1	Minor party (1)
Liberal Democratic Party	288	12	8	New Party Harbinger (4) Democrats (3) Japan Socialist Party (1)
New Frontier Party	235	65	20	Independent and minor (14) Democrats (6)
Democrats	143	157	26	Independent and Minor (13) New Party Harbinger (6) New Frontier Party (6) Liberal Democratic Party (1)
Socialists	43	257	10	New Party Harbinger (5) Liberal Democratic Party (3) Independent (2)
New Party Harbinger	13	287	45	Democrats (18) Socialists (16) Liberal Democratic Party (10) Independent or minor (1)

Note: Party support of independent or minor party candidates often results in major party cooperation, as multiple parties often support the same independent or minor party candidate.

vious three years. Rengō unions had their members as candidates in the New Frontier Party, the Socialist Party, and the Democratic Party. The coalition government among the LDP, the Socialists, and the New Party Harbinger opened doors for cooperation among those parties. Socialist-affiliated unions had for years been building strong relations with LDP legislators having expertise in their specific fields; now, the opening of doors to the LDP allowed them to formally support some of these friends. The one party axis of no cooperation was the LDP and the New Frontier Party. These two parties are the closest in ideology and temperament, but their mutual aspiration to become the dominant party left little room for cooperation. Where cooperation was possible, it did not occur. In those districts, it was instead more common for the New Frontier Party to refrain from putting up a candidate, allowing its party's support to flow to the non-LDP candidate as part of a common "anti-LDP" front.

This varied pattern of electoral cooperation is more a creation of the opportunities created by the large number of parties than an inherency in the electoral system. If the single-seat districts had the effect that its founders intended and only two major parties had emerged, there would be no room for electoral cooperation, just as there is little room for that kind of cooperation in the United States. However, if the multiple-party system is sustained, cooperation will continue to play a significant role as a halfway station that parties can use, thereby easing the pressure to merge created by single-seat districts. Indeed, since the 1996 elections, the pattern has been for increasing defections rather than for mergers. Multiple defections, culminating in the disbanding of the New Frontier Party, resulted in a plethora of new parties with such names as Sun Party, From Five, New Peace Party, and the Liberal Party.

Perhaps in preparation for the next election, scheduled to be held in late 1999 or 2000, a countertrend of consolidation began in 1998, with the Liberal Party moving into alliance with the LDP and most of the other parties consolidating under the leadership of the Democratic Party. The former Clean Government Party members remain uncommitted to any alliance. Perhaps they will follow the strategy of working with all possible partners, depending on the local situation, to maximize their seats won. The Communists still remain committed to an independent, noncoalitional strategy.

After a postelection period of defection and regrouping, the parties have largely settled into the electoral alliances that they are likely to use in the next election. This consolidation has reduced the need for electoral cooperation. It will still occur between the LDP and the Liberals, and it will be important to the former Clean Government Party members. The Democratic Party, even if it runs candidates in most districts, will also rely on cooperation in helping elect like-minded independents and minor party candidates. Electoral cooperation could also increase in importance if there are more defections or party splits. Electoral cooperation probably will remain an important and useful tool of parties in Japanese elections.

5

Party Cooperation and Strategies of Party Reorganization

In 1970, a Japanese journalist wrote an account of the events surrounding the formation of the two coalition governments of 1947–1948, which included the Socialist Party. Unfortunately, the author could find no publisher for his work. At that time, there was little interest in two brief coalition governments of the late 1940s, coalition governments that seemed to have been aberrations, given the long, uninterrupted rule of the LDP and its conservative predecessors. Interest in the manuscript rose, however, with the LDP's loss in the 1989 House of Councillors election. Coalition governments then seemed a possibility, and the revival of the Socialist Party made a study of its only period in power especially relevant. The manuscript was published in 1990 (Matsuoka 1990).

Similarly, the various opposition plots to seize power from the LDP, to split the LDP, or to join with the LDP have not been the subject of scholarly attention or analysis. The machinations of an ostracized, largely irrelevant opposition, though interesting, did not seem particularly noteworthy, given the strong rule of the LDP and the need to better understand the LDP's complex processes of decision making and governing practices.

Events of the late 1980s and the 1990s have likewise changed these attitudes. The story of coalition building in the postwar period gives a historical context to the events of the 1990s. More important, this story sheds light on Japanese party relations, on opposition failure and success, and on the likely success or failure of future coalition governments. As with the elections described previously, each of the events described in this chapter is full of specific, idiosyncratic factors that defy general-

ization. My analysis acknowledges this rich contextual knowledge while
distilling out important patterns and commonalities.

Common Themes

Four themes emerge from the history of coalition efforts. First, the splitting of the LDP and the creation of a non-LDP coalition government,
along with proposals for electoral reform and for reducing the influence
of money in politics, all have their roots in the coalition efforts of the
1960s, 1970s, and 1980s. Plots and schemes similar to those of the 1990s
were ubiquitous throughout the postwar period. The strategies of 1993
were not created in a vacuum; rather, they were the final fruition of one
of these many nascent plans. The Socialists' coalition with the LDP in
1994, and their support of an LDP minority government after the 1996
elections, also have rich historical precedents.

Second, though the number of cases is small, the evidence suggests
that governing coalitions follow the same essential numerical logic that
electoral coalitions follow. The opposition parties vacillate among the
three available strategies: building a party unilaterally, working toward
an opposition coalition government, or jockeying for position as the
junior member of an LDP coalition government. When the LDP has a
bare parliamentary majority, or when the LDP is facing an election in
which it could likely lose its parliamentary majority, talk of coalitions, defections, and party reformulations is common. When the LDP
is ascendant and strong, such plans are shelved, and opposition parties
concentrate on building their own bases or on cooperating electorally to
reduce the LDP majority.

Coupled with this numerical logic is the logic of personal ambition.
LDP politicians who had lost a battle for power within the LDP were
prime candidates for defection proposals, because they were considering all options to increase their power. Therefore, the prime time for discussing LDP defections was when the LDP faced both an election in
which it might lose its majority, and some powerful losers from an internal leadership battle.

A third lesson to be learned from this history of coalition efforts is the
relative success that the opposition has had in bringing the LDP to a vulnerable position and exploiting splits in the LDP to their advantage. Just
as the LDP exploits divisions within the opposition camp, the opposition
can and does exploit factional divisions within the LDP. The failure of
the opposition to bring any of its schemes to fruition does not negate

its successes in bringing the LDP to the brink of chaos on multiple occasions.

Last, this chapter illustrates well the bargaining advantage that is the key to LDP success in staving off the opposition challenge. When party relations are fluid and interchangeable, the LDP enjoys the great advantage of playing off the opposition parties against each other. In contrast, if a rigid division exists between the LDP and the opposition, the LDP has fewer options and cannot divide the opposition so easily. The fluidity of party relations varies from year to year, but for most of the postwar period, LDP relations with each of the opposition parties were as strong as relations among the opposition parties. Before moving into the more context-rich discussion of the various coalition plots, I will give a few illustrations of close relations between the LDP and Socialist, Clean Government, and Democratic Socialist Parties.

Close Relations between the LDP and the Opposition

That close ties existed between the non-Communist opposition parties and the LDP is not a matter of debate. The ties between Kanemaru Shin of the LDP and Tanabe Makoto of the Socialist Party were famous. Though they denied the existence of specific deals to pass legislation, they admitted to meeting regularly and discussing legislation.[1] The accusations hurled at Tanabe went well beyond those of simple legislative logrolling. An official of the Socialist Party confided that he refused to accept any gifts from Tanabe, despite their friendship, because he was convinced that the ultimate source of such funds was money passed to Tanabe from Kanemaru.[2]

A similar cozy relationship between the two parties was exposed in Shiga prefecture in the 1970s. When the opposition mounted a credible challenge to the incumbent LDP governor, the governor used his ties with the leaders of the prefectural Socialist Party to get them to try to sabotage the cooperative arrangement. The three prefectural party leaders prevented the Socialist Party from joining the opposition coalition, insisting that the party run its own candidate. They hoped this strategy would divide the opposition vote and allow the LDP incumbent to be reelected; instead, other Socialist officials understood what was happening and voted to expel their own party leaders. Interestingly, the opposition candidate for governor was Takemura Masayoshi, who later joined the LDP, then in 1993 led a group of LDP defectors to form the New Party Harbinger. Though there was no clear evidence of such deals or transfers of money between the LDP and the Socialists at the national level, the existence of such relations was accepted as fact. The parties worked closely together.

The Democratic Socialists and the LDP maintained even closer ties. Because an important tool of the opposition parties is the boycotting of Diet proceedings, the Democratic Socialists' reluctance to join such boycotts clearly reflected their close ties with the LDP. When the opposition and the LDP were disputing, the Democratic Socialists could often obtain amendments to a bill by voting with the LDP for the bill, or at least by attending the parliamentary session. Through this exchange, the Democratic Socialists gained influence on, and could take credit for, revisions in the legislation while the LDP could preserve the facade of a consensus between itself and at least one opposition party. The significance of this relationship between the Democratic Socialists and the LDP declined as the Democratic Socialists' parliamentary power shrunk. The LDP's 1989 loss of control of the House of Councillors graphically exposed the Democratic Socialists' weakness. Even if the party had joined with the LDP in a House of Councillors vote, the two parties would not have had a majority.

LDP–Democratic Socialist relations extended beyond the parliamentary arena. Much of the Democratic Socialist vote came from conservatives, and in this sense, the LDP and Democratic Socialists shared a common support base. In elections, the Democratic Socialists typically moved to the right to shore up their conservative base.[3] Both parties also relied on the support and finances of big business. Though the Democratic Socialists were seen as union politicians, they conducted what are called business-enmeshed campaigns. Businesses having Democratic Socialist–affiliated unions were the most important factors in turning out campaign workers and voters; they also provided campaign funding. Because Democratic Socialist–affiliated unions were typically on good relations with their companies, both union and management worked to provide campaign resources. Thus, the management side was important in turning out resources during a campaign.

The Democratic Socialists and the LDP, therefore, were quite vulnerable to inroads from each other. Democratic Socialist candidates could siphon off some of the conservative vote to the opposition, but the LDP could shut down a Democratic Socialist candidate by putting pressure on business donors and conservative organizations to withhold support.[4] The LDP did not control the Democratic Socialists, but close relations decreased the latter's enthusiasm for challenging the LDP too strongly and increased its expectations of eventually becoming the LDP's coalition partner.

The Clean Government Party and the LDP also maintained close, informal relations. In legislative matters, the Clean Government Party helped pass LDP legislation by giving tacit or explicit support on many occasions. Journalists alleged Clean Government Party–LDP exchanges of money and votes, and LDP protection of Sōka gakkai from government inquiry. One of the first of these allegations was that the Clean Government Party used its ties with the LDP's Tanaka to control damage in the wake of its first big scandal—the 1971 book-publishing scandal (Aochi 1970, 114). Such allegations were common; a more recent example was the rumors of shady financial practices that arose from a tax investigation of Sōka gakkai (*Shūkan Asahi* 1991). Critics also accused the Clean Government Party of shifting votes to LDP candidates in open districts in exchange for money or LDP votes in other districts.

Separating fact from fiction in these allegations is difficult. Clean Government Party leaders categorically denied all of them. Even political scientists or commentators who knew of such practices were precluded from talking about them because of the Japanese expectations of loyalty once a confidence is extended. One political observer told me of a Clean Government Party leader's confidential admission that, in a close gubernatorial election, the LDP candidate had persuaded the party leader to shift three thousand votes during the final days of the campaign in exchange for money. Yet this observer swore me to strictest secrecy, saying that if he were discovered in betraying this confidence, it would ruin all his relations with Clean Government Party politicians.

Another anonymous Rengō official refused to criticize the Clean Government Party directly, but he did describe how the party's support of Rengō-sponsored candidates in the 1991 prefectural assembly elections suddenly disappeared. He then insinuated that the party and the LDP had agreed to shift Clean Government votes to LDP candidates in certain crucial districts. Another political observer (who also wished to remain anonymous) described to me how the Clean Government Party exchanges votes and lists of supporters with the LDP in national elections, just as it does with the opposition-affiliated labor unions. The manager of an LDP incumbent's local campaign organization likewise repeated a rumor that in the 1986 election, another LDP incumbent in the same district had "bought" Clean Government Party votes (there was no Clean Government candidate running in the district). The votes were rumored to have cost $1 million (100 million yen).

Separating fact from slander in the unlit world of backroom politics is a difficult task in any nation. It is especially difficult with the Clean Government Party because of the extreme degree to which the party was attacked and vilified during its history. Party officials understandably were very guarded about who they talked to, and once a relationship existed, these officials were more sensitive to criticism than the activists and politicians of the other political parties. This dynamic limited the amount of reliable information on Clean Government Party–LDP relations that was made public.

The extreme form that criticism took when someone came out and openly attacked the Clean Government Party also muddied the waters. Such critics claimed that they often were subjected to extreme pressure or harassment from the party or from Sōka gakkai. However, the complete rupturing of relations that occurs between the party and a critic, as well as the assured media market for another exposé of the party or Sōka gakkai, gave these critics every incentive to exaggerate their claims. In such an atmosphere of boundless recriminations, judging the credibility of the assertions becomes difficult.

For analytical purposes, however, the truth of these accusations need not be proved. Rather, it is sufficient to show that some Clean Government Party leaders maintained close ties with the LDP, just as certain members of the Socialist and Democratic Socialist Parties did. Members of the LDP strike deals with leaders of each of these parties on a wide range of issues. Though rarely acknowledged publicly, some money flowed from the LDP to at least some members of all three parties. In addition, all three parties relied on the LDP for political leverage, on the LDP or big business for some financial support, and on the LDP or the conservative-oriented bureaucracy for information.

Cultural Explanations of Close Party Relations

These ties between the LDP and the opposition parties existed, and likely will continue to exist, under the new, reformulated party system. The newly reformed Clean Government Party maintains its close ties with the LDP, and many of the politicians in the Democratic Party are former members of the LDP, or are opposition politicians who have shown a willingness to work closely with the LDP. It seems incongruous, especially with regard to the supposedly ideologically rigid Socialist Party, that the opposition could work so closely with the LDP. Why would the opposition be so flexible in its arrangements with the LDP while at the same time losing its chance to take power by being inflexible in its ideology?

The most common explanation is simply the LDP's long-term dominance of the Japanese political system. The LDP's long rule has given it a monopoly on political influence, money, and information, which forces the other parties to compromise with the LDP to have any political influence. This explanation, however, must be supplemented by a discussion of cultural attitudes in Japan and of the light these attitudes shed on the multifaceted relationships between the LDP and the opposition.

Compromise with the LDP was not the opposition's initial course of action. The first postwar decade saw disputes within the Socialist Party over whether to compromise with or fight against the conservatives; with the rise of the Socialist left wing in the 1950s, the party had several violent disputes with the LDP on issues that culminated with the 1960 United States–Japan Security Treaty demonstrations.[5] Thereafter, both sides refrained from vitriolic confrontation, and they established more amicable relations in the 1960s.

The form that this cooperative arrangement took was influenced by Japanese cultural notions of what is acceptable. In the political arena, the compromises took the form of ritualized confrontation that followed a script written before the dispute. The LDP and the Socialists worked out in advance such things as the length of the Socialist boycott of Diet proceedings.

This style of compromising, while maintaining all the trappings of confrontation, seems culturally influenced because of the extreme degree to which the hypocrisy of the situation is tolerated. Secret deals between politicians who oppose each other publicly occur in any political arena; Japan is not unique in this regard. However, the extent to which the farce of political confrontation is accepted by most Japanese, even though it is known to be a farce, reflects certain features of the Japanese culture. In both private and public matters, the Japanese are quick to accept a dichotomy between the real intentions or rationales for an action *(honne)* and principles under which the system is supposed to operate *(tatemae)*. The *tatemae* is not simply a facade or a lie; rather, it is the accepted framework or principles under which a system operates. Therefore the *tatemae* is rarely challenged publicly, even though in private it often is conceded that it does not reflect reality accurately.

This dichotomy between the *honne* and the *tatemae* has taken many forms in Japan's ancient and modern politics. The tradition of a figure-head ruler who is manipulated by the holder of real power is best exemplified by the strictly symbolic role of the emperor in Japan. The Meiji oligarchs who established the modern Japanese state initially ruled directly from ministerial positions, but they continued to control the Japanese state even after they resigned from their formal positions of power. This tradition continues in the modern LDP; many times the prime minister is not the most powerful person in the LDP, but is controlled to some degree by a more powerful faction leader of the LDP.

The dichotomy of the *honne* and the *tatemae* appears throughout Japanese politics. One of the key political activities of the Japanese Diet is interpellation of the prime minister and other ministers by Diet members. However, the questions the minister is asked are almost always communicated to the relevant ministries in advance, to give the minister's bureaucratic underlings a chance to prepare an appropriate answer.

These examples show that Japan is different from many Western democracies, because of the degree to which the *tatemae* can continue to operate despite universal recognition of its inaccuracy. In Japan, the believability of the *tatemae* is not its important feature; rather, the acceptance of the *tatemae* as a framework for action is key.

The movement of the opposition parties to positions subordinate to the LDP, to obtain some of the benefits of power, is not unique to Japan, but the form this subordination takes is. In any country, a subordinate party might preserve its public stance of independence, but in Japan, the gulf between the public stance of confrontation and the private stance of compromise is exceptionally wide. The disparity can be explained by other factors, but the cultural factor is crucial. The Japanese have a greater tolerance for a *tatemae*-like deviation from reality, as long as the deviation provides a set of operating principles on which all of the participants can agree.

Other cultural explanations of coalition behavior are less persuasive. For example, it is true that the negotiation style and relationships between Japanese politicians are unique to East Asia, if not Japan. However, there is little evidence that these cultural norms were more influential than the numerical incentives to form coalitions. For example, in Japan, personal networks are heavily influenced by common schooling, familial, or experiential ties. Thus, it might be expected that patterns of cross-party alliances could be explained by such ties. On examination, however, it appears that the network of ties is so complex that a link can be made to any party or politician through this network. In other words, though potential coalition partners are approached through this Japanese system of networking, the networks do not seem to significantly constrain the strategic choice of potential coalition partners.

Coalition Building before 1955

With this background of LDP-opposition relations and of the cultural attitudes that affect those relations, an analysis of party-relation patterns becomes possible. Party relations like these have a long history; coalitions between parties, and between parties and elements of the bureaucracy, were prominent in the politics of prewar Japan. Richard Mitchell (1996) and Najita Tetsuo (1967) document in excellent detail the various types of deal making that went on during this period. Interestingly, prewar coalitions formed during the multiple debates over Japan's electoral system. As in the postwar period, the type of electoral system was a charged, much-discussed political issue. Politicians in the prewar period responded to numerical incentives in building coalitions to pass electoral reform legislation much like politicians who participated in the 1994 vote on electoral reform.

The most prominent electoral reform was the 1925 decision to implement the medium-sized constituency system (districts with magnitudes of three to five seats). This was the final prewar electoral change culminating three decades of debate about the electoral system. In the 1890s, Japan had used an electoral system based mainly on single-seat districts. In the first two decades of the 1900s, Japan used large, multiseat districts that corresponded generally with Japan's prefectures. Immediately before the 1925 reforms, Japan used a mixed system of many single-seat districts with some two- and three-seat districts.

The motivations and coalitions for each reform are interesting. The large-district system was implemented with the support of a coalition between the Liberal Party in the Diet and the bureaucracy, the branch of government controlled by the founders of the modern Japanese state.[6] The bureaucratic elite hoped that districts of large magnitude would encourage the proliferation of political parties, thus splintering their power. The elite wanted to create a niche for a small, bureaucracy-dominated party.

In a reaction to this system, the dominant political party, the Seiyūkai, made several proposals from 1911 on to restore the single-seat district system of the 1890 election law. The Seiyūkai hoped to cement in place its dominant position in Japan's party system by winning most of the proposed single-seat districts, as opposed to taking only a proportion of the seats in multiseat districts. The Seiyūkai's proposals clearly served its interests, and though these proposals were implemented in the early 1920s, they were reversed in 1925 as part of a package deal to grant universal male suffrage and reinstate multiseat districts of medium magnitude.

The 1925 reforms advantaged the major political parties because they allowed each major party to win a seat while raising the bar for smaller parties that might have won seats under a more proportional electoral system.[7] Leaders of the three major parties were most worried about the possible growth of socialist parties with the granting of universal male suffrage. The 1925 reform reduced some of the negative effects of large-magnitude districts on the major political parties while making it harder for new political parties to challenge the entrenched political parties. Because the reform did not give an enormous advantage to any one of the major parties, it was acceptable to all of them.

The Allied Occupation of Japan, which began in 1945, set the stage for coalition building in the postwar period by encouraging the proliferation of political parties. Initially, the Occupation's two main goals were to democratize and demilitarize Japan. Occupation authorities allowed the suppressed and banned leftist parties to freely organize; women were given the vote; and the Japanese government removed the advantages of incumbency by redrawing the boundaries of election districts and reinstating the large district election system used from 1900 to 1920 (Soma 1986, 208). These and other reforms were significant, incubating the fledgling parties of the Left and creating a fluid, complex political situation. The first postwar decade saw many party mergers and divisions, as well as active coalition building.

Figure 5.1 shows how successful these changes were in "democratizing" the Japanese political system. The parties of the Left, the Socialists and the Communists, advanced rapidly, gaining 20 to 30 percent of the vote. The rise of the Communists, however, ended abruptly because the Socialists soon began to dominate the Left both in the political and labor movement arenas. The Communist Party declined because of tactical errors, the rise of anti-Communism in the United States, and a conservative backlash in Japan to Communist advances (see fig. 4.1).

One of the first failures of the Communist Party was its inability to consolidate its early postwar domination of the Japanese labor movement. Scalapino sees the failed general strike of 1 February 1947 as the peak of Communist labor influence. He blames the subsequent decline partly on the subordination of workers' interests to the broader political objectives of the Communist Party and partly on the alienation of potential allies by the conspiratorial nature of the Communist organization (Scalapino 1967, 74).

The Communists made a grave tactical error in the political arena, too. In October 1951, the party bowed to pressure from Peking and Moscow by replacing its postwar "peaceful revolution" platform with

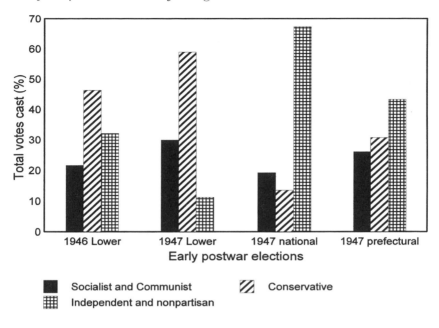

Figure 5.1 Combined leftist vote in Japan's first postwar elections

more orthodox revolutionary rhetoric, in a policy called the 1951 Thesis. Richard Boyd (1986, 176–177) states that this policy shift cut the popularity of the party, encouraged its suppression, and increased the factionalization within the Communist movement. As Scalapino (1967, 87) observes, "The party rapidly became a symbol for extremism and all except the most firmly committed fell away."

Occupation authorities also hastened the decline of the Communists. They objected to Communist excesses, such as the call for a general strike in 1947, and their attitudes reflected the rising tide of anti-Communism in the United States. By the late 1940s, the Occupation's labor policies were decidedly anti-Communist. Communist leaders were also purged from positions in the union movement and politics.

The Occupation's anti-Communism was encouraged and applauded by the conservative elite in Japan's government and big business. These conservatives had already reintroduced medium-sized election districts in 1947 in response to Communist advances under the large districts of the 1945 reforms (Soma 1986, 241–245). Business also worked with moderate elements in the labor union movement to hasten the decline of Communist labor influence.

The initial democratization push of the Occupation not only jump-started the parties of the Left, but it also created an environment of new political opportunities and uncertainties. In the first postwar decade, there were many political parties and a fluid atmosphere of coalition formation. Until 1955, the antecedents of the LDP were divided into at least three political groups, whose names changed with each factional defection or merger. The two main conservative parties were the Liberal Party and the Democrat Party, but even these two parties changed their names several times. The Socialists were also divided at times into three different political groups. This period resembles the post-1993 period of fluid politics in Japan. During both periods, politicians changed parties frequently and parties changed names frequently.

Similar to the 1990s, during the first postwar decade the various political groups considered and discussed coalitions. The right wing of the Socialist Party approached the conservatives after the first election and proposed a coalition. The plan was rejected, though, and the left wing of the Socialist Party became suspicious of Socialist proponents of a coalition government, especially right-wing leaders Nishio Suehiro and Hirano Rikizō, because they seemed too eager to form a coalition government (Matsuoka, 1990).

Japan's first postwar party government was a conservative coalition led by Yoshida Shigeru and backed by the Liberal and Progressive Parties.[8] Nishio and Hirano's plan for a coalition government involving the Socialists came to fruition after the next election, when the Socialists emerged as the largest parliamentary party. With the encouragement of the Occupation authorities, the new prime minister was the Socialist Katayama Tetsu, and his government was supported by the Socialists, the Democrats, and the smaller National Cooperative Party.[9] The initial coalition negotiations even included the Liberals, but they pulled out when the Socialists refused to meet their demands to cut off the left wing of the Socialist Party. This coalition government lasted from June 1947 to February 1948, but was then replaced by another coalition government, with Ashida Hitoshi as the prime minister, which again was supported by the Democrats and the Socialists. The Socialist-Democrat coalition again proved unstable; in October 1948, Yoshida became prime minister with the backing of an expanded Liberal Party, which had changed its name to the Democratic Liberal Party.[10]

Though this was a period of fiercely ideological politics in Japan, all the parties (except the Communists) actively courted each other as coalition partners. Ideological differences, though important, did not stand in the way of considering potential coalition partners. For example, Yoshida Shigeru, leader of the Liberals, was willing to consider coalitions with all parties except the Communists. The left wing of the Socialist Party, though it eventually brought down the Katayama government, still initially supported a coalition with one of the conservative parties. It is even rumored that the right wing Socialist leader, Hirano, talked to Yoshida about splitting the Socialist Party and bringing out right-wing members to join with the defectors from the Democrats in a coalition government led by Yoshida's Liberals (Matsuoka, 1990).

Ideology mattered, of course—Yoshida was talking to a right-wing leader in the Socialist Party, and the two coalition governments were put together largely through ties between the right wing of that party and the Democrats. Similarly, the right wing of the Socialist Party ruled out any possibility of a coalition with the Communists, just as Yoshida had done. Ideology also mattered in the Katayama government's insistence on a bill to nationalize the coal industry, the one piece of Socialist legislation in a legislative agenda that was otherwise indistinguishable from a conservative one. Passage of this bill was important in driving some of the more conservative members of the Democrats into defection and an alliance with the Yoshida Liberals. However, even though ideology limited the actions and potential coalition partners, these limits were few.

The events of this period also highlight the incentive structures that influence elite behavior toward coalition opportunities. For example, the creation of the Democrat Party resulted from a leadership struggle in the Liberal Party. After the war, both Ashida and Yoshida were competing to dominate the Liberal Party, and Ashida was losing. When the opportunity came to defect and lead his defectors into a merger with the existing Progressive Party, he took the chance. The new merged party became the Democrat Party, and Ashida became its leader. Matsuoka (1990) cites Ashida's rivalry with Yoshida as a major reason for the formation of the Katayama and Ashida coalition governments. After the defection, for Ashida to go back to the Liberals would have meant his being subordinate to Yoshida again; as a result, Ashida actively pursued all other coalitional opportunities. Yoshida, in a defensive maneuver, also was forced to pursue coalitional options, to strengthen his hand against Ashida.

For the Socialists, the choice from the beginning was either to remain united, hoping to elect a future parliamentary majority, or to pursue some form of coalition government. The left wing tended to favor the first option, the right wing the second. The party never resolved this issue, but because right-wing representatives were the majority, they pushed the party toward the coalition option, ensuring the cooperation of the left wing by supporting the left-wing Katayama's bid to become prime minister.

Though the failure of this government is often cited as a reason for the electorate's long support of LDP governments, it does not appear to have left as bad a taste in the mouths of the participants as some would suggest. For example, Masaru Kohno (1997) documents how in 1955, when the LDP was created, another alliance with the Socialist Party was still a viable option. Similarly, the Democrats continued to build electoral alliances with the Socialists in gubernatorial races across Japan in the years following their coalition government. For example, in the 1951 unified local elections, the Socialists and the Democrats backed joint candidates for governor in seven of Japan's prefectures. Prospects of cooperation with the Socialists still existed, even as the Liberals and Democrats moved toward unification and the Socialists began their long exile from power.

Opposition Party Fragmentation

The first decade of postwar politics ended in 1955 with two significant party mergers. The right and left wings of the Socialist Party agreed to merge in 1955. The conservatives, in response, merged into the Liberal Democratic Party, because they feared the growing power of a united Socialist Party and were being pressured by big business to unite. In one stroke, the complex multiparty system became a two-party system. Politicians labeled this model of two-party politics the 1955 System, after the year in which it first took shape.

Emergence of the Democratic Socialist Party

The 1955 System lasted in its pure form for only five years. In 1961, the Communists formally renounced violent revolution and regained the popularity they had enjoyed immediately after World War II. The Socialists, acknowledging the growing political power of the Communists, agreed to work with them to fight the extension of a revised United States–Japan Security Treaty. In addition, a movement began within the Socialist Party in 1958 to expel a leader of its right wing, Nishio Suehiro.[11] The expulsion vote threw the party's September 1959 convention into disorder, and Nishio and his followers left the party in October. In January 1960, Nishio and fifty-six other members of the Diet formed the Democratic Socialist Party. This split of the Socialist Party was not, however, a clean split between the left and right wings of the party. Many right-wing Socialists remained Socialists.

The creation of the Democratic Socialists opened another window of opportunity for coalitions. The Democratic Socialists presented a tempting option for would-be LDP defectors. It was closer ideologically to the LDP, and its leader, Nishio, was the architect of the Katayama and Ashida coalition governments. LDP leaders immediately considered this option. The first opportunity came after the bruising battle within the LDP for leadership in the wake of Prime Minister Kishi Nobusuke's resignation. The battle pitted the "bureaucratic" group of representatives against the "politician" group. Protégés of Yoshida Shigeru led the bureaucratic faction; they were generally politicians who had previously worked in the bureaucracy. Their opponents were "true" politicians who lacked previous careers in the bureaucracy and whose leaders, like Kōno Ichirō, had been politicians before and during World War II. The politician group lost this battle for leadership. Shortly thereafter, in August of 1960, Kōno Ichirō told his faction members that their leaving the LDP was inevitable. He was, however, talked out of this plan by the members of his faction and by his ally Ono Bamboku (Tominomori 1994, 157).

The next public surfacing of this LDP defection option came in 1966, again involving an antimainstream LDP politician, Nakasone Yasuhiro. This time, involvement with the Democratic Socialists was explicit. Nakasone was one of the most conservative members of the LDP, evidence again that ideology was not the primary barrier to such coalitions.[12] Nakasone worked against incumbent prime minister Satō Eisaku in the December 1966 LDP president's race. When Satō won, Nakasone was relegated to the antimainstream group, an informal opposition group within the LDP.

Shortly after the election, Nakasone happened by chance to meet Democratic Socialist official Sasaki Ryōsaku on the train. This significant and coincidental meeting on the train shows the willingness of Japanese politicians to go beyond their existing network and pursue opportunities when they exist. There the two men hatched a plan to dissolve the Diet and create a new centrist coalition. They planned to bring down the government and force an election. Their goal was to limit the LDP in that election to fewer than 270 seats. At that level, the LDP would retain a parliamentary majority, but with a margin so slim that it would be lost if Nakasone brought thirty defectors out of the LDP. The plan had potential, because the LDP was in the midst of a scandal, which was sapping conservative strength and popularity. Sasaki and Nakasone then hoped to use these defectors and the Democratic Socialists as the nucleus of a new centrist coalition. The centrist coalition was to include Socialists, though the left wing of that party was to be excluded. This new coalition would then build its strength in future elections to the point where it could alternate in power with what remained of the LDP (Sasaki and Kunimasa 1989, 253).

The plan died on the vine when the Satō-led LDP won 277 seats in the January 1967 elections, thereby ruling out any possibility of a Nakasone-led defection that would deprive the LDP of power. Nakasone saw that the opportunity had passed; he later told Sasaki he intended to rejoin the mainstream of the LDP by accepting a cabinet post—an action he took in the cabinet reshuffle of November 1967.

Electoral Debut of the Clean Government Party

The debut of the Clean Government Party onto the national political stage in 1964 further splintered the opposition. As the political arm of the religious organization Sōka gakkai, the new party progressed, rapidly winning twenty-five seats in the 1967 House of Representatives elections and forty-seven seats in 1969.[13] The Clean Government Party became the second largest opposition party, winning more seats in 1969 than the Democratic Socialists and the Communists combined. The LDP now had two centrist coalition options; additionally, the possibility remained of working with the Socialist Party. Incentives to negotiate also increased because the rise of the Clean Government Party (along with the revitalization of the Communist Party) sapped both the LDP and the Socialists' strength. By the 1970s, the LDP was in such a vulnerable position that even a minor defection could take away its parliamentary majority and open the door to a non-LDP coalition government. LDP leaders were well aware of their potential need for a junior coalition partner. Each election of the 1970s raised the question, What would happen if the LDP lost its majority?

Despite these favorable circumstances for the opposition, opposition unity became more difficult to create and maintain, because there were now four opposition parties. Unlike the climate of the 1950s, when the Socialists were the only viable opposition party, two Socialist parties, produced by the Socialist disunity, were now joined by the Clean Government Party and the reemerging Communists. Numerically, it made sense to include the Communists in any anti-LDP coalition, but for ideological and organizational reasons, some insisted that the Communists be excluded.

The first coalition proposal involving the Clean Government Party developed in the wake of a scandal that stopped the meteoric rise of the new party's power. Fujiwara Hiroshi wrote a book criticizing Sōka gakkai. He and reporter Naitō Kunio accused the Clean Government Party and Sōka gakkai of harassing them and blocking the publication of this and later publications.[14] Politicians of all parties, especially the Democratic Socialists and the Communists, attacked the Clean Government Party, primarily alleging that it was merely a political front for the religious organization Sōka gakkai. Some alleged that the Clean Government Party and Sōka gakkai were the same organization, run by the religious leader of Sōka gakkai, Ikeda Daisaku. In response, the party and Sōka gakkai severed all formal ties in May 1970. Rumors also circulated that the Clean Government Party had asked Tanaka Kakuei of the LDP to help moderate LDP attacks on the party (Hrebenar 1986, 154).

A third prong of the Clean Government Party's response was to temper the attacks of the Democratic Socialists by secretly proposing a Clean Government–Democratic Socialist coalition. A high official of Mitsubishi Bank, where Sōka gakkai was an important banking customer, approached Democratic Socialist leader Nishimura Eiichi with the coalition proposal.[15] Nishimura did not immediately accept it, because he was wary of Clean Government Party promises to clearly separate religion and politics and to move away from the LDP. Throughout 1970, the Clean Government Party courted Nishimura, with Nishimura waiting to see the results of the next party conference. When he was satisfied, Nishimura announced a plan for a new political party. His initial proposal was for the Clean Government Party and Democratic Socialists to merge, forming a new centrist alternative between the conservatives and the Communists. This plan was vehemently opposed by Nishio Suehiro, who was leading the Democratic Socialist attack on the Clean Government Party. Other procooperation Democratic Socialists, such as Kasuga Itsukō and Sasaki Ryōsaku, urged Nishimura to include the Socialists in his proposal. They were concerned that an alliance with only the Clean Government Party would be summarily rejected by anti–Clean Government Party members of the Democratic Socialist Party.

The proposed new party, as announced to the public, included the Socialists, Democratic Socialists, and the Clean Government Party. Nishimura proposed that these parties merge by 1972, hoping to win a parliamentary majority by 1975.

The proximate cause of the Clean Government Party–Nishimura proposal was the party's overtures to Nishimura in the wake of the scandal about its attempt to quash negative publications. All the parties involved, however, had complex motivations for accepting the proposal. The political environment had changed, and coalition proposals were now easier to pursue. First, the Socialist Party suffered a devastating loss in the 1969 House of Representatives election, falling from 140 to 90 seats. Half the lost seats went to the LDP, but the other half went to the Clean Government Party and the Communists. As a result, Socialist leaders were receptive to cooperation and coalition proposals. The openness to centrist proposals was further augmented by changes within the Socialist Party. Eda Saburō, a proponent of centrist cooperation, was mounting a challenge to Socialist Party leaders. His challenge, though ultimately unsuccessful, forced the leadership to take a more neutral stance regarding cooperation either with the Communists or the centrists.

Second, the Democratic Socialist leadership changed. Nishio Suehiro, who was understandably antagonistic to the Socialist Party, retired in 1966. Nishimura Eiichi replaced him as chairman, and Kasuga Itsukō became vice-chairman.[16] Nishio remained influential within the party, however, and continued to oppose the procooperation initiatives of Nishimura.

Nishimura had multiple motivations for pursuing electoral cooperation so aggressively. He feared isolation by the increasingly successful Socialist-Communist cooperation in municipal and gubernatorial elections. In addition, he saw an opportunity to join with the Clean Government Party and part of the Socialists to create a viable, centrist political alternative to the LDP. This was, at the time, the only realistic path to political power, and after ten years of Democratic Socialist stagnation, Nishimura was ready to set aside old animosities in his pursuit of power.[17] Nishimura also saw an opportunity to become a political broker. By bringing the Clean Government Party and the moderate Socialists together, he hoped to occupy a pivotal role in this new political party.

The Clean Government Party was motivated by a desire to mute criticism, and Nishimura was enticed by the prospect of augmenting his own personal power. The timing was ripe for coalition discussions. The

Socialists had just been defeated, the bloc of LDP seats was smaller, and the rise of the centrists gave hope to the possibility of a new coalition option. Again, ideology played a role in excluding the Communists, but ideological desires to exclude the Socialists were overruled by those who saw no hope for success without including the Socialists. The potential stigma of allying too closely with the larger Clean Government Party forced Nishimura's plan to include the Socialists in order for it to be seriously considered.

Though Nishimura's proposal had much grander designs, its implementation was cut short by his untimely death (while watching televised election returns), so the effort never got past the stage of electoral cooperation discussed in the previous chapter. A prominent figure in these discussions, Sasaki Ryōsaku (1991), suggests that Nishimura's plan was flawed from the start because he overestimated the ability of the Democratic Socialists to dominate in an alliance with the Clean Government Party.

Eda Saburō and the Socialist Response

As part of the Nishimura plan, Secretary General Sasaki Ryōsaku of the Democratic Socialists approached his counterpart in the Socialist Party, Eda Saburō, in early 1970, shortly after the 1969 election. Eda initially rebuffed Sasaki. But later that year, Eda and Sasaki coincidentally met on a train—as had Nakasone and Sasaki—and began cooperation and coalition discussions. These informal discussions became regular, secret meetings between Eda, Sasaki, and their counterpart at the Clean Government Party, Yano Junya. Eda began these meetings immediately after he lost in his attempt to become a Socialist Party leader in August 1970. In these meetings, Sasaki persuaded Eda to become an important conduit into the Socialist Party for planning and implementing the Nishimura plan. They succeeded in implementing their first goal—electoral cooperation between the Socialists, Democratic Socialists, and Clean Government Party in the 1971 House of Councillors election.

The next step of the plan was for Eda to bring a large number of Socialist representatives out of that party and combine them with the centrist party members, and possibly with defectors from the LDP. The new party envisioned by Nishimura would be formed. It was understood that the left wing of the Socialist Party would not join in the merger. Eda would split the Socialist Party.

The planners envisioned several opportunities by which Eda could leave the party over a divisive issue. One was the Socialist Party decision not to boycott the Diet session on the reversion of Okinawa in December 1971. The December 1972 House of Representatives election was another opportunity; in preparation for Eda's defection and the new party's contesting of this election, the planners even drew up the new party's organization and its lists of candidates. A third opportunity came in April 1974, over the Socialist Party decision to back the reelection of the incumbent governor of Kyoto, Ninagawa Torazō.[18]

Eda's goals were different from those of his centrist counterparts, however. His main goal was to reform the Socialist Party without destroying it; he had a long history of fighting to reform the party. In the 1960s, Eda had led the call for structural reform with his famous Eda Vision. He failed. In 1970, he again led an unsuccessful battle for reform and moderation in his bid for party leadership. After this, his centrist allies expected him to split the party, but reluctant to do this, he declined at each of the opportunities presented. From the outset of the negotiations, Eda had stressed his desire to unify the labor unions before pursuing political restructuring, but Sasaki and Yano pushed political reorganization first. Finally, the Sōhyō labor unions also weighed in to quash any talk of defection. The political restructuring that did occur in the 1990s was pushed by the labor unions, which had undergone their own restructuring several years earlier; interestingly, this is precisely the path to political reform that Eda had advocated two decades earlier.

Eda's failure to carry out the plan was met with disgust by some of his colleagues. Democratic Socialist Kasuga said that Eda was not a samurai (Mainichi shimbun seijibu 1993, 55). Years later, former chairman of the Clean Government Party Takeiri Yoshikatsu (1991) referred to Eda's failure to split the party with obvious contempt. Eda finally left the party, in 1977, but he took only a few colleagues with him. His action was too little, too late.[19]

Throughout this period of negotiations with Eda, the opposition parties built and refined the electoral cooperation links discussed in chapter 4. Without the hoped-for split in the Socialist Party, however, the centrist parties turned away from the Socialists and began to focus their attention on coalition opportunities with the LDP. Though Eda was not the only Socialist willing to negotiate with the centrists, other Socialist leaders were even less enthusiastic about the idea of a party restructuring than Eda had been. These leaders accepted electoral cooperation efforts with the centrists, but the Socialist Party itself was torn between those who advocated more cooperation with the centrists and those who favored electoral cooperation with the Communists. This issue was not resolved in favor of centrist cooperation until 1980. Until that time, the Socialist Party took the compromise stance of promoting all-opposition cooperation, which meant that the Socialists would cooperate with all other opposition parties. This stance effectively ruled out the possibility of extensive cooperation efforts with the centrists.

Selection of Prime Minister Miki Takeo

The centrists regained interest in cooperating with the LDP at the same time as a fortuitous (for coalition purposes) split developed in the LDP. A bitter leadership battle occurred over who would replace resigning Prime Minister Tanaka; the centrist parties played an important, possibly deciding, role in this decision. Their extraordinary influence did not materialize into any specific benefit for them.

Prime Minister Tanaka was forced to resign on 24 November 1974, for his part in several scandals. During the battle over his successor, many in the LDP feared the very real specter of an LDP split, with the defectors joining the opposition parties. This fear had several sources. One was the formulation over the past three years of the Nishimura plan, which had led to opposition electoral cooperation and to regular meetings between Eda, Sasaki, and Yano, leaders in the three non-Communist opposition parties. Another reason was that some defectors had already left the LDP to form the New Liberal Club. A third source of fear was the recent incident of LDP defectors cooperating with the opposition, which had occurred in the House of Councillors. In the July 1971 election for speaker of that House, the opposition parties had backed a renegade candidate from the LDP who defeated the LDP's designated candidate. He won the post, combining his support among part of the LDP with the opposition support. Lastly, Tanaka and Miki had nearly come to war in the summer of 1974, during a House of Councillors election in Miki's home prefecture of Tokushima. Miki's favored candidate was denied the LDP nomination in favor of Tanaka's favored candidate, Gotoda Masaharu. Miki's man nevertheless ran as an independent. Before the election, Tanaka made repeated campaign visits to the prefecture, and Miki threatened to do likewise in support of his independent. Through this action, Miki risked censure and expulsion from the party, because Miki's candidate, unlike Tanaka's, was not an official candidate of the LDP. Though Miki tempered his acts to avoid this penalty, he placed himself squarely in opposition to Tanaka by resigning his post in the Tanaka cabinet.

With Tanaka's resignation, the obvious candidates for the next prime minister were the main faction leaders, Ōhira Masayoshi, Miki Takeo, Fukuda Takeo, and Nakasone Yasuhiro. Party elder Shiina Etsuzaburō was given the task of picking a successor. Shiina could choose one of the four faction leaders, or he could pick a party elder to serve as a caretaker prime minister. Ōhira ruled out the caretaker option by publicly attacking it. It quickly became clear that if Shiina did not come up with a compromise candidate acceptable to a majority, then the selection would go to an election by LDP parliamentarians. In such a party election for party president (and hence, prime minister) Ōhira had a numerical advantage; he could count on the support of his own large faction and the support of the even larger Tanaka faction.

On 1 December 1974, Shiina was to announce his decision. Some expected the designation to go to Ōhira; in the past, such designations went to the largest faction. Even if Shiina failed to build a consensus in support of a designation of Ōhira, Ōhira would likely win if the decision were thrown to an internal party election. In preparation for either result, Nakasone was working out plans with members of the Fukuda and Miki factions to leave the LDP and form a new party (Mainichi shimbun seijibu 1993, 12–15). Their plan was to enlist 90 defectors and then to boost that number to 150 in a subsequent election. They began their plotting in earnest on 30 November, but late that night, Nakasone received word that Miki would be the designated candidate. The plotting ended as quickly as it had begun.

Fukuda was also contemplating defection. His mentor, Kishi Nobusuke, had urged him the previous summer to resign from the Tanaka cabinet and risk being expelled. Kishi told Fukuda to simply form his own party and take his case to the people in an election (Mainichi shimbun seijibu 1993, 110–111). Fukuda also agreed in principle to consider defection, should the selection go to an election process. However, he was lukewarm to Nakasone's plans on the night of 30 November because he, unlike Nakasone, already had word of Shiina's designation of Miki. Fukuda, too, had previously hatched plans to form a new party with the Clean Government Party and Democratic Socialists, called the Liberal Progressive Party (Jiyū Kakushintō) (Naka 1990, 247).

Miki also considered the option of using the opposition parties, and he played it to his advantage in obtaining Shiina's designation of him to be Tanaka's successor. Unlike the others, Miki pursued this option with greater vigor, making his threat of defection more credible. On 26 November, Miki and Sasaki met and decided to pursue defection if the LDP leadership battle went to an election. Sasaki reports their agreement that if Miki could bring out thirty defectors, the opposition could provide the rest of the votes needed to elect Miki as prime minister (Sasaki and Kunimasa 1989, 205–208). At this meeting, Miki said that Japan needed two parties that could regularly alternate in power; without such a change, he said, both the LDP and Japan would sink. They agreed that in a coalition government, such contentious issues as the United States–Japan Security Treaty would be set aside. Their discussion shows a willingness to set aside ideological barriers when incentives to cooperate were strong. They also agreed that if Shiina succeeded in designating an acceptable compromise candidate, they would both deny any such plans to split the LDP and form a new party.

Sasaki's task was to prepare the opposition parties to be ready to work with Miki and others from the LDP, if they defected. Many of the preparations for this possibility had already been accomplished. Several months earlier, in September, Eda Saburō had caused a stir in the Socialist Party by urging it to be ready to cooperate with defectors from the LDP. By November, the secretary general of the Socialists, Ishibashi Masashi, had endorsed this position. Sasaki met with Democratic Socialist Chairman Kasuga, and they mapped out their strategy to contact opposition leaders. Sasaki met with Eda, who was initially cool to the idea because of his need to defer to Socialist Party leaders. Chairman of the Socialist Party Sasaki Kōzō had previously extended a public invitation to begin talks with the Democratic Socialists about a possible reunification. When Kasuga contacted him about a meeting, he responded positively and did not rule out the possibility of working with LDP defectors.

Kasuga, however, was working his own angle for the new coalition (Mainichi shimbun seijibu 1993, 51). Rather than supporting Miki for the prime ministership, he preferred to support Kōno Kenzō, the speaker of the House of Councillors, who had previously won that office with the support of the opposition parties and a group of LDP councillors who broke party ranks. After electing Kōno as the next prime minister, Kasuga planned for this support coalition to form a parliamentary group with the name either of Democrat Club (Minshū Club) or Society Club (Shakai Club). They would one year later fight an election together and then formally merge into a new centrist party. Kasuga was pushing this option through his own ties to the LDP in the Nakasone faction.

Though myriad plans existed, and though each faction head had the option to use the defect threat to gain Shiina's designation, only Miki succeeded in using the threat to his advantage. Miki's threat was the most credible, and his ties to the opposition were better. He was a member of the last coalition government with the Socialists, in 1947–1948, and he played a role in the so-called *bakayarō* dissolution of the Diet in concert with the opposition parties.[20] A strong pacifist, he was closer to the opposition ideologically, but those ties alone did not make his threat credible. Miki spoke out unmistakably against selecting the prime minister by election, and he made sure that Shiina learned of his meetings with Sasaki and others. The night Shiina found out about Miki's plotting (29 November), he decided to designate Miki as Tanaka's successor. Miki could show unequivocally that failure to consider his interests would result in a split of the LDP, whereas other contenders at that time could not present similar, concrete plans for defection.

Miki's credible threat to defect explains Shiina's anomalous decision to designate someone other than the strongest faction leader. If Shiina had chosen Ōhira or Fukuda, the designation probably would not have been accepted. In the bitter ensuing battle, the party would have split, and Shiina's legacy would be as the man who had destroyed the LDP. Designating Miki allowed the party to stay together by avoiding a contentious election battle.

The plotting surrounding Miki's selection also indicates that ideological and networking factors influenced Shiina's decision. These factors were not as constraining as they are often assumed to be. Every contender for the position was plotting with the opposition. Ideological differences among the candidates were not a significant barrier to the discussion of such plots. Both Nakasone and Fukuda were involved in their own schemes, and in later years, Ōhira went on to become closely intertwined with opposition politicians in coalition negotiations. Miki's closer historical ties to the opposition provided him with the advantage of greater credibility, but each of the other leaders in the LDP had his own ties to various members of the opposition camp. Networks did not limit such ties; they were easily created even when networks did not exist. The weakness or lack of such ties did not prevent an active schemer from approaching the other side.

The 1980 Election

Sasaki Ryōsaku noted that the abandoned Miki plot could lay the foundation for the next strategic move (Mainichi shimbun seijibu 1993, 79). The opportunities for such a move were not long in coming. In choosing Miki's successor, Ōhira and Fukuda fought the battle that Shiina had avoided in designating Miki. The ill will from this battle created another split in the LDP that presented opportunities for the opposition.

Throughout this period, the centrist parties began to consolidate their move toward the LDP. They moved beyond talk of just defection from the LDP and began to work closely with the LDP and its leaders. A first step closer to the LDP came about by allying with LDP candidates in important local races, such as governorships of major prefectures. In Tokyo, the Socialist-Communist–backed incumbent was defeated by a new coalition of the LDP and centrist parties. The prelude for this upset was the mayoral race in Kushiro. There, Sasaki met with LDP representative Nakagawa Ichirō and persuaded the LDP not to put up a candidate. It became a race between the Socialist-backed incumbent and the centrist candidate, who received conservative support. The centrist candidate won; this began the trend of centrist-LDP cooperation in local races.

Later, Sasaki, Ōhira, and Takeiri, chairmen of the Democratic Socialists, LDP, and Clean Government Party, respectively, held secret meetings to choose a coalition candidate for the upcoming Tokyo gubernatorial race. In January 1979, they selected their candidate, who went on to win. This pattern was repeated in prefectures and cities around the country. In April 1979, Sasaki called for a policy agreement with the LDP; he had given up on opposition party coalitions and was firmly committed to joining the LDP in a coalition government. In November 1979, the Clean Government Party and the Democratic Socialists announced their intentions to work with the LDP if it lost a parliamentary majority. They also agreed in private that they would work together with the LDP in a coalition, not allowing the LDP to divide them against each other.

Throughout this period, the centrists repeatedly negotiated with LDP Prime Minister Ōhira Masayoshi, whose policy for dealing with the opposition was called a "partial coalition." He would work with the centrist parties on selected issues or local races, but he refused to create a formal coalition government. At one point, he actually accepted a centrist proposal to modify the 1980 budget bill, but he reversed his position the next day because he was afraid it would have led to a formal coalition between the parties and the LDP. He saw no consensus within the LDP to move toward such a coalition government. A coalition with the LDP would come about only when the LDP lost its parliamentary majority.

Shortly thereafter, this prospect became a near reality: Turmoil arose within the LDP. An important block of LDP representatives abstained in a no-confidence vote; the government of Prime Minister Ōhira fell, and an election was called. The Democratic Socialists were torn over the best strategy in this situation. Kasuga urged support of the Ōhira government in the no-confidence motion in exchange for future coalitional concessions from Ōhira. Sasaki called for building two political parties, which could alternate in power. He envisioned defections from the LDP and party reorganizations. The decision became moot, however: The LDP went on to a spectacular electoral victory that made partial or parliamentary coalitions irrelevant.

The debate and the events of 1980 helped push the Socialists even closer to accepting the possibility of working with LDP defectors in a coalition government. The Socialists also seized this opportunity to abandon their decade-long policy of endorsing cooperation with both the Communists and the centrist parties. The failure of coalition efforts in 1980 put a damper on cooperation discussions for several years, but 1980 represented a turning point for the Socialist Party. The party had finally committed to the path that Eda had outlined a decade earlier, and this change of policy helped pave the way for the events of 1993.

The Nikaidō Affair

The 1983 elections again opened the door to coalition speculations. The LDP lost its majority in the House of Representatives, retaining control of the chamber only by entering into a coalition government with the New Liberal Club, the group of LDP defectors who had left the party in the wake of the Tanaka scandal. Even with the addition of the New Liberal Club, the LDP had only a razor-thin majority. In addition, a leadership battle was brewing in the LDP. The prime minister was Nakasone Yasuhiro, elected with the strong support of the Tanaka faction. The question was whether Nakasone's term should be extended for another year. Though Tanaka was still nominally in control of his faction, forces were at work to wrest control from him. Some Tanaka faction members wanted to return the prime ministership to their faction. Other factions wanted their turn at the top spot.

In the midst of this plotting, Suzuki Zenkō began to organize support for Tanaka faction member Nikaidō Susumu as the next prime minister. Suzuki approached Clean Government Party leader Takeiri and asked him for his party's support if it were a close battle. Suzuki later contacted

Sasaki Ryōsaku, and in the days leading up to the LDP decision, the two opposition party leaders waged a feverish battle to mobilize politicians in support of Nikaidō.

The centrist participation in this battle was at first distrusted. Because Tanaka's close ties to the Clean Government Party were well known, party motives were suspect. Was the effort to promote Nikaidō part of some secret Tanaka plot? Why would the loyal Clean Government Party back one of Tanaka's own lieutenants in a bid for the prime ministership that would increase Nikaidō's power over the Tanaka faction at Tanaka's expense? Indeed, when told of the centrist support of Nikaidō, Tanaka reportedly boasted he could end that support with one phone call to the Clean Government Party. Party leader Yano (1994) defended his stance as necessary to rein in the extremism of the Nakasone prime ministership. He further defended his moves as being in Tanaka's best interests, because the real plotters against Tanaka within his faction lay elsewhere; Nikaidō was still loyal to Tanaka.

At the suggestion of other Tanaka lieutenants, notably Kanemaru Shin, Tanaka crushed the Nikaidō plot, but in hindsight, Yano was correct. Kanemaru eventually would lead an internal faction revolt against Tanaka with his ally Takeshita Noboru. Kanemaru feared that selecting this prime minister from the Tanaka faction would preclude selecting another prime minister from the same faction for several years. Because Kanemaru was working to support Takeshita he could not allow Nikaidō to become prime minister, for that would block Takeshita's future path to the same position. Kanemaru gained the future support of Nakasone and his faction by supporting another term for Nakasone at Nikaidō's expense (Naka 1990, 188).

In these maneuverings, the two centrist parties, especially the Clean Government Party, played a crucial role. The Clean Government Party and the Democratic Socialists signaled early on their willingness to support Nikaidō's bid for the prime ministership. Part of their desire can be explained simply as a strategic opportunity to gain a seat at the coalition table. Though the Clean Government Party opposed the nationalistic policies of the Nakasone administration, their ostensible ideological concerns seem questionable; Nakasone had been involved with political plots in the 1960s and 1970s, and he had been a nationalist then, too. Moreover, the party ignored the ideological difficulties of choosing Nikaidō as a coalition candidate. Nikaidō had been tainted in the Tanaka scandals, but the Clean Government Party justified its support by saying essentially that Nikaidō was the lesser of two evils.

The Democratic Socialists' participation was also problematic. Initially, Sasaki was troubled by the plot against Nakasone, his former partner in scheming. Former party chairman Kasuga was close to Nakasone, meaning Sasaki's efforts on behalf of Nikaidō had to be kept secret from Kasuga as well. Neither Sasaki nor the Clean Government Party leaders let their stronger ties to other LDP politicians preclude their alliance with Nikaidō and Suzuki when offered a seat in a coalition government in exchange for their support.

The plot failed, and Sasaki and the Clean Government Party leaders were severely criticized for plotting with the LDP. Centrist party officials were upset that the agreement with Nikaidō had been struck without prior consultation.[21] However, Sasaki and Takeiri defended their actions, claiming that it was correct to exploit opportunities to become part of a coalition government.

Rengō and the 1989 Election

After the Nikaidō affair, stability returned to the LDP. Nakasone continued in power and led the LDP to a spectacular victory in 1986. The next leadership transition was smooth: The prime ministership rotated back to the former Tanaka faction, now under the leadership of Takeshita Noboru. The opposition had no role to play; the LDP parliamentary majority was solid and the succession struggle was relatively peaceful.

Hence, the opposition parties returned to their efforts to build opposition cooperation and reduce the LDP majority. Electoral cooperation moved up on the agenda, stimulated in large part by the revival of twenty-year-old efforts to unify the politically divided labor union movement. When these efforts culminated in the creation of a new labor federation, Rengō, unions that previously had been aligned with either the Socialist or Democratic Socialist Parties became members of the same labor federation. Rengō leadership pushed hard for the constituent unions to set aside their differences and work together, and for the respective political parties to set aside their differences as well. They urged and sponsored electoral cooperation and a plan of opposition coordination. Their plans for opposition unity resembled the plans of twenty years earlier and foreshadowed the events of 1993. The Rengō plan for victory urged the cooperation and then merger of the Socialist Party, the Democratic Socialist Party, and the minor Social Democratic League into one party. As part of this merger, everyone acknowledged that the left wing of the Socialist Party would not want to participate. Union leaders urged the Socialist Party to get rid of this left-wing faction, just as the unions had lost their Communist-affiliated members when the Socialist-affiliated unions had joined the more moderate Rengō federation.

The Rengō plan also acknowledged the participation of LDP defectors in the plan to take power, thinking it unlikely that the opposition could reach majority status without some defectors from the LDP. Their plan also counted on Clean Government Party support as a cooperative partner, though not as a constituent part of the new political party. Rengō's sponsorship was based on a common union base, and the Clean Government Party, with its religious affiliations, was too different to become part of the newly envisioned political party. In addition, the organization distrusted Clean Government Party activists and feared what might occur, should they be included.

As in previous, similar plans, the Rengō initiative did not advance beyond the stage of electoral cooperation, but Rengō-sponsored cooperation proved a great success in the 1989 House of Councillors election. Rengō's success, coupled with a massive swing in the electorate from the LDP to the Socialist Party, deprived the LDP of its majority in the House of Councillors for the first time since the creation of the LDP in 1955. Though budget bills, treaties, and the selection of the prime minister did not have to pass the House of Councillors, all other legislation had to pass that house or be passed in the House of Representatives by a two-thirds majority. With the exception of budget legislation, the LDP had lost its legislative majority.

Ironically, these successes were the root cause of the failure of cooperative efforts to advance beyond electoral cooperation. Much of the Socialist advance in the 1989 election seemed to come at the expense of the centrist parties, and the tendency was even more apparent in the 1990 House of Representatives election, when the LDP held its own and the Socialists advanced at the expense of their centrist allies. Cooperative efforts yielded disparate benefits, and the centrist parties became disenchanted. The problem was exacerbated by the increasing confidence of the Socialist Party, which had actually won more votes than the LDP in 1989. Some Socialist Party members saw the possibility of becoming a majority party without centrist cooperation; these members naturally supported all Socialist efforts to win more seats, even if those seats came at the expense of centrist allies.

A second problem of success is that with the LDP's loss of its legislative majority, it began to court the opposition parties in building legislative and electoral coalitions. The centrist parties and the Socialists were now actively being wooed by the LDP. The incentives to continue active opposition cooperation declined when it appeared that such cooperation had achieved its goal of rendering the LDP vulnerable. Plotting and scheming now focused on act 2 of the drama: who would become the LDP's coalition partner. It was in this setting that Kanemaru Shin and his protégé, Ozawa Ichirō, began their proposals of party reformulation and electoral reform.

Kanemaru Shin and Plans to Split the LDP

Shortly after the 1990 elections, LDP kingpin Kanemaru Shin met secretly with Rengō union leader Yamagishi Akira and Socialist Party leader Tanabe Makoto. Kanemaru told them the LDP needed to split, forming a new party with the centrists and part of the Socialists. Kanemaru said he would not leave the party, but the younger generation, led by his protégé Ozawa Ichirō, would—he compared Ozawa to Mikhail Gorbachev, someone who could change things. In other secret meetings, Kanemaru said that Japan was in its worst situation since the United States had forced Japan to open its borders in 1854. He also urged a grand coalition of the LDP and the Socialists (Tanabe 1997).

Kanemaru's views were not new. Miki had said nearly the same thing twenty years earlier. The desirability of two large, moderate parties that alternated in power was a recurring theme in Japanese politics. That Kanemaru picked up this theme is not surprising; the LDP was in dire straits. It had lost its majority in the House of Councillors, and it was being hammered by repeated scandals. In the foreign policy arena, Japan's political power and political will did not seem commensurate with its growing economic influence.

The importance of Kanemaru's sponsorship of these ideas is that it laid the groundwork for the actual split of the LDP in 1993. Kanemaru's support and his ties to Tanabe explain Tanabe's predictive powers when in the spring of 1993 he warned of a possible breakup of the LDP, a breakup that occurred six months later. Yamagishi's ties to Kanemaru also explain why Yamagishi played a crucial role in pulling together the opposition parties, throughout the negotiations over the electoral system and in the new coalition government. As Kanemaru faded from the scene, Ozawa Ichirō took up the mantle of change. Ozawa implemented change using political reform as a vehicle. Electoral reform was the institutional change necessary for permanent defection from the LDP, and for the structural changes necessary for the LDP and Japan.

Conclusion

Every interaction between these parties is heavily colored by the idiosyncrasies of the individual and the situation. Though no single explanation fits every story, common themes run through the narrative. First, the idea of saving Japan by breaking up the LDP and forming two new parties was a recurring theme; it was part of the Nishimura proposal, and it was shared by the opposition reformists who succeeded him. Miki clearly stated it in 1974; Fukuda, Kasuga, and Sasaki also shared this goal (Naka 1990, 209); Kanemaru became a vocal proponent of it; and finally, Ozawa Ichirō used it to justify his actions.

Second, the patterns of negotiations, schemes, and cooperation generally operate according to incentives that are recognizable in any society. These patterns are not unique to Japan. Coalition opportunities are driven first by numbers. Defections become more likely when a group has a notably slim majority; the smaller the majority, the greater the power wielded by small groups of defectors. Similarly, a leadership struggle within a group, or simply a leadership rivalry between two strong politicians, opens doors for outside participation. Takeover plots will not always occur whenever there is a leadership struggle or whenever a party has a small majority, but they are more likely under these circumstances. A split in the LDP could still have occurred when the LDP was strong and ascendant and there had been no leadership struggle, but such occurrences are rare. Each political plot can be traced to these two circumstances; politicians, we can safely conclude, respond to tangible incentives in leadership struggles and coalition negotiations.

Though ideology has an effect in limiting potential coalition or alliance partners, the rhetoric that surrounds the importance of ideology is much stronger than its punch. In the Japanese example, ideology was repeatedly set aside to make way for a potential coalition. Though observers expressed shock at the cavalier manner in which coalition partners in the 1990s turned a blind eye to ideological differences, the historical record shows that similar actions had been taken in the coalition cabinets of the late 1940s, and that Miki and Sasaki had planned to do something similar in the 1970s. Clean Government Party leaders and Democratic Socialist leader Sasaki had been roundly criticized by their party members for their willingness to join forces so quickly with the

LDP at the time of the Nikaidō plot. There is, therefore, historical precedent for the Socialist decision to disregard ideological differences in order to be part of the Hosokawa coalition government in 1993, and for Socialist leader Murayama's decision to unilaterally revise objectionable Socialist policies to obtain LDP support for a Socialist prime minister in 1994.

Similarly, a strong historical precedent was in place for parties to reach past their normal networking ties and ideologically proximate partners, if necessary, to build winning coalitions. Socialist participation in the initial Hosokawa government was accomplished through the expected routes, the more moderate faction and leaders of the party. When the LDP began courting the Socialists, though, in 1994, it used ties through the party's left wing. The left-wing leader, Murayama, became a strong proponent of the coalition with the LDP. Similarly, left-wing leader Kunihiro Masao actively worked for this LDP alliance after having been part of the defection of Socialist legislators that defeated the electoral reform bill initially in the House of Councillors vote. The incongruity of the left wing of the Socialist Party teaming up with the LDP was noticed by all, but it too has its historical precedents. Within the LDP, some of those closest to the opposition have been those ideologically furthest from it. Consider Nakasone's strong involvement in plots with the opposition, despite his strong nationalism; or Tanaka, Kanemaru, and Ozawa's strong ties with the opposition parties despite their reputations as the most corrupt of LDP politicians.

Finally, the historical record shows that the former opposition parties were not incompetent or complacent in their actions. They pursued with vigor a variety of options, both among themselves and with the LDP. Their failure can be attributed to miscalculations or to their inherently inferior strategic situation, not to an absence of desire or talent. I will never forget my interview with Sasaki Ryōsaku when he was in retirement, suffering from Parkinson's disease. This dean of cooperative efforts and coalition scheming said he was ready to throw in the towel. He had reason to be discouraged, after more than twenty years of unsuccessful efforts, but he had never given up. His dream came true only a few years after his retirement.

6

Successes and Failures
of the Opposition Parties

SUPERFICIAL EVIDENCE seems to suggest that the Japanese opposition has utterly failed. The LDP ruled Japan for thirty-eight uninterrupted years, until 1993, and it returned to power in 1994, reconstructing its parliamentary majority in 1997. Hrebenar (1986, 83) presents succinctly the common stereotype of opposition failure and incompetence. With regard to the Socialist Party, he states, "Many Japanese regard it as poorly organized, indifferently led, narrowly based, doctrinaire and irresponsible in policy, lacking in autonomy, poor in human talent, and overly prone to ideological and factional division." Hrebenar's statement is based on the common explanations for opposition failure—poor leadership and ideological rigidity.

The growing school of rational-choice literature on Japan reaches a similar conclusion. Cox (1996, 1997; Cox and Niou 1994) explains LDP longevity in power by citing its relative electoral efficiency. The LDP's greater access to resources allows it to better coordinate its electoral efforts than the opposition camp, thus winning more seats. Matthew McCubbins and Frances McCall Rosenbluth (1995) seem to agree. Though inefficient, LDP coordinative efforts seem to compare favorably with the even less efficient methods of the opposition camp. This school of analysis explains LDP success by looking at the institutions and resources available.

I present a contrasting view of opposition efforts. Opposition parties repeatedly came close to facilitating a breakup of the LDP in the 1970s and 1980s. They cooperated in elections to win seats from LDP candidates. In 1993, their support was crucial in the Ozawa-led defections from the LDP. Since 1993 these parties have gained influence on legislation, and their members have served in cabinet posts and as prime minister. The parties have increased their contacts with the bureaucracy, and they are regular and consistent players in legislative discussions. Opposition politicians have recast their popular image and created new parties. They now reach out to, and receive, the support of a much broader cross-section of the electorate.

These two characterizations of the opposition seem contradictory, yet the difference can be reconciled by correctly identifying the goals the opposition was pursuing. If the only goal of the opposition was to increase its share of the electorate so as to become a parliamentary majority, then the conclusion that it failed, and failed starkly, is indeed inescapable. However, if analysts recognize the multiple goals of the opposition, then it becomes possible to see areas where the opposition achieved its goals, though it did not wrest power from the LDP.

The designation of goals or standards by which performance is measured is crucial. In campaigns, for example, the battle over such measuring sticks is vital to the success of a candidate. Campaign staff in the United States will try to lower expectations before a debate or a primary election so that even a mediocre performance can be claimed a "victory." Thus a candidate might say that coming in second in a certain primary will be a "victory" because of the large advantage of the opponent in that state. If the candidate can persuade the media to use his or her standard, then a second-place finish will be touted as a victory, and the candidate will gain momentum.

In a similar but more disinterested manner, the standard by which the efforts of the Japanese former opposition parties are judged should be closely examined. These parties did achieve their goals, if their goals are allowed to include such things as enticing divisions within the LDP, reformulating the opposition parties, gaining legislative access, and maximizing seat shares through interparty cooperation. It is true that the opposition lost every election from 1948 to 1989, a sobering record of defeat. Focusing on only these defeats, though, obscures the more interesting story of the opposition's efforts and successes.

A Rational-Choice Perspective on Events

The two competing stereotypes of the opposition, and their reconciliation, can be restated from a rational-choice analytical perspective. The opposition parties' goals have been to increase their seats in the Diet and to take control of government. However, they have repeatedly failed to take power from the LDP, and they have failed to make the changes necessary to take power. Two of the proffered explanations for these failures, that the opposition politicians were complacent or that they were too consumed with petty ideological jealousies, would seem at face value to be evidence of irrational behavior.

The conclusion that opposition leaders were working at cross-purposes against their own stated goals would be surprising, if not shocking. Faced with such a conclusion, practitioners of rational choice would make one of two possible analytical moves. First, they might look at the supposed irrationality and posit other goals that the actors were actually pursuing. When these other goals are considered, the supposed irrational behavior is revealed as rational, that is, goal oriented. An example of this analytical shift is Kathleen Bawn's (1993, 965–989) analysis of electoral reform in the former West Germany. At one point, the Social Democrats supported proportional representation rather than single-seat districts, despite the fact that single-seat districts would have given them, as one of the two largest parties, a greater share of seats in the Bundestag. Bawn, however, shifts the analysis from the goal of maximizing seats to the alternative goal of maximizing favorable policy outcomes by making coalition governments more likely. This other goal justifies support of a proportional representation system.

Alternatively, a rational-choice theorist is likely to analyze the strategic incentives in the supposed irrationality. An analysis of these incentives could well lead to the conclusion that a coordination problem exists. In this situation, rational actions by individuals can lead to suboptimal results for the group. The group may fail, even though the actions of individuals have been quite rational and the downfall of the group was predictable.

My analysis makes a similar reexamination of Japanese opposition goals and coordination dilemmas. I followed this analytical path not because an overarching assumption of rational behavior dictated such a conclusion. Rather, my empirical work in the field with opposition politicians led me to reject the stereotype of opposition incompetence, complacency, and deficiency. I turn now to an evaluation of each of three popular explanations of opposition failure.

Poor Leadership and Complacency in the Opposition

In 1988, when I began my field work on the topic of opposition electoral cooperation, I thought my research would help document the findings of opposition incompetence and complacency that are common in the literature. I expected to find ample evidence of the several most often identified pathologies of the opposition. To my surprise, I found in interviews that opposition leaders were competent, intelligent, and enthusiastic in their plotting and scheming of how to take power from the LDP. I remember Takeiri Yoshikatsu's emotional description of Eda Saburō's failure to divide the Socialist Party. It was clear more than a decade later that he still felt very strongly about these issues. Sasaki Ryōsaku, a skilled orchestrator of cooperative efforts and schemes to divide the LDP, spoke with emotion and intensity despite his frail physical condition. Ishibashi Masashi was extremely animated as he described his efforts to reform the Socialist Party. Not one of these leaders seemed complacent with his position in the opposition. Each of them had devoted a career to devising and hatching new schemes for taking power from the LDP. They were politically savvy, intelligent, and articulate. I was puzzled. How could the failings of the opposition be laid at the feet of complacent, incompetent leaders, if the leadership of these parties was energetic and effective?

MacDougall (1982) presents a sophisticated argument that deals with the incongruity of opposition failure coupled with energetic and competent leaders. He focuses the blame on party structures that make it difficult for good leaders to actually lead their parties. His explanation shifts the focus to the complacence or ideological rigidity of the rank and file of the parliamentary party, a group that allegedly resists and obstructs innovative party leaders.

MacDougall's shifting the blame for complacency from the opposition's leaders to its rank and file in the Diet is better supported by the evidence. The complacency of opposition representatives can be traced to the multiseat districts of the electoral system used from 1948 to 1993. Opposition politicians could be elected with as little as 10 or 15 percent of the vote in some districts. In addition, the importance of organizations in highly circumscribed electoral campaigns created incentives for opposition politicians to rely largely on organizational support in elections. In many districts, these politicians came to have what the Japanese called *shiteiseki*—a reserved seat in the Diet. These politicians could be elected easily with their organization's votes. In contrast, many LDP representatives feared another LDP challenger rising up in an attempt to build a stronger personal support organization. Even though the LDP would usually not give such challengers the party nomination, they could run as independents, and if they won, they would get the LDP party nomination in the subsequent election instead of the defeated incumbent.

This difference in electoral threat led to an organizational dominance of candidate selection within the opposition. Union leaders were "promoted" to the Diet as a reward for their long years of service to the union. Such politicians often were complacent, merely enjoying the perks of elective office. They were not required to make sacrifices to gain election as most leaders in the LDP were.

I saw evidence of this attitude among Socialist Party representatives. One man reluctantly explained his decision to run for the House of Councillors as resulting from a bargain he had struck with the party. He agreed to run only if the party agreed to support him for two terms. This commitment was important because that length of service was necessary for receiving a pension as a Diet member.[1] Many officials in the Socialist Party criticize their own members on these grounds. Clearly, a gulf divides the enthusiasm of party leaders and that of rank-and-file representatives. This problem was most severe in the Socialist Party.

Yet this explanation alone is not persuasive. A complacent parliamentary rank and file can explain some of the opposition's problems, but not all. For example, complacent representatives might account for resistance to changing electoral lineups of candidates or to encouraging greater electoral cooperation, but they should not have obstructed efforts to moderate party policies or to plot with LDP renegades. The opposition of party supporters or of such support groups as unions might explain the failure of the initiatives, but would not the complacency of Diet representatives make it easier for party leaders to undertake these initiatives, even facilitating party reform or coordination efforts?

Furthermore, the attitude difference between opposition party leaders and their Diet representatives mirrors a similar attitude gap in the LDP. The history of the LDP's attempts to craft electoral reform illustrates this point best. Single-seat districts would be to the LDP's advantage and occasionally were favored by party leaders, but in every instance, internal opposition from individual LDP representatives blocked such reforms. In this situation, personal political interests stopped the party from enacting a change that would be unambiguously advantageous to the party. This dynamic in the LDP drove Ozawa Ichirō to leave the party and to advocate a new political alignment that would solve this problem. The alleged incompetence of the opposition is similar to the coordination dilemmas that also existed in the LDP.

Ideology

A second explanation of opposition failure derives from the observation that the opposition parties were consumed in irrelevant ideological squabbles, which prevented them from taking more effective action. This ideological predilection arguably comes from any of three sources. A structural explanation focuses again on the multiseat districts and the opposition's need to divide the vote among multiple candidates. Ideological differentiation was a useful method for the opposition parties to efficiently divide the electorate among multiple candidates. This useful device then works against the same parties: They are less flexible because of the clearly staked out ideological positions they have taken. A second structural explanation begins with the irrelevance of the opposition in Japanese politics. Because of this irrelevance, parties were free to let meaningless ideological squabbles consume their time and energy. Last, a historical explanation focuses on the prewar history of ideological divisions that continue to affect opposition efforts to achieve unity.

These explanations are supported with ample evidence. Eda Saburō's efforts to reform the Socialist Party ran aground on the shoals of ideological divisions. All subsequent efforts to reform that party were blocked by ideologically based opposition. Socialist–Democratic Socialist cooperation was blocked throughout much of the 1970s by ideological differences. Ideology clearly matters, and it has hampered efforts by the opposition to take power from the LDP or to reduce LDP influence.

Party leaders also used ideological differences as an excuse for stymied cooperative innovations. Whenever cooperation broke down, it was easier for parties to blame the ideology of the other side than to admit that parochial concerns of party advantage were the real reason for the breakdown. When the benefits of cooperation were great, or coordination dilemmas blocking cooperation were solved, parties suddenly could deal with ideological differences that previously were, or subsequently became, intractable problems. For example, in 1971 the Socialists and the Democratic Socialists managed to achieve a satisfactory level of cooperation. At repeated intervals in the 1970s and 1980s, Democratic Socialists set aside ideological differences and approached Socialist leaders about possible coalitions involving LDP renegades. Yet, after 1971, these same two parties could not cooperate electorally, ostensibly because of ideological differences. Ideological differences allegedly blocked all efforts to cooperate electorally, but these differences could be set aside to form a coalition government. Party leadership finally did set aside ideological differences and formed the Hoso-kawa and Murayama governments.

Ideology does matter. It makes certain linkages more difficult to create. Ideological distance can strain cooperative relationships, but it was not the ultimate factor in determining the outcome of party coop-erative efforts. These efforts were more significantly influenced by calculations of party advantage than by ideological differences.

The Opposition Lacks Resources

Cox (1996, 1997; Cox and Niou 1994) presents a third explanation of opposition failure that does not rely on a lack of initiative or intelligence on the part of opposition party leaders or members. He claims that in the realm of electoral cooperation, the opposition has fewer resources available—it cannot craft government policies as well as the LDP to reward supporters and more efficiently divide the electorate in support of multiple candidates. Cox presents significant quantitative data to show the LDP's electoral advantage, and he concludes that the LDP stays in power because of this electoral advantage. Cox's explanation is similar to T. J. Pempel's (1990, 16) broader explication of the "virtuous cycle." A party in power can structure political discourse and reward supporters to make its rule self-perpetuating.

A more refined examination of Cox's evidence, however, indicates an opposite conclusion. The LDP is not more efficient than the opposition in the realm of electoral coordination. The LDP has no electoral advan-tage; in fact, it performs worse than the opposition parties when those parties are cooperating fully. Thus, the LDP stays in power not because of its electoral efficiency but despite its electoral inefficiency.

Arguments Supporting a Claim of LDP Electoral Efficiency

Electoral efficiency under the former Japanese electoral system con-sisted of doing two tasks well. Because a party or coalition of parties often ran multiple candidates in the same district, they needed to run the optimal number of candidates in a district, and to divide the vote equally between those candidates. Failure in either task resulted in a party or alliance winning fewer seats than it could have. A camp that ran three candidates when it had the votes to elect only two risked dividing its vote so thinly that only one candidate was elected. Furthermore, even if the camp correctly ran three candidates when it had the votes to elect all three, if one candidate won a lopsided share of the camp's votes, perhaps only that one of the three would be elected. Thus, both the conservative and the opposition camps in Japan faced two serious coordination dilemmas.

Cox (1996, 1997) acknowledges that each camp possessed different resources in solving these coordination dilemmas. He claims, however, that the LDP had the advantage of being the party in power. It could distribute money, cabinet posts, and pork-barrel projects to help solve both dilemmas. If there were too many candidates in a district, the party could mediate negotiations between faction leaders to equitably restrict the number of candidates in certain districts. Any remaining discrepancies could also be smoothed over by distributing money, cabinet posts, and pork-barrel projects to a side that felt cheated in the party nomination negotiations. The LDP could efficiently parcel out nominations because party leaders could centrally coordinate this process. The resources available to the LDP made it possible for the party to extract sacrifices from candidates and factions; these sacrifices could be compensated for by side payments to factions. Cox and Rosenbluth (1994) and Cox and Matthew Shugart (1995) also describe how the efficiency of LDP nomination procedures has increased over time.

The Achilles' heel of LDP nomination procedures is the incentive that exists for party factions and candidates to cheat on party decisions. Despite its central control over nominations, the party effectively abdicates such control after elections by its policy of welcoming conservative independents into the party and giving them the LDP nomination in the next election (Christensen 1995, 580). Disgruntled candidates and their factional allies know that if they can win the election as an independent, opposition to their candidacy or place in the party will become irrelevant. Cox and Rosenbluth (1994) examine this phenomenon; they conclude it is not a significant barrier to LDP efficiency, since the number of affiliated independents has declined in tandem with greater LDP efficiency in parceling out the optimal number of nominations. They do note, though, that the number of affiliated independents rose in the 1980s and that these independents consistently numbered between 7 and 20 percent of the conservative camp's candidates.

In its second task, dividing the electorate, the LDP has relied largely on a decentralized approach. The distribution of money and pork-barrel projects, as well as memberships in LDP-sponsored, sector-specific committees, allows multiple candidates in districts to differentiate themselves sectorally (McCubbins and Rosenbluth 1995; Cox 1996, 1997).

For example, a candidate will stake out a position with an important support group such as local transportation companies. Once elected, that candidate will take a position on the LDP transportation committee and will claim credit for all government support of the transportation sector in the election district. Another LDP candidate will stake out a position with another LDP support group, such as small shopkeepers. McCubbins and Rosenbluth (1995) show that party committee assignments reduce overlap in districts, helping to ensure that each candidate exploits different niches in the conservative electorate. These actions ensure that votes are distributed among multiple candidates.

The Achilles' heel of this coordination mechanism is that there is no central coordination. Exploiting niches ensures that the electorate gets divided, but it does not ensure that the electorate is divided equally. Each candidate competes to gain as much support as possible. Nothing in this competitive process assures that anything other than a rough, unequal division of the electorate will occur. In addition, the loyalty of supporters and support groups to specific candidates means that no influential person or group in the electoral process has an incentive to shift votes from an LDP candidate assured of victory to a struggling LDP candidate. McCubbins and Rosenbluth (1995, 42) recognize this inefficiency and thus label LDP coordination strategies as a "second–best solution." Cox (1996, 1997) recognizes that opposition parties also have distribution strategies that might also be efficient. Nevertheless, all authors conclude that whatever deficiencies exist, the LDP is still more efficient than the opposition.

Explanations of Opposition Electoral Efficiency

The opposition's method of coordinating its number of candidates is similar to the LDP's method. Party leaders meet together to negotiate which party's candidate will stand down and which will run, in much the same manner that LDP faction leaders negotiate. Opposition leaders lack the resources available to the LDP that could be used as side payments to gain cooperation in these negotiations, but they enforce their decisions much more effectively than the LDP. Each of the opposition parties has little tolerance for unauthorized candidacies by party members running as independents. Strong party organizations and closely affiliated support groups whose loyalty is to the party, not to individual candidates, make failure likely for a renegade, independent candidacy of an opposition party member. Thus, opposition decisions on candidate numbers are rarely undone by unauthorized candidacies. In contrast, similar decisions by the LDP are regularly inflated by 7 to 20 percent by the candidacies of affiliated independents.

The efficiency of the opposition camp depends on each party's willingness to negotiate. Perhaps it can be argued that the LDP's resource advantage explains why the LDP can coordinate in every election—in contrast to the opposition, which only began to cooperate nationally in 1971 and only reached full cooperation levels in 1979. Though it may be true that opposition cooperative efforts are more slowly initiated and more quickly undone than similar efforts in the LDP, the opposition has, with time, moved to partial cooperation and full cooperation. This development of efficient mechanisms of electoral cooperation mirrors the LDP's gradual development of greater efficiency. The LDP began coordinating in 1958, becoming more efficient over the next decade; the opposition's need to cooperate was not great until the late 1960s. Within a decade, these parties had developed an efficient method of coordinating candidacies.

The opposition also developed a coordination mechanism for the task of dividing the vote equally among multiple candidacies. The opposition's methods are radically different from the LDP's; it relies on a coordinated (thus more efficient) division of the vote than the LDP's decentralized approach.

The opposition electorate is initially divided along workplace (union) affiliations or religious lines. If the opposition parties stopped here, their efforts most likely would be more inefficient than the LDP's. Even with electoral agreements, many opposition voters would be reluctant to bridge the deep gulfs that separate these parties. Cooperation attempts would flounder (as they did in the early 1970s), as many opposition voters would ignore party instructions to vote for the candidates of other parties.

Opposition party leaders and leaders of important support groups recognized this problem. They used core voters of each organization who reliably followed an organization's instructions to vote for the candidates of other parties. By directing the votes of these core members, it became possible to fine-tune electoral cooperation efforts. The bulk of opposition voters could vote sincerely for their preferred candidates. Opposition leaders could then calculate at the margins how many votes needed to be shifted to equalize the distribution of votes among multiple candidates.

Both the opposition and the LDP use a blunt method to divide the electorate initially. The opposition advantage comes from their refining this initial division using reliable, core members of important support groups. These voters' organizational loyalty makes them willing to follow instructions and vote strategically across party lines. The opposition can do this fine-tuning because it has support groups with strong, hierarchical organizations that are committed to the party rather than to specific candidates. Thus, the organizations actively seek out opportunities to equalize votes between candidates and thus elect as many of their candidates across the nation as possible. LDP support organizations, which are loyal to a specific candidate, have much weaker incentives to shift votes to other candidates in the same district.

Evaluating the Comparative Efficiency of Electoral Coordination Efforts

The first task in comparing coordination efficiencies is to make sure that opposition efforts to cooperate are evaluated appropriately. The opposition's attitude toward cooperation varies from election to election. In the late 1950s, the opposition was not fragmented, so cooperation was not needed. This changed in 1960 with the splitting of the Socialist Party and the creation of the new Democratic Socialist Party. The opposition task of coordination became even more daunting with the debut of the Clean Government Party in the mid-1960s and the revival of the Communist Party. The opposition camp became diverse; the coordination problem of running the optimal number of candidates was tremendous. We would therefore expect that the opposition camp would have developed a poor record of coordination by the late 1960s.

In 1971, opposition cooperation took a new turn as the parties began to actively coordinate not only party nomination strategies but also vote distribution strategies. Chapter 4 shows that the coordination efforts began small but grew until, in the late 1970s, the unions began cross-party cooperative efforts that transcended party barriers to cooperation. With the exception of the Communists, the opposition made increasingly effective efforts to turn seats into votes throughout the 1970s and into the 1980s.

Thus, in comparing the efficiency of opposition electoral efforts with those of the LDP, the best and most appropriate comparisons are the years of full-scale opposition electoral cooperation (1979–1986). Comparisons of other years, such as the years of partial cooperation (1971–1976 and 1990) or the years of noncooperation (1958–1969), do not help answer the question of whether the LDP gains an advantage in electoral coordination because of its superior resources. Comparisons of these years measure only the difference between an LDP that is coordinating its efforts and an opposition that is not trying to cooperate, or is cooperating in only a few districts. The years 1972, 1976, and 1990 are years of partial cooperation for the following reasons. In 1972, cooperative efforts had just begun, and little informal cooperation occurred between unions. In 1976, informal cooperation was still not widespread, and Clean Government Party leaders decided to test their party's appeal by running a record number of candidates. Finally, in 1990, the Socialist Party, in the wake of its astounding victory in the previous year's House of Councillors election, put forth many new candidates and rejected most opportunities for electoral cooperation. Cooperative agreements existed, but in many districts, new Socialist candidates went head-to-head with centrist incumbents. These elections are not appropriate for a comparison of the opposition and the LDP's cooperative efficiencies.

A first test of the resource explanation can be achieved with aggregate electoral data. This test casts initial doubt on the resource explanation of opposition failure. The opposition parties have been as successful as the conservative camp in coordinating their candidates and supporters to maximize the share of seats they can win, given the number of votes they receive. The effectiveness of cooperative efforts becomes especially apparent when elections are viewed longitudinally (fig. 6.1).[2] In 1958, the opposition does as well as the conservative camp because the opposition essentially was just the Socialist Party. There was only a minor coordination problem because the Socialists, the single significant opposition party, could manage the number of candidates in a district as well as the LDP could. In subsequent elections during the period of noncooperation (1958–1969), however, the conservative camp outperforms the opposition camp. The opposition camp often outperforms the conservatives in the periods of partial and full electoral cooperation (1972–1990).

Cox (1997), however, accurately points to a pitfall in using such aggregate data. He suggests a "task-specific" approach to measuring the electoral efficiency of the two camps. The problem he identifies can be illustrated by the following example from a hypothetical United States Senate election. Suppose that going into the election, the Democrats hold sixteen and the Republicans hold seventeen of the seats up for election that year. All sixteen of the Democrat incumbents are running for reelection. However, only ten Republican incumbents are running

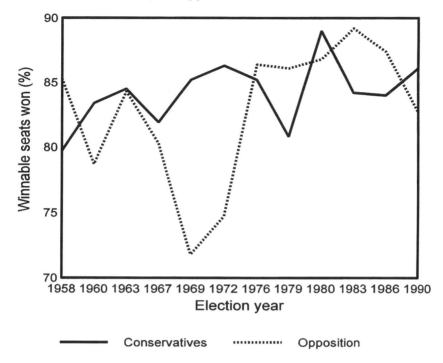

Figure 6.1 Comparison of electoral efficiencies

for reelection; the other seven have retired, creating open races in those seven seats. Because of the advantages of incumbency, the Republicans face the more difficult task of holding on to all seventeen seats when seven of them are open seats. The Democrats have an advantage—they have incumbents running in all their sixteen seats. Suppose that, in the election, the Democrats win all sixteen of their seats and manage to take one of the open Republican seats. The ten incumbent Republicans also win, and the Republicans manage to hold onto six of the seven open seats.

Which party did better in the election? The obvious answer, given by aggregate data, is that the Democrats did better. They won seventeen seats and the Republicans won only sixteen, for a net gain of one to the Democrats. If we look at the advantages of incumbency, though, the Republican victory in six of seven open seats suggests that the Republican Party or its candidates ran more effective campaigns than the Democrats. Under this task-specific analysis, we can conclude that the Republicans "won" the election. Though both parties elected 100

percent of their incumbents, the Republicans won 85 percent of the
open seats.

The evaluation depends on the question asked. If the question concerns control of the Senate, the conclusion that the Democrats won is
better, because the net change in seats was in the Democrats' favor. If
the question is which party ran the better campaign, it is appropriate to
conclude that the Republicans won, because they did better than the
Democrats when equivalent tasks were compared.

In this same manner, Cox points out that the LDP in Japan typically
had the more difficult coordination problem, for in many districts it had
the votes to win three or four seats, whereas the non-Communist opposition camp had more districts in which it could win only one or two
seats. Thus, it was easier for the opposition camp to parlay its votes into
seats than it was for the LDP to do so. In comparing the efficiency of

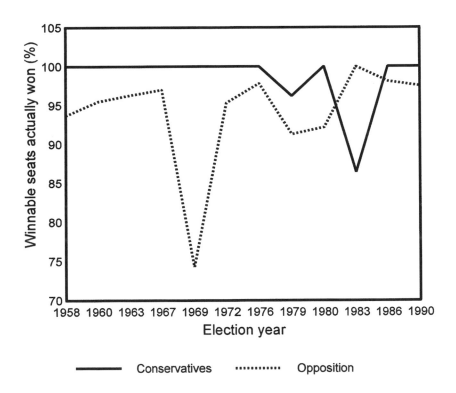

Figure 6.2 Comparison of conservative and opposition electoral efficiency in districts where one seat was winnable

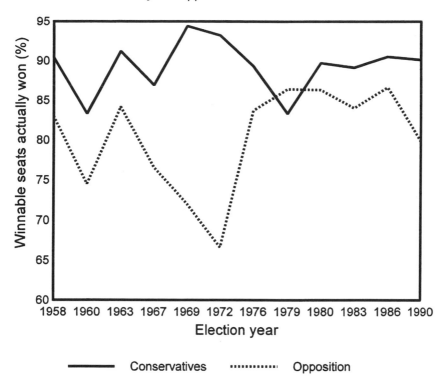

Figure 6.3 Comparison of conservative and opposition electoral efficiency in districts where two seats were winnable

opposition cooperation efforts to similar conservative camp efforts, Cox's suggestion to compare equivalent tasks is appropriate.

In contrast to the conclusion suggested by the aggregate data, Cox (1997, 247) claims that when the task is held constant, the LDP always outperforms the non-Communist opposition camp. In the twelve elections from 1958 to 1990, both the conservative and the opposition camps had districts in which they could have won one, two, three, four, or even five seats if they ran the optimal number of candidates and divided the vote equally among those candidates. When the opposition and conservative records are compared for districts where each could win at most one seat, the conservatives win a greater percent of its possible seats than the opposition camp does. The conservatives similarly outperform the opposition in those districts in which two, three, or four seats could have been won. The difference between the conservative performance and the opposition performance reaches levels of statistical significance

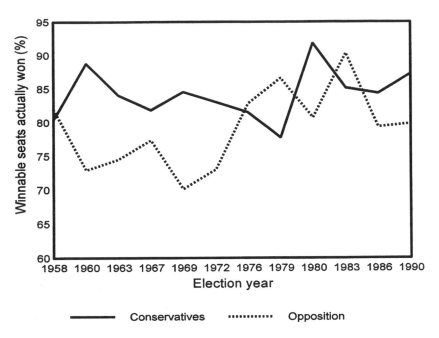

Figure 6.4 Comparison of conservative and opposition electoral efficiency in districts where three seats were winnable

in the districts where two or three seats could have been won. When Cox considers only the period of electoral cooperation (1972–1990), the LDP advantage remains, though it is considerably smaller in districts with one, two, and three seats that could have been won.

Cox's analysis glosses over some important trends in the comparative efficiency of opposition cooperation. A more detailed view of the data by years reaffirms the importance of electoral cooperation efforts in improving the electoral efficiency of the opposition parties. Cox is correct that, on average, the conservatives outperform the opposition when the task is held constant, but as Cox notes, the advantage declines when the opposition parties begin cooperating (figs. 6.2, 6.3, 6.4, and 6.5). In several elections, the opposition outperforms the LDP, assuming task held constant.

To best compare the efficacy of opposition and LDP efforts to cooperate, data from the years of opposition cooperation, especially the years of full cooperation, should be used. The data for periods of partial cooperation (1972–1990) and especially the period of full cooperation

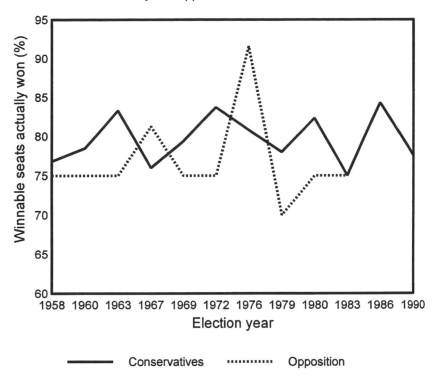

Figure 6.5 Comparison of conservative and opposition electoral efficiency in districts where four seats were winnable

(1979–1986) indicate that the conservative advantage is muddled. Cox presents a measure of the significance of the difference in electoral efficiency. I have replicated his calculations in figure 6.6 for each election year. Figure 6.6 gives a rough estimate of how many seats in each election the opposition camp lost or gained because of differences in its electoral efficiency, contrasted with the conservative camp. One line gives the number of seats the opposition camp won in each election. The other line calculates how many seats the opposition camp would have won in each election, had it translated votes into seats with the same electoral efficiency as the conservative camp. If the opposition had performed with the same electoral efficiency as the conservative camp, task held constant, during the period 1972–1990, it would have gained a net average of 9.2 seats in each election. During the period of full cooperation, the opposition would have had an average gain of only 1.6 seats in each election, if the opposition camp had coordinated with the same effi-

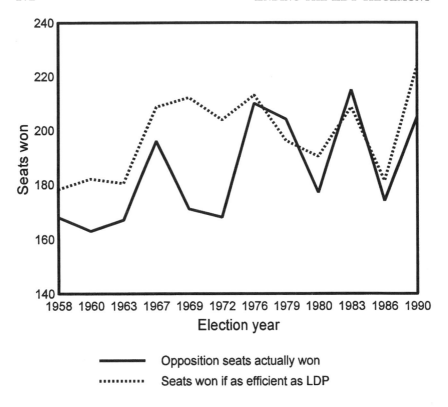

Figure 6.6 Comparison of seats won by the opposition and at rates of LDP efficiency

ciency as the LDP camp. In fact, in two of the four elections of this
period (1979 and 1983), opposition efficiency was greater than LDP
efficiency. The opposition would have lost 7.9 and 6.4 seats, respectively, in these elections, if it had performed at the level of the more
inefficient LDP.[3]

The best years for a comparison are the years of full cooperation:
1979, 1980, 1983, and 1986. Even in these years, however, measurements of the efficacy of cooperative efforts are skewed by swings in
turnout that gave an advantage to one camp or the other. In 1980 and
1986, the LDP held House of Representatives elections simultaneously
with House of Councillors elections. This tactic raised turnout, which
helped the LDP. The LDP scored impressive victories in these years,
and as a result, the electoral efficiency of the opposition dropped significantly. In contrast, the LDP did poorly in 1979 and 1983; not surprisingly, in these years the opposition outperformed the LDP in electoral

efficiency. The results of 1979 and 1983 do not prove that the opposition outperformed the conservative camp, and the results of 1980 and 1986 do not prove the conservatives were more efficient. If task is held constant, in these four elections the conservatives were more efficient in three elections for districts where either camp could win only one seat. For districts with two winnable seats, the conservatives again outperformed the opposition in three of four elections. In three-seat districts, the opposition was more efficient than the conservatives in two of four elections. In four-seat districts, the conservatives outperformed the opposition in two elections, and in one election the two camps had identical electoral efficiencies; in the remaining election, the opposition had no districts where it could have won four seats. Task held constant, the LDP outperformed the opposition in these four elections that are crucial for comparative purposes, but the level of conservative advantage is minuscule. The loss to the opposition because of its inefficiency in these elections was only an average of 1.6 seats in each election.

These results challenge the conclusion that the LDP is always more efficient than the opposition camp in electoral coordination. They show that when the opposition camp cooperates extensively, it can be as efficient as the LDP. Comparisons based on years of noncooperation (1958–1969) or partial cooperation (1972–1976 and 1990) do not isolate and measure the efficiency of opposition cooperative efforts. Rather, these comparisons also measure the effect of the opposition decision not to cooperate. Thus, they give no reliable information about the comparative efficiency of opposition efforts to cooperate.

This muddled conclusion concerning the comparative electoral efficiency of both camps can be clarified by an analysis of the type of errors committed by the two camps. Various authors suggest that greater resources give the conservatives advantages in negotiating the optimal number of candidates and in apportioning the vote optimally between those candidates (Cox 1996, 1997; Cox and Niou 1994; McCubbins and Rosenbluth 1995). However, the opposition parties and their support groups have characteristics that should facilitate their efforts to run the optimal number of candidates, and opposition methods to fine-tune vote divisions should have greater accuracy than the decentralized approach to vote division used by the LDP.

In keeping with Cox's observations, an analysis of these two separate tasks of electoral coordination should be made with task held constant. It is more difficult to run the optimal number of candidates when the optimal number is four than when the optimal number is one. Similarly,

**Table 6.1 Percent of Districts Where the Optimal Number
of Candidates Ran**

Number of Winnable Seats/Camp	Years of Noncooperation 1958–1969	Years of Partial Cooperation 1972–1976, 1990	Years of Full Cooperation 1979–1986
1/opposition	34.4	**61.5 (opposition)**	**53.1 (opposition)**
1/conservatives	**39.1 (conservative)**	18.2	25.6
2/opposition	46.4	**58.7 (opposition)**	**59.3 (opposition)**
2/conservatives	**55.2 (conservative)**	50.7	53.2
3/opposition	**59.2 (opposition)**	**72.8 (opposition)**	**83.8 (opposition)**
3/conservatives	51.5	51.6	57.6
4/opposition	**61.9 (opposition)**	**83.3 (opposition)**	**62.5 (opposition)**
4/conservatives	50.4	47.4	53.0

Note: **Bold** indicates the camp that performed better in each pairing.

it should be more difficult to divide the vote equally among five candidates than it is to divide the vote equally between two candidates.

Table 6.1 presents the data on running the optimal number of candidates, task held constant. The opposition camp in ten of twelve categories outperforms the conservative camp. During the years of partial or full cooperation, task held constant, the opposition camp always runs the optimal number of candidates in a greater percent of districts than the LDP does. The LDP outperforms the opposition only during the period of noncooperation and only in districts with one or two winnable seats. The data also show that as the opposition began to cooperate, the percent of districts where it ran the optimal number of candidates increased.

The results of table 6.1 are surprising. I did not expect the opposition to outperform the LDP so clearly and convincingly. I was especially surprised at relative opposition efficiency in years of noncooperation and partial cooperation. Perhaps these results are explained by the policies of the opposition parties to unilaterally restrict party nominations even in districts where they did not cooperate. With few exceptions, the non-Communist opposition parties ran candidates only in districts where their candidates had a chance of victory. Perhaps this practice, coupled with the bleak prospects of success for an unauthorized independent candidacy from the opposition camp, made the opposition better at running the optimal number of candidates than the LDP, even when the opposition parties were not cooperating.

The second coordination problem, of apportioning the vote equally between multiple candidates, is addressed in table 6.2. I have excluded districts where only one seat was winnable; the vote-apportioning problem does not exist in those districts. Table 6.2 shows the results of three tests of opposition and conservative efficiency in apportioning the vote equally among candidates. For each of the three tests, data are presented to compare similar districts. The districts where the opposition could have won a maximum of two seats and actually ran two candidates are compared with districts where the conservatives, too, could have won two seats and actually ran two candidates.

Table 6.2 Vote-Apportioning Efficiency of the Conservative and Opposition Camps in Districts Where the Camp Ran the Optimal Number of Candidates

Number of Winnable Seats/Camp	Test 1. Winnable Seats Actually Won (Average)			Test 2. Deviation of Candidates' Votes from the District Mean for Their Camp (Average)			Test 3. Effective Number of Candidates		
	Degree of Cooperation			Degree of Cooperation			Degree of Cooperation		
	None	Partial	Full	None	Partial	Full	None	Partial	Full
2/opposition	1.65	1.58	**1.73**	**.115**	.124	**.079**	**1.956**	1.956	**1.976**
2/conservatives	**1.84**	**18.2**	**1.77**	.125	**.109**	.122	1.947	**1.959**	1.951
3/opposition	2.31	2.41	2.58	**.134**	.158	**.100**	**2.906**	2.890	**2.953**
3/conservatives	**2.59**	**2.61**	**2.62**	.150	**.136**	.126	2.890	**2.989**	2.918
4/opposition	3.23	3.33	2.80	**.138**	.196	**.173**	**3.873**	3.731	**3.797**
4/conservatives	**3.32**	3.33	**3.29**	.152	**.130**	.195	3.847	**3.881**	3.743

Note: **Bold** indicates the camp that performed better in each pairing.

The first test is a simple success rate: What is the average number of candidates that each camp actually elected? This test shows how the performance of the opposition camp generally improved with the advent of cooperation, but it also shows that conservatives outperform the opposition in every category during periods of noncooperation, partial cooperation, and full cooperation. During the period of full cooperation, the opposition comes close to matching the LDP success rate in districts where two and three seats were winnable. The test one data, like Cox's data, suggest that the LDP marginally outperforms the opposition in the task of dividing the vote equally, even in periods of full cooperation.

The results of test one and Cox's analysis are misleading, however, because they conflate LDP superiority in winning more votes than the opposition with the comparative efficiency or inefficiency of the LDP in dividing its votes equally among its candidates. A better test of electoral efficiency is to measure how evenly the votes are distributed among a camp's candidates in a given election district. This efficiency can be measured directly, unlike the indirect measurement of efficiency used in test one and in Cox's analysis. This indirect analysis measures victories and implies that a greater number of victories results from a more optimal division of the vote.

The second and third tests in table 6.2 present a much more direct test of vote-apportioning efficiency, and both tests support the conclusion that the opposition camp is more effective than the conservative camp at dividing the vote optimally among multiple candidates. The second test calculates the average vote for all the candidates of a camp in a district. Each candidate's actual vote is subtracted from this average and the absolute value is taken. This measurement is the deviation of each candidate's vote from the district average for the camp. These deviations are then averaged for each of the categories presented in table 6.2.[4] The data from this second test show that opposition camp candidates divided the vote more equally among themselves in all three categories of districts in the periods of noncooperation and full cooperation. In periods of partial cooperation, the conservative camp divided the vote more equally among its candidates.

The third test supports the conclusions of the second test. In the third test, the effective number of candidates was calculated for each of the camps.[5] For example, a district where three candidates split the vote at 35 percent, 35 percent, and 30 percent will have 2.98 "effective" candidates. A district where the vote is split 60 percent, 30 percent, and 10 percent will have 2.17 "effective" candidates. Thus, districts with a more equal division of the vote will have an effective number of candidates that is closer to the actual number of candidates. These calculations in table 6.2 show that again the opposition camp outperforms the conservatives in all categories of districts, in periods of noncooperation and of full cooperation. The conservatives, however, outperform the opposition in all categories during the period of partial cooperation.

The direct measurements of vote division efficiency in tests two and three contradict Cox's results and the results of test one. It must seem incongruous that the opposition can run the same number of candidates and divide the vote more efficiently than the LDP but still win fewer seats. Table 6.3 resolves this incongruity. This table shows the percent of the vote that each of the camps had in its districts. In every category of district, the conservative camp had a greater percent of the vote than the opposition camp, even though both camps could have won the same number of seats. Because the conservative camp on average had more votes, it still won more seats, even though the opposition camp did a better job of apportioning the votes equally among its candidates.

The following results from the fourth district of Hokkaido in 1986 illustrate this difference. In this five-seat district, the LDP could have won three seats; the opposition also could have won three seats, if it had

Table 6.3 Conservative Advantage in Votes Received, Comparing Districts Where A Camp Ran the Optimal Number of Candidates

Number of Winnable Seats/Camp	District Vote Average (%)		
	Years of Noncooperation	*Years of Partial Cooperation*	*Years of Full Cooperation*
2/opposition	35.8	37.6	37.1
2/conservatives	**46.9**	**45.0**	**49.1**
3/opposition	44.3	46.6	48.2
3/conservatives	**59.9**	**58.6**	**60.7**
4/opposition	55.1	56.5	50.1
4/conservatives	**63.8**	**59.2**	**64.7**

Note: **Bold** indicates the camp that had an average greater percentage of the vote in each pairing.

divided its vote more equally. The results follow, with the winners in
bold:

Party	Votes Won
LDP	**100,297**
LDP	**93,001**
Socialist	**87,603**
Socialist	**87,539**
LDP	**84,626**
Democratic Socialist	83,022

The opposition could have won the fifth seat, relegating the last LDP
candidate to the losing sixth position, if the two winning Socialist candidates had transferred 1,700 of their excess votes to the struggling
Democratic Socialist candidate. In other words, the opposition could
have won three seats if they had divided the vote more equally among
their three candidates. The opposition, though, was already dividing the
vote more equally among its three candidates than the conservative
camp was. In this district, the opposition's average deviation from the
mean is 2.3 percent, in contrast to the conservative camp's score of 5.8
percent. The effective number of candidates for the opposition camp is
3.00; for the conservatives it is 2.99. The conservative camp won the fifth
seat, despite its relative inefficiency at dividing the vote equally, because
this camp had more votes. Conservative candidates won 19,000 more
votes than the opposition. They could be less efficient than the opposition and still win more seats.

The findings of table 6.2 can be extended to every election district,
not just those where the optimal number of candidates actually ran.
Table 6.4 presents similar results for all the election districts, again running all three tests of vote-apportioning efficiency. In number of seats
actually won (test one), the LDP again outperforms the opposition in
seven of nine categories, and this LDP dominance exists in periods of
noncooperation, partial cooperation, and full cooperation. Test two, the
average deviation from the mean, shows that the opposition outperforms
the LDP in seven of nine categories; the LDP does better only in the
category of two winnable seats in the periods of noncooperation and of
partial cooperation. The calculation of effective number of candidates,
test three, shows similar results; the opposition camp outperforms the

Table 6.4 Vote-Apportioning Efficiency of the Conservative and Opposition Camps in All Districts

Number of Winnable Seats/Camp	Test 1. Winnable Seats Actually Won (Average)			Test 2. Deviation of Candidates' Votes from the District Mean for Their Camp (Average)			Test 3. Effective Number of Candidates		
	Degree of Cooperation			Degree of Cooperation			Degree of Cooperation		
	None	Partial	Full	None	Partial	Full	None	Partial	Full
2/opposition	1.56	1.53	**1.72**	.178	.172	**.131**	**1.848**	**1.870**	**1.903**
2/conservatives	**1.80**	**18.2**	**1.77**	**.177**	**.159**	.172	1.845	1.863	1.849
3/opposition	2.24	2.37	**2.55**	.166	.187	**.122**	**2.826**	**2.818**	**2.906**
3/conservatives	**2.48**	**2.52**	2.54	.198	.201	.183	2.752	2.743	2.782
4/opposition	3.10	**3.33**	2.88	**.160**	.196	**.139**	**3.816**	**3.731**	**3.864**
4/conservatives	**3.18**	3.23	**3.18**	.181	2.00	.207	3.759	3.696	3.717

Note: **Bold** indicates the camp that performed better in each pairing.

LDP in all categories, in all three periods. Again, in all twelve categories, the LDP's percent of the vote was higher than the opposition's; thus the difference between test results.[6]

The test of all districts is a less accurate test because it conflates the mistakes made in running the correct number of candidates with mistakes made in apportioning the vote equally among candidates. In districts where parties undernominate candidates, the optimal division of the vote still requires that the vote be divided equally between competing candidates. In districts of overnomination, an equal division of the vote is suboptimal only when it is clear that overnomination has occurred. Because the optimal number of candidates is calculated in hindsight and is affected by the other camp's mistakes, many cases of overnomination are not apparent until after the election results were in. Thus this test of all districts provides a crude test of the relative efficiency of vote-apportioning strategies, conflated as it is with a camp's other task of running the optimal number of candidates. This test also shows that the results presented in table 6.2 for only those districts where parties ran only the optimal number of candidates can be extended to all other election districts.

In summary, the conservatives outperform the opposition, task held constant, in terms of electing more people, but this advantage disappears or is small in the periods of full cooperation. Furthermore, this advantage is based partly on the fact that the LDP on average receives more votes than the opposition in similarly situated districts. When this LDP advantage of winning more votes is held constant by separately evaluating the tasks of running the correct number of candidates and dividing the votes equally between those candidates, the opposition camp generally outperforms the LDP.

These results suggest that though the LDP has greater resources and a mechanism for dividing candidacies and dividing the vote, this mechanism is not more efficient than the opposition's methods of coordination. The LDP is perhaps less efficient than the opposition because of two deficiencies in its coordinating mechanisms. In the realm of running the appropriate number of candidates, LDP policy actually rewards a disgruntled potential candidate who bucks a party decision and runs as an independent. In the realm of vote division, the LDP lacks a coordinating mechanism that stands above the interests of specific candidates.

Conservative voters and support groups can reach an optimal allocation of the votes among multiple candidates, however. With proper information, less-personally committed conservative supporters can flow to a conservative candidate who is struggling, thereby helping to shore up that candidacy. Conservative voters can shift support to another conservative candidate more easily than shifting votes across party, religious, and ideological lines within the opposition camp. The opposition outperforms the LDP only because its leaders strategically use core members from each of the important opposition support organizations in an effort to fine-tune an equal division of votes among opposition candidates. A division like this can be maneuvered in the conservative camp, but personal loyalties to specific candidates have blocked these same efforts toward vote division.

Electoral Efficiency under the New Electoral System

Events that have taken place since the enactment of the new electoral system illustrate the different flexibilities of the two camps. With the creation of single-seat districts, LDP candidates must now merge previously competing personal support organizations behind a single candidate. Similarly, the former opposition parties are now combining with other groups to back a single candidate. Interviews with campaign activists in Hokkaido, Ibaragi, and Nara revealed that LDP candidates have had a difficult time overcoming personal differences that divided the core supporters of LDP candidates who were previously rivals. These efforts in the conservative camp are hampered by long-standing financial links between groups of supporters and a candidate. Two rival construction companies will have long supported two different LDP candidates in their same district, for instance. They each have relied on their candidate for lucrative public works jobs. Now one candidate is gone, and they are supposed to consolidate under the leadership of the single remaining LDP candidate. This has worked well in places like Ibaragi, where the LDP is strong. However, in Hokkaido, where the Democratic Party effectively challenges the LDP, some affiliated companies and personal support group backers would rather deal with the Democratic candidate than support their old LDP rival.

Cooperation is further hindered by personal ties and jealousies among competing organizations. In Nara, Takaichi Sanae challenged the secretary of LDP incumbent Okuno Seisuke in the new Nara first district.[7] Takaichi beat the secretary and later joined the LDP, but she cannot expect Okuno supporters in Nara 1 to join her organization (Takaichi 1997). Similarly, in Asahigawa, Democratic candidate Sasaki Hidenori got some supporters of an LDP prefectural assembly member, a rival of the LDP candidate. They see it as more advantageous to support a candidate of another party than to help their longtime rival consolidate his control over the local LDP organization. These rivalries can become extremely self-defeating. Most LDP candidates were double listed on the proportional representation list; the LDP listed most of these candidates in the same post position, with ties to be broken by whoever had the highest percent in their losing district. As a result, in some districts today, supporters of a former rival will refuse to vote for the sole LDP candidate in their district because they want to hold down his percent of the vote. By so doing, they increase the chance that their favored candidate, who is now running in a neighboring district, will be elected on the proportional-representation list.

The opposition parties have experienced similar difficulties. For example, the Federation of New Religions abandoned any formal support of Democratic Socialist candidates when that party merged with the Clean Government Party into the New Frontier Party. In isolated instances, the Federation still supported individual candidates, but across-the-board support was ruled out by the competition between this organization and its rival, Sōka gakkai. Similarly, some of the opposition-affiliated labor unions have begun supporting LDP candidates in certain districts. Their support is policy oriented, though, and not the result of jealousies or inflexibilities. For example, the postal workers union (Zentei) still supported all but one Democratic Party candidate in the 1996 elections. Their support for LDP candidates was only in districts where no Democratic Party candidate ran.[8]

Failure of the Opposition to Restructure the Electorate

The opposition has three paths to power, and it has primarily followed the two coalition paths rather than the path of building a majority party. Why did the parties eschew the more visible, obviously more desirable path to power—building an attractive, dominant party—in favor of the more questionable coalition alternatives, which put the parties in a disadvantaged bargaining position compared to the LDP? Why in Japan, unlike other countries, did the opposition parties give up so quickly on the option of inducing a favorable shift in the electorate? This option was abandoned after several attempts.

The attempts all failed because the voting preferences of the Japanese electorate in Japan are exceptionally difficult to influence, due to the strong organizational nature of Japanese elections. A substantial chunk of the electorate casts its votes according to the policies of the organization they are connected with; moreover, members regularly lobby and cajole friends, family, neighbors, business associates, and so on, to vote a certain way. In essence, much of the electorate is persuaded to vote not by policy appeals, or by the direct appeals of the candidate, but by a friend, relative, or colleague's affiliation with an organization. The type of organization varies considerably by party. Conservative candidates generally use agricultural and business organizations; they also rely on their own personal support groups and the personal support groups of affiliated local politicians. Opposition candidates rely mainly on the support of labor unions and religious groups, gaining secondary support from smaller personal support groups.

The importance of organizations in campaigns is no accident or quirk of Japanese culture. Campaign regulations in Japan are so strict as to render it difficult to influence or reach voters. Advertising by candidates is not allowed; door-to-door appeals are not allowed. Direct mail and literature distribution are circumscribed within government-dictated numerical limits and formats. The location and size of campaign posters is strictly limited. One of the few unregulated areas is phone calls, and phoning is a popular campaign activity. Another area beyond the pale of the strict regulations is the activities of organizations. It is illegal for a candidate to go from door to door, but a candidate with a list of organization members can approach each member under the guise of an organizational introduction. Organizations can include campaign information and appeals in their literature; these do not come under the strict regulations that govern the distribution of direct mail and other campaign literature. For the former opposition parties, these organizations were preexisting groups that had an interest in politics. Conservative candidates have the support of some preexisting organizations, but they also build their own personal support organizations, through which they can access the electorate.

A large number of voters remain uninfluenced by organizations. The Japanese call these "floating voters," and politicians regularly complain about their existence. This may seem odd. What Japanese politicians complain about is the same crucial block of voters who are arduously courted in other electoral democracies—the swing voters. Japanese politicians dislike these voters because there is no effective way to reach out to them in an election. The best that candidates can do is to give speeches in front of train stations, hoping that somehow their image of perseverance might resonate with some of the floating voters. In contrast, in other countries, swing voters can be targeted with direct mail, advertising appeals, door-to-door appeals, and neighborhood community meetings—methods limited in Japan.

The different types of organizations in Japan do have a different effect on a candidate's limited ability to reach unaffiliated voters. Conservative candidates can use their large, effective personal support organizations to bring them in and turn them into organizational voters. Members can recruit friends and relatives to join the organization, thus expanding its influence in the electorate. Through this process, floating voters, besides being persuaded to vote a certain way, are converted to being organizational voters. Conservative candidates therefore have at least some methods of expanding their appeal with the electorate.

In contrast, opposition candidates have an even more difficult time expanding their level of support from the electorate. Their organizations are not going to recruit new members solely on political grounds. They may cast a wide net in an attempt to influence the votes of friends and family, but they cannot easily increase the size of their main support organizations. The same organization members contact the same circle of friends in each election. These friends do not become members of the organization, because the organization is a labor union or a religion, not a personal support organization. Thus, the number of voters that a union or religion can mobilize is stable and is limited by the size of the organization.

Because of the importance of organizations, and the opposition's difficulty in widening its appeal with the electorate, the opposition parties by 1970 had largely given up on the strategy of taking power by increasing electorate appeal. The one way to expand such appeal, by enlarging a personal support organization, had been effectively exploited by the conservatives. Even if the opposition parties could overcome the ideological and funding limitations to build up personal support organizations, they likely would not be very successful; each district already had several competing personal support organizations of conservative candidates.

By 1970, the opposition parties focused more on the other obvious path to power: recombining existing political units to form a new political party that would have the strength to win a parliamentary majority. They never gave up entirely on the prospect of increasing their share of support in the electorate, but they viewed this strategy as only a bonus for their party reformulation efforts. In assessing a reformulation scheme, plotters would count how many representatives each group could bring to a new coalition government. They would then often add a few more seats to that number to account for what they hoped to gain in the next election. This attitude has not changed much, even in the more relaxed campaign environment of the new electoral system. One loser in a recent round of elections blamed his too-heavy reliance on appeals to unaffiliated voters and his failure to nurture personal support organizations and other organizational ties (Sakata 1997). Another strategist for the Democratic Party says that the party's only hope for growth is to entice other representatives to join. An effort to increase party size by running candidates would be doomed to failure, because the party lacks the organizational support to elect such new candidates (Matsuda 1997).

Therefore, the path to power for the opposition in the 1970s and 1980s and for the Democratic Party in the 1990s was to encourage defection and recombine existing units to create a new majority party. The different strategies for joining the opposition parties together or joining an LDP-led coalition, pursued in the 1970s and 1980s, were described in chapter 5, and they are contradictory. But the two commonalities of these strategies are that they relied very little on changing the support patterns in the electorate, and they aimed to reduce inefficiencies in the opposition camp by better cooperation.

It would be a mistake to conclude from this discussion that floating voters are irrelevant, or that elections in Japan are not decided by swings in the electorate. Floating voters are extremely important in deciding Japanese elections; the electorate can be quite volatile. Japanese politicians, however, lack the means to effectively influence the decisions of such voters. If Japanese politicians could target floating voters more effectively, they most likely would; as it is, they influence the elections by making appeals to voters through organizations, a method that, unlike advertising, direct mail, and door-to-door campaigning, is not banned.

The United States illustrates the opposite phenomenon. Both organizational appeals and direct appeals are legal, but with the growth of television advertising, direct appeals have eclipsed organizational appeals. Both avenues are possible in the United States, but one form has become dominant with the growing perception that television ads win campaigns.

In Japan, organizational appeals triumph because they are favored by strict campaign legislation. Direct appeals to the voters are allowed only through circuitous, ineffectual routes. Thus, opposition parties enter into a downward spiral of organizational reliance. They rely on organizations to get the vote out and win elections, but these organizational ties and restrictions on direct appeals hinder their efforts to persuade floating voters. In a self-fulfilling prophecy, the organizational ties of the party further weaken the party's efforts to expand its appeal beyond its core of organizational voters.

The effects of the restrictions and limitations I have just described became apparent in the following examples. The Democratic Socialist Party was never able to expand beyond its initial appeal, primarily centered on moderate union members. Nor did the Clean Government Party, despite decades of effort, expand beyond its organizational base. In the mid-1970s, the party tested the waters by expanding the number of districts where it ran candidates, but this effort failed, and the party reverted to its more cautious strategy. The Socialist effort in 1990 to expand its electoral roster met strong internal party resistance; the effort was rejected after it facilitated the LDP's victory in that election. Even more instructive is the fate of the minor parties, which lacked a significant organizational base. Both the New Liberal Club and the Social Democratic League were formed by incumbent politicians who had their own personal support organizations, which helped them win re-election despite their having switched parties. However, these politicians were unable to transfer their popularity to other election districts. The New Liberal Club enjoyed an initial boom as it attracted floating voters in the wake of LDP scandals, but in subsequent elections, the party fell back to its core base, the personal support group vote of its incumbent politicians.

The problem is not unique to the opposition. The LDP regained its parliamentary majority in the 1990s by changing the electoral system and enticing representatives back into the party. The LDP has tried to increase its share of the vote, but as figure 6.7 shows, it has failed. The

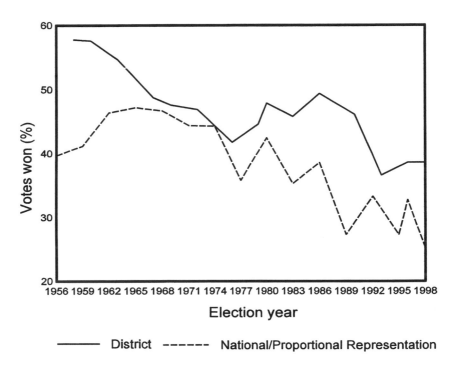

Note: The label "National/Proportional Representation" includes proportional representation and national constituency races in the House of Councillors and the 1996 proportional representation race of the House of Representatives. The label "District" refers to non-proportional races of the House of Representatives.

Figure 6.7 LDP share of the popular vote

LDP regained its parliamentary majority not by increasing its share of the popular vote but by enticing sitting representatives back into the party.

The electoral reforms of 1994 hold the potential to change the balance of Japanese elections, now strongly weighed to favor organizational elections. The simultaneous proportional representation race allows for extensive party media advertising. Over time, these advertisements could grow in importance. They could become an effective tool for parties to use in swaying floating voters. If so, the option of the Japanese opposition to pursue power by increasing the size of the party, rather than by coalition building, could become much more attractive and realistic.

The creation of single-seat districts in the new electoral system might also influence opposition calculations. In the previous, multiseat districts, LDP incumbents were relatively impervious to swings in the preferences of the floating voters. Though the LDP would lose seats when it was unpopular, one LDP incumbent in a district might lose while two others were reelected. Furthermore, the incumbent might be replaced as often by a conservative independent as by an opposition challenger. The inherent proportionality of the electoral system limited the amount of damage suffered when floating voters deserted the LDP.

In contrast, single-seat districts accentuate the importance of swing voters. The LDP cannot weather a significant shift in public opinion against it and come anywhere close to winning a parliamentary majority. The new electoral system not only has opened up paths to influence floating voters, it also has increased the magnitude of the prize that can be won if the floating voters shift significantly.

The 1996 elections did not show a great divergence from campaign methods used under the former electoral system. If change occurs in the next election, to be held in late 1999 or 2000, it is most likely to appear in the following areas: (1) a greater reliance on party-based media campaigns, (2) a growing ineffectiveness of existing campaign methods in urban and suburban districts, and (3) increased LDP vulnerability in those districts; the 1998 House of Councillors election showed this vulnerability in the LDP's complete defeat in Japan's urban prefectures.

Opposition Successes

Do the coalition governments of the 1990s actually represent a success of the former opposition? The opposition has done well in developing electoral efficiency through electoral cooperation. How well has it achieved its second goal—reformulating the party system? I have argued in previous chapters that the opposition acted strategically in the many takeover plots of the 1960s, 1970s, and 1980s. They finally succeeded in restructuring the party system in 1993, but have their efforts been truly successful?

A not unreasonable answer is no. The Socialist Party is decimated. Many LDP renegades have returned to the LDP or are in close alliance with it. Few significant policy differences separate the Democratic Party and the LDP. Nothing appears to have changed in Japan except for a few party labels.

I disagree with this answer. Significant political change *has* occurred; the net gain to the former opposition parties is often overlooked in superficial analyses of which party has gained or lost seats. These parties and their supporters now sit at the table of power. Their views have meaningful influence on the policy-making process. In fact, their status and influence are enhanced by the positions they have gained in cabinets and in new parties.

The former opposition parties could be considered the big losers of the 1993 reforms. Socialist strength in the Diet dropped precipitously from 136 seats before 1993 to 69 seats after that election. After the 1996 election, the party became nearly irrelevant, winning only fifteen seats. Such analysis ignores the move of a majority of Socialist Party supporters and representatives to the new Democratic Party, however. In 1996, twenty-five former Socialists were elected on the Democratic Party ticket, totaling forty Socialists and former Socialists elected on the tickets of two different parties in 1996.

The former Clean Government Party and Democratic Socialist Party also did well under the label of the New Frontier Party. The Clean Government Party elected fifty-two members to the House of Representatives in 1993. Forty-nine of these incumbents ran for the New Frontier Party in 1996, and thirty-seven were elected. They were joined by six new representatives who had close ties to the former Clean Government Party. Forty-three New Frontier Party representatives were from the former Clean Government Party. The Democratic Socialists fared similarly well. Of the fifteen elected in 1993, thirteen ran in 1996 on the New Frontier Party label. Ten were successful. They were joined by eleven new representatives, totaling twenty-one former Democratic Socialists in the New Frontier Party.

Though the number of conservative legislators has increased under the new political and electoral system, the shift in formal power, as defined by the number of seats won, is not as great as is commonly assumed. Opposition party or former opposition party members still occupy about 30 percent of the seats in the House of Representatives. As with the Communists and Socialists, the Democratic Party contains few members formerly of the LDP. Those with opposition party pedigrees won approximately 150 of the 500 seats contested in 1996.

The formal power of seats won tells only part of the story. Though the long-suffering veterans of the opposition wilderness did not take power directly and at the exclusion of the LDP or LDP defectors, they have more influence and power over legislation and government policy than they have had at any time since the late 1940s. Their members are chairing committees, becoming ministers, and sitting at the policy negotiation table. The views of their supporters are now more directly reflected in legislation and government policy. This monumental accomplishment should not be overlooked in assessing their efforts. Nor should we overlook the opposition's success in accomplishing two of their strategic options: They broke up the LDP and formed a coalition with LDP defectors that held power for one year and continues to be a contender for power. The Socialist Party remained in power in coalition with the LDP for two additional years. Moreover, the former opposition parties, working with LDP defectors, have denied the LDP a parliamentary majority in every national election since 1993. Judging by their own criteria, the former opposition parties have been notably successful in the 1990s.

Opposition and LDP Failures

Having shown the ways in which the opposition succeeded, it is also important to note their failures. First, the opposition failed for twenty years, despite planning and scheming, to bring about a party reformulation. Indeed, the fruition of their plans came at the initiative of an LDP renegade, not an opposition reformer. Similarly, the multidecade effort to reform the Socialist Party brought forth few tangible results in the 1970s and 1980s. Again, the most significant changes came only when the LDP, not the opposition, offered the prime ministership to that party. The superior bargaining position of the LDP, and the opposition's reliance on support organizations that initially blocked internal party reforms and cooperative efforts, can explain, but not erase, this failure.

Second, the opposition could have cooperated better than it did. Cooperation often degenerated into acrimony and distrust. Again, there are explanations. These supposedly cooperative allies were in intense competition in many districts. Ideological differences, workplace hostilities between supporters, and enticements from the LDP were additional impediments to effective cooperation. Again, though, they could have cooperated more effectively.

Third, some elements of the opposition miscalculated in their 1993 and 1994 maneuverings after the splitting of the LDP. For example, some members of the Socialist Party who opposed the party reformulation efforts blocked the passage of an electoral reform bill. They were successful only in the short term. As a direct result of their actions, the coalition government was forced to compromise with the LDP and accept changes in the reform bill that made it even more difficult for the Socialist Party to remain an independent, autonomous political organization. The Socialists mistakenly thought that by defeating the bill, they might possibly block the passage of all such legislation—an obvious tactical mistake.

Proponents of political reform within the Socialist Party overestimated their ability to mold the new political party into their image. Much of their initial enthusiasm for political reform waned as it became increasingly apparent that the new political party would be largely controlled by Ozawa Ichirō and his allies in the former Clean Government Party. The Socialist reformists failed to control the new party's evolution to be amenable to their policies and attitudes.

The LDP has had similar failings, both historically and recently; for example, its decline in voter support has been mitigated only by turnout manipulations. Figure 6.7 shows that the LDP has been unsuccessful in significantly raising its share of voters.

Similarly, the LDP did not develop efficient methods of dealing with coordination problems under the old electoral system. The party's major role was to ensure the optimal number of nominations, but it often failed at this task, relying on the crude, though effective, tool of giving the nomination mainly to incumbents. This tool is effective because it allows the official nomination to be largely in line with the optimal number of seats the party could win, but it is crude because it actually encourages suboptimal challenges. Those aspiring to a Diet seat under the LDP label know that if they can win an election as an independent, they can then join the party and obtain the nomination in subsequent elections. Therefore, there are often suboptimal challenges of LDP incumbents by other LDP politicians who have recently been denied the LDP nomination. This LDP free-market policy of nominations has the advantage that only the fittest survive to gain the LDP nomination in the next election, but it has the disadvantage of encouraging suboptimal challenges. It is difficult to admire this policy for its efficiency—it is at best a blunt instrument that only partially solves the coordination problem faced by the LDP.

The LDP's lack of an efficient mechanism for allocating nomination slots can be explained as follows. Like the opposition, the party was forced to deal with the internal competition created by the use of multi-seat districts. With the frequent turnover rates in these districts, welcoming independent newcomers into the party was more advantageous than barring their entrance. Though understandable, LDP nomination policies were a partial success and a partial failure at solving the coordination dilemma. These policies continue under the new electoral system. For example, in Nara, Takaichi Sanae repeatedly petitioned for the LDP nomination and was denied it. Undaunted, she ran and finally won as an independent. In her new single-seat district, the LDP gave its nomination to someone else, so Takaichi joined the New Frontier Party. After defeating her LDP opponent, however, the LDP welcomed her. LDP practices mean that a strong, conservative challenger to a formally nominated LDP candidate faces few incentives to stand down in a campaign.

Finally, the LDP also made grave miscalculations in its actions after the 1993 election. It lost out in the bidding process to gain the support of the Japan New Party and the New Party Harbinger in an LDP-led coalition government, paying for this mistake by spending nearly a year out of power. Similarly, all the events of the 1990s were set off by miscalculations rendered by LDP leaders. Prime Minister Miyazawa miscalculated his ability to bring an electoral reform bill to passage. Those opposing the electoral reforms miscalculated the extent of the negative reaction within the LDP to blocking reform legislation in early 1993.

The LDP and the opposition have both enjoyed successes. And as historical record shows, neither has been free of errors.

7

The Future of Japanese Politics

HOW DOES THIS analysis of opposition efforts and interparty cooperation help predict the future trajectory of Japanese politics? Prediction is a difficult task in politics. Because I claim that explanations of events share some commonalities and are not entirely idiosyncratic, though, some general forecasts should be possible. This type of forecasting has been successful in the past. Hrebenar (1986, 47) accurately foresaw in 1986 that "most likely to occur in the next decade is a complete change in the electoral devices for house elections." In this same spirit, I put forth the following possible scenarios for the future.

First, there is little reason to expect stability in the party system in the near term. The incentives to merge into a stable system of two competing major parties remain weak in Japan. Single-seat districts exist, but 40 percent of the seats in the House of Representatives are won by proportional representation. Similarly, the majority of the seats in the House of Councillors, prefectural assemblies, and city councils are also elected in multiseat or proportional representation districts. This mixture of electoral systems dilutes some incentives for parties to merge. Moreover, district campaigns in Japan are candidate centered. The 1996 elections showed that prominent politicians could win their districts easily, regardless of the national weakness of their party or their lack of a party affiliation. Only for weaker candidates is there an incentive to merge into a nationally viable party.

For these reasons, I expect a continuation of patterns manifested in the 1996 election. Before an election, there will be a flurry of coalitions, alliances, and mergers as parties and candidates respond to the incentives created by single-seat districts. After an election, these incentives will disappear, and divisiveness and defection will become common. This tendency will be strongest, as it was in past decades, when the LDP has a small parliamentary majority. Possible scenarios for defection and coalition multiply when no party has a majority or when the majority is fragile.

Despite these incentives for fragmentation, coalitions and alliances should become more stable and mergers more common with the passage of time. This should occur because there is a cost (even if it is smaller in Japan than elsewhere) for switching parties and changing party names. Voters can become confused or cynical by these frequent switches. Furthermore, the campaign finance system introduced in 1994 provides significant government funding of existing parties twice a year. Defectors from an existing party usually do not get to take money from their former party with them, and they do not receive government money until the next payment cycle arrives. More important, perhaps, will be the stability that will come about as a result of the track record of specific parties or alliances. If a certain party or alliance does well in successive elections, potential defectors from that party or alliance will be encouraged to remain with a winning electoral entity. Defections are common when the LDP is unpopular, but rare when the LDP is popular and powerful.

Stability will be more likely if the LDP or another party can win parliamentary majorities successively. Though it is possible that the LDP can win a parliamentary majority, the countercurrents that pull the Diet toward coalition governments are probably stronger. The LDP share of the vote has not significantly improved despite the change in electoral systems. It still wins only 35 percent of the proportional representation seats in the House of Representatives. At these rates, a bare parliamentary majority can be won if the LDP wins 180 of the 300 single-seat districts. A victory is within the LDP grasp, but it will be difficult to achieve. LDP candidates would have to win a significant share of urban and suburban seats to reach that level, and so far they have not had great success in those areas.

Second, the rise in prominence of the Communist Party is likely to continue. All things being equal, I would not expect the Communists to advance their appeal beyond the temporary boost they received from the disintegration of the Socialist Party, which caused much of the electorate on the left to switch to Communist support. However, if a popular alternative to the LDP fails to arise, the Communists may inherit the Socialist mantle. As the primary or only opposition to the LDP, they could continue to grow, garnering the votes of all those dissatisfied with the status quo. In elections of the 1990s, the Japan New Party, the New Frontier Party, and the Democratic Party have each acted as receptacles for anti-LDP votes. If the Democratic Party falters, then it is possible that the Communists might make a major advance as the main opponent of the LDP.

Also of interest is the related question of what the Communists will do with their enhanced position and potential advances in their position. For ideological and tactical reasons, one would not expect the party to enter into coalitional or cooperative arrangements with other parties easily. Though the party's ideology is not extreme, it has a long history of taking principled stances on issues and of refusing to cooperate. At a tactical level, a party that benefits by its image as the only true opposition to the LDP would damage that image by associating too closely with the LDP or any other existing political party. Besides these problems, the existing parties themselves have long refused to cooperate with the Communists. Communist power probably will not pose a threat to continued LDP dominance of the system, because the possibility of cooperation between the Communists and other non-LDP parties is small. This means that even LDP minority governments will rule Japan with ease.

The lessons of history show, however, that the Communist Party was not anathema in the late 1960s and early 1970s, when it was ascendant; the Clean Government Party and the Socialists managed to cooperate with them. The ideological and even stylistic objections to cooperating with the Communists, which are voiced universally as supporting the lack of cooperation, would most likely fade away if an alliance with them became advantageous to the other parties. If the Communists continue to win a substantial share of the vote, I expect some cooperative overtures to the Communists.

Third, even with the demise of the New Frontier Party, the potential for new alliances or political reformulations remains high. Additional defections from the LDP are still possible. The Democratic Party could fall apart or lose significant numbers to defection. Though the Clean Government Party has moved closer to the LDP, it has positioned itself in the middle (as it did in the late 1970s and 1980s) to take advantage of all coalition opportunities.

The Clean Government Party might reassess its close ties with the LDP. These ties are strained by issues that divide the two parties. Many Sōka gakkai members support policy issues that have not been traditionally identified with the LDP. Former Clean Government Party representatives have already split into a small, pro-Ozawa group and a larger, autonomous group. Further division could occur if leaders move too close to the LDP. Also, wariness of Sōka gakkai power and influence might limit the organization's ability to tie too closely with other opposition parties. The best stance for the organization might be to continue cultivating cooperative relations and a good relationship with the LDP and the major opposition alliances. This can be accomplished easily by continuing the policy of supporting a variety of candidates in the single-seat districts.

One stumbling block to this preferred strategy is that incumbents with close ties to Sōka gakkai cannot win on their own power. They must build a broader coalition of support in their districts. Because many of them could not do so, they were elected in 1996 on the proportional representation lists of the New Frontier Party. In the election, to be held in 1999 or 2000, some of these incumbents will go down to defeat unless they form alliances with other groups. This clear and close cooperative linkage with the LDP would be difficult, and all the current opposition parties clearly reject this option. When the next election approaches, though, the incentives to merge or create such alliances will become greater; what is unimaginable now will become possible then. That is why Sōka gakkai support of some opposition alliance is a likely alternative, along with an equally likely possibility that the organization will run its own proportional representation lists. Alternately, the organization may farm out its candidates to multiple lists. Some incumbents who have close relations to the LDP could join that party; others could run on the lists of the opposition parties or alliance.

I have discussed in the previous chapter how the new electoral system may alter the organizational structure of Japanese campaigns. If these changes make floating voters a more accessible and more important target of campaigns, it will enhance the viable options for an opposition party such as the Democrats. Organizations and personal support groups would continue to be crucial components of any successful campaign, but the balance would more often be tipped to party leaders' generic appeals to floating voters, and away from individual candidates' appeals in specific districts.

To the extent that these changes occur, I would expect the Japanese opposition to come to resemble more closely the Social Democratic parties of Europe that Kitschelt (1994) describes. Japanese opposition parties would have a realistic option of repositioning themselves to take advantage of shifts in the preferences of the voters. Coalition building would be an important path to power, but there would be additional alternatives for parties to follow.

The future of Japanese politics is exciting; drastic change in the party system is almost a given. The lessons of history teach us that Japanese politicians are highly pragmatic in forming alliances. Though this tendency is typically castigated as unprincipled, it bodes well for Japanese democracy. Flexibility is a virtue in a system of coalition governments. Fluid party systems and flexibility have their deficiencies and inefficiencies, but it is preferable to the alternative of a polarized party system. The rhetoric of Japanese politicians may appear to indicate a higher degree of polarization and ideological rigidity than is actually present. As we have seen and will continue to see, political parties can overcome differences and build ruling political alliances.

Notes

Chapter 1. Stereotypes of Success or Failure in Japanese Politics

1. Chalmers Johnson made these comments during a class lecture at the University of California, Berkeley, in September 1987. He confirmed their accuracy in a personal communication with the author in May 1999.

2. These parties are called the "former" opposition parties because in 1993 three of them lost their opposition status when they became part of a coalition government. For easier referencing, I will generally refer to these parties simply as the opposition parties. Similarly, I will refer to the Socialist Party by this name rather than its new name, the Social Democratic Party of Japan. I use the older name because much of my discussion is historical and because the new name invites confusion with other parties that have similar names.

3. The one exception to this record was the LDP's coalition with the New Liberal Club from 1983 to 1986. Though the New Liberal Club received cabinet posts as part of the coalition agreement, the party disbanded in 1986, and almost all its members rejoined the LDP. For this reason, I do not consider this coalition government significant.

4. The best comparative discussion is found in T. J. Pempel (1990).

Chapter 2. The LDP Fall from Power

1. The number of districts and their magnitude changed slightly with each of several limited reapportionments of the system. These reapportionments occurred at roughly ten-year intervals. The deviations from the three-to-five magnitude rule were minor. There was one single-seat district, and in the latter years of the system, two six-seat and several two-seat districts were created.

2. The classic in this discussion is Gerald Curtis (1971). See also Yanaga Chitoshi (1956) and J. Mark Ramseyer and Frances McCall Rosenbluth (1993).

3. I use the term *conservative* to mean LDP politicians and independents who are affiliated with the LDP. Similarly, the term *opposition* includes independents affiliated with those parties. When I speak of opposition cooperation or the opposition camp, I am including the Socialists, the Clean Government

Party, the Democratic Socialist Party, and the Social Democratic League, a minor party.

4. This and all subsequent calculations assume an exchange rate of 100 yen = $1.

5. The Japanese version of the system is semiproportional only in the aggregate, however. Rein Taagepera and Matthew Shugart (1989) posit that the system itself should produce superproportionality, meaning that larger parties would get fewer seats than they would be entitled to under a system of pure proportionality. Gary Cox (1996) counters that the resource advantage of ruling parties allows them to win more seats than Taagepera and Shugart's analysis would suggest.

6. *Asahi Shimbun* (Tokyo), 28 January 1994, 1.

7. Bradley Richardson (1997, 94) also puts forth an incentive-based explanation for the 1993 LDP split. He emphasizes the numerical incentives to form coalitions and the sagging popularity of the LDP, and includes factors such as interpersonal relations.

8. As early as 1989, officials of the Ministry of Home Affairs made clear their preferences for a new election system, similar to the one that was ultimately adopted (*Asahi Shimbun* [Tokyo], 27 April 1990, 1). In 1989, the five main private-sector economic organizations in Japan issued a joint call for public funding of elections, full disclosure of the donors of all campaign contributions, and channeling of corporate contributions to political parties rather than to individual politicians (*Asahi Shimbun* [Tokyo], 29 April 1990, 1).

9. For example, in the 1990 House of Representatives election, 125 of 512 victors were elected from the same area that had previously sent their fathers or other close relatives to the Diet.

10. *Asahi Shimbun* (Tokyo), 26 January 1994, 9.

11. In 1993, Rengō had 7.8 million members. The Communist-affiliated federation had 860,000 members.

12. *Asahi Shimbun* (Tokyo), 26 March 1993, 4.

13. As early as 1990, an LDP opponent of Ozawa commented on Ozawa's sponsorship of political reform, calling it the "beginning of politics of fear by an Ozawa LDP" (Ozawa Jimintō no kyōfu seiji ga hajimaru). *Asahi Shimbun* (Tokyo), 23 November 1990, 2.

14. *Asahi Shimbun* (Tokyo), 12 January 1994, 3.

15. For example, see *Asahi Shimbun* (Tokyo), 15 January 1994, 9.

16. Ibid., 27 January 1994, 22.

17. Ibid., 26 March 1993, 4.

18. Ibid., 26 January 1994, 2.

19. Rumors of defections ran rampant in the days preceding final approval of the legislation. Proreform leader Gotoda Masaharu made an equivocal statement that was widely interpreted to indicate that he would lead a revolt from the party. In response, the stock market rose sharply. Former Prime Minister Kaifu said that the government bill was like giving "a previously miscarried child another chance to be born through in-vitro fertilization." *Asahi Shimbun* (Tokyo), 28 January 1994, 2.

20. See *Asahi Shimbun* (Tokyo), 27 January 1994, 2; 26 March 1993, 4.

21. The convention ended in a draw, with both prorealignment and anti-realignment forces agreeing to withdraw their resolutions without a vote. This allowed the Socialist Party leadership to continue in their prorealignment tilt, but it did nothing to resolve the divisions within the party. *Asahi Shimbun* (Tokyo), 12 January 1994, 3.

22. *Asahi Shimbun* (Tokyo), 28 December 1993, 3.

23. Two months earlier, the government and the LDP had almost reached a compromise, breaking off talks only when they could not resolve differences over the number of seats to be assigned in each election system. In late December of that year, there were calls from within both the LDP and the coalition government for a compromise between these two groups. Foreign Minister Hata said that compromise with the LDP was inevitable. One week before the vote in the House of Councillors, the LDP began drawing up its demands in the event of a reopening of compromise negotiations. See *Asahi Shimbun* (Tokyo), 28 December 1993, 3, 5; 11 January 1994, 1; and 13 January 1994, 3.

24. The enacted law works against small parties because they have to win seats in regions, rather than nationally; in contrast, the government bill used a national proportional representation district. Minor parties that have a strong regional base can still do well under the new system, especially parties based in urban areas, where the number of seats available is larger and hence the threshold for victory is lower. In the Kinki region, only 3 percent of the vote is needed to win a seat. Most minor parties, however, would have been better off with a national district, in which they would need to win only 2 or 3 percent of the vote nationwide to win a seat.

25. Kunihiro Masao (1996) corroborated this version of events. Kawato Sadafumi (1996) presents a similar explanation, focusing on the incomplete information these legislators had at the time they voted to defeat the government bill in the House of Councillors.

Chapter 3. Strategic Dilemmas and Options of the Opposition

1. I calculated the number of wasted votes in this proportional representation system using the following formula: $[V_i-S_i(V_l+1)]$, where V_i is the number of votes cast for the ith party and S_i is the number of seats won by the ith party. V_l is the number of votes that the party winning the last seat in the district had when it was awarded that last seat. In a ten-seat district, if the tenth seat went to a party that won a total of three seats, then V_l is that party's total vote divided by three.

2. Richardson (1997, 94) emphasizes this variation in his explanation of the events of 1993.

3. Duverger (1965, 325) argues that electoral coalitions will occur in single-seat districts and in nonintegrated proportional representation systems, systems that allocate seats proportionally only at the district level. Because such systems create remainders, or dead votes, in each election district, the number of dead votes and hence the potential benefits of electoral cooperation are greater than in integrated proportional representation systems.

4. For the extremist party, however, associating with an electoral coalition

can have significant benefits. By linking with a mainstream party, extremists can downplay their extremism and broaden their appeal to the electorate.

5. Michael Laver and Kenneth Shepsle (1990) explain how the assignment of ministerial portfolios can operate as a monitoring device.

6. Tsebelis (1990, 191) suggests this short time lag is a hindrance to cooperation, contrasting the short campaign week in France with the months that intervene between primary and general elections in the United States. In France, however, different parties are trying to cooperate; in the United States, each party is healing its internal wounds. Interparty cooperation does not require as much time to heal wounds and is perhaps better served by a shorter election period.

7. Tsebelis (1990, 219) argues that in the coalitions of the Left, Socialist districts have considerably weaker Communist parties than Communist districts, where the two parties tend to be more evenly situated. A comparison of districts with similar levels of leftist competition (i.e., those of similar party strength) would help support his claim. In addition, Tsebelis' calculation of his variable "cohesion" needs to account for the fact that coalitions between evenly situated parties should do relatively worse in votes transferred, simply because they have more votes to transfer.

Chapter 4. Electoral Cooperation in Japan

1. Isolated examples of formal cooperation occurred on the prefectural level. See Ellis Krauss (1980, 393–395).

2. Nishikawa Nirō (1991) provided this explanation. He should be an expert on this phenomenon—he has run unsuccessfully in twelve elections, ranging from village mayor to the House of Councillors.

3. Communist official Yoshioka Yoshinori (1991) praises Sasaki's leadership of the Socialist Party. He credits Sasaki for engineering the coalition victory in the Tokyo gubernatorial race and for initiating Socialist-Communist cooperation.

4. Though the Socialist-Communist coalition won impressive victories, their advance was not as uniform as is often assumed. Coalition candidates in 1967 and 1971 also went down to defeat in such opposition strongholds as Hokkaido, Fukuoka, and Kanagawa. Despite putting up thirty-three coalition candidates for mayor in 1971, the opposition won only eight of the forty-six new mayorships. Furthermore, a large group of the coalition mayors were incumbent Socialists who accepted Communist support in their reelection campaigns. See *Asahi Shimbun*, 27 April 1971.

5. House of Representative electoral data are most appropriate in this urban-rural comparison because they closely approximate the actual electoral strength of the parties. A comparison based on gubernatorial elections or on the prefectural constituency vote of House of Councillors elections would be skewed by the large number of cooperation districts in each. Another option is the national constituency vote of the House of Councillors, but this vote underestimates the electoral strength of the Socialists and the LDP.

6. The socialist parties appear more unified in the House of Councillors elections than in the House of Representatives elections, but this reflects the number of each type of election held only during the period that the Socialist

Party was most severely divided. Three House of Representatives elections took place during this time, but only one House of Councillors election.

7. The Clean Government Party followed a different pattern of expansion. It put up candidates in its strongest districts and slowly expanded into marginal districts. This was a strategic use of the party's finite support base. Party leaders could accurately predict voter support levels before the first election; a limited expansion program would not discourage potential voters in excluded areas, because they were already committed to the party by their religious identification.

8. See Krauss (1980, 398) for a description of how the progressive governor of Kyoto turned down an offer of LDP support.

9. The issue was much more complex than this cursory summary indicates. Many left-wing Socialists also opposed cooperation with the Communists (Kunimasa 1973, 102–106). However, these radicals also opposed cooperation with the centrists, so the all-opposition cooperation platform suited them well. It prevented the Socialist Party from making a substantial cooperation commitment either to the centrists or to the Communists.

10. For a description of the events of this period, see *Sekai* (1973).

11. See Ishigami Yamoto (1984, 134). Ishigami contends that Nishimura's greatest motive in proposing Socialist-centrist cooperation was to stop the rising tide of Socialist-Communist cooperation.

12. In later years, it was the Clean Government Party that was the most afraid of isolation, because of that party's religious affiliations. In 1971, however, both the Socialists and the Communists saw the Clean Government Party as a prime coalition prospect. Only Democratic Socialist leaders excluded themselves from this potential coalition by their virulent anti-Communism.

13. An example of how the Democratic Socialists feared Socialist-Communist cooperation is revealed in the following quote. A Democratic Socialist bureau chief, commenting on the unified local elections, said that the party did well, but "The possibility has emerged that Socialist-Communist cooperation will become routinized along the lines of the Communist's policy positions. The effect of such an event would be immense. The Democratic Socialists must consider strategies and tactics to deal with this attack." He added that the party would reconsider its campaign slogan for the upcoming House of Councillors election and its policy of never supporting another party's candidates. Both reforms were expressly aimed at making it easier for the Democratic Socialists and the Socialists to cooperate. (*Mainichi Shimbun* [Tokyo]), 14 April 1971).

14. See Ueda Kōichirō (1971, 297–304) for the Communist position on this dispute and Yokoyama Taiji (1971) for the Socialist position.

15. Ishibashi Masashi (1991) cites this reason when he says the Socialists should not have abandoned all-opposition cooperation in 1980.

16. See *Yomiuri Shimbun* (Tokyo), 2 June 1971.

17. See *Asahi Shimbun* (Tokyo), 20, 21, 22, and 24 May 1971.

18. *Mainichi Shimbun* (Tokyo), 19 June 1971.

19. See *Asahi Jānaru* (1971, 127–128).

20. *Mainichi Shimbun* (Tokyo), 19 June 1971.

21. The numbers add up to nine because Tochigi prefecture (one of the

three Socialist-centrist cooperation districts) is a two-seat district, so it is not included in the total of the eight single-seat districts that the Socialists won.

22. See *Mainichi Shimbun* (Tokyo), 29 June 1971; *Asahi Shimbun* (Tokyo), 28 June 1971; and Yomiuri *Shimbun* (Tokyo), 29 June 1971.

23. *Mainichi Shimbun* (Tokyo), 26 June 1971.

24. The decline in Nakamura's vote is most easily explained by the presence of two conservative candidates in the race. Nakamura may have calculated that many of the centrist voters would go to one of the conservative candidates, so he opposed centrist cooperation to encourage left-wing Socialist voters' support of him rather than their defecting to the Communist candidate. Perhaps it was Nakamura's opposition to cooperation, rather than the support of the centrist parties, that won him the race.

25. See *Asahi Shimbun* (Tokyo), 4, 8, and 15 July 1971.

26. The order of Diet interpellations before the election was Socialist, LDP, Socialist, Clean Government Party, and so on; the centrists wanted it changed to Socialist, LDP, Clean Government Party, Democratic Socialists, and so on. In the management committee, according to Takeiri (1991), the Socialists continued their old pattern of deciding the agenda of the Diet in exclusive consultation with the LDP. The centrists expected to be included in such consultations after the elections.

27. Initially, the December 1972 election ruptured Socialist-Communist ties when the Communists attacked Socialists as "partners in collusion" with the LDP during the election campaign. By February of 1973, this dispute was smoothed over. See Indō Kazuo (1977, 140) and Iizuka Shigetarō (1973, 11).

28. The move began in the June 1972 Clean Government Party convention, in which the party switched to being in favor of a "quick" repudiation of the United States–Japan Security Treaty and a resumption of diplomatic relations with Communist China. In 1973, the party strengthened its anti–Security Treaty stance to the "immediate" rejection of the Treaty.

29. According to my interview with an anonymous Democratic Socialist official, the centrist barter arrangements are always exchanges of equal numbers of votes rather than equal numbers of districts. The number of cooperation districts is unequal because the number of votes transferred varies from district to district; some of the cooperation districts are purposely kept secret, even though their vote totals are included in the overall exchange.

30. In a 1973 interview, Secretary General Ishibashi of the Socialist Party expounded on the Socialist's all-opposition stance in a manner that hinted at this shift. He said that the Socialists envisioned only the four opposition parties working together. An opposition coalition government would require only two or three of the four opposition parties to actually participate in the government. He acknowledged that the voters did not want a Socialist-Communist coalition government (*Ekonomisuto* 1973a).

31. Ishibashi (1991) cites this last reason as an explanation for why the Socialists ultimately went with centrist cooperation in 1971. Communist votes are concentrated in the cities and therefore can provide less benefit to Socialist candidates in rural prefectures. The Clean Government Party is also weak in rural areas, but Sōka gakkai has committed members in every locality.

32. The parties also cooperated regularly in Okinawa, but cooperation on Okinawa is a special case because of the existence of an independent, Okinawa-based opposition party.

33. Most Sōhyō support of the Clean Government Party candidate in Gifu 1 came from the Meitetsu union, a private railway workers union. This was in exchange for informal Clean Government Party support of a Meitetsu Socialist candidate in neighboring Aichi 4. Kokurō, the public railway workers union, also agreed to support the Clean Government Party in Gifu 1 in exchange for Clean Government Party support of a Kokurō Socialist candidate in Miyazaki 2. Other exchanges with other unions were proposed, but agreements to cooperate with those unions were not reached. *Mainichi Shimbun* (Tokyo), 13 and 28 November 1976.

34. See *Asahi Shimbun* (Tokyo), 1 November 1976, which quotes Ishibashi as saying disparagingly that the cooperation plan is just something that "Yamamoto and his cohorts in the Eda faction have done." The article continues, stating that not only Ishibashi but the entire leadership of the Socialist Party is cool on the idea of Socialist-centrist cooperation because the idea and plan originated with the Eda faction.

35. Clean Government Party Chairman Takeiri (1991) criticizes Eda in retrospect for not being able to make up his mind about leaving the Socialist Party, claiming that Eda decided to leave the party after it was too late. Eda left only after he had already been defeated within the party, and then he persuaded only one other person to leave with him. (The three others who left the party did so independently of Eda.) Tanabe Makoto (1997) paints a different picture of Eda's departure, claiming that Eda urged his supporters to stay in the Socialist Party rather than risk defeat by joining him in trying to build a new party.

36. See the analysis of Ishikawa Masumi (1979, 6–7), one of the few political analysts to recognize and highlight the revival of the LDP.

37. A double election makes cooperation more difficult because it forces parties in the same election districts both to cooperate and to compete simultaneously in different races. For example, in Shiga prefecture in 1980, the Socialists and the Democratic Socialists backed the independent, Yamada Kōzaburō, in the House of Councillors race, but they also competed against each other in the House of Representatives race in which each party had an incumbent running. In such a circumstance, both parties hold back on their cooperative efforts so as to put the majority of party resources into the campaigns of their House of Representatives candidates. In addition, party leaders shore up their support bases in the competitive race by attacking the candidate and policies of the party closest to them, their cooperation partner. Such attacks typically spoil the joint efforts to back a coalition candidate. In double elections, the interests of the coalition candidates are always subordinated to the interests of the party candidates in the more important and more competitive House of Representatives races.

38. *Mainichi Shimbun* (Tokyo), 1 June 1977.

39. For a discussion of this factor in the context of opposition party relations, see Takagi Ikurō (1989, 75).

40. See *Asahi Jānaru* (1979), for a brief summary of these factors.

41. Initially, the Socialists had urged the Clean Government Party to choose a coalition candidate for Oita prefecture. When negotiations in Oita broke down, party leaders preserved the token barter nature of the cooperation agreement by running a Democratic Socialist–affiliated independent in Kōchi prefecture.

42. See *Yomiuri Shimbun* (Tokyo), 23 June 1980.

43. This announcement was not a surprise. The Democratic Socialist stance was well known. See *Asahi Shimbun* (Tokyo), 9 October 1979. The prominent and public nature of the announcement during an election campaign gave Sasaki's speech its significance.

44. Secretary General Yano (1984, 206) of the Clean Government Party called the election an "extremely painful experience." Chairman Takeiri (1991) shook his head as he described the 1980 election as "unforgettable." He severely criticized the stupidity of the Socialist leader Asukata Ichio and the Democratic Socialist leader Sasaki for engaging in such a harmful dispute during an election campaign. Even Ishibashi (1991) criticized his colleague Asukata's handling of the dispute as "amateurish."

45. This clause was meaningless; it didn't stop Sasaki from publicly stating his willingness to work with the LDP in a coalition government (Nihon Shakaitō 1986, 552, 612).

46. Double elections and the threat of double elections discouraged cooperation in the 1980s by forcing parties to cooperate and compete simultaneously in the same districts, and by intimidating the Clean Government Party, which feared the high turnouts of double elections, therefore concentrating all its resources on its own candidates rather than on supporting coalition candidates.

47. An anonymous Democratic Socialist official gave an example of this problem during an interview. The Democratic Socialist candidate in Nagano 4 faced the perennial problem of finding a Clean Government Party district to pair with. In 1976, the Clean Government Party ran a candidate in Nagano 1, solving his problem for that election by allowing a vote exchange between two districts in the same prefecture. In 1990, facing a tough race, he tried to work out an arrangement for receiving Clean Government Party votes in exchange for his union (Shōwa Denkō) giving votes to the Clean Government Party candidate in Kanagawa 2. The Clean Government Party refused to sanction this exchange because it regarded its seat in Kanagawa 2 as safe. Lacking any district to pair with, the candidate did not receive Clean Government Party support and lost the election.

48. For a brief narration of these events, see Nihon Shakaitō (1983, 618).

49. Anonymous interview with a high official of a Socialist affiliated union. I received this information on the condition that I not reveal the name of the union, the name of the interviewee, or any specific dates or place names that would allow the union to be identified.

50. Ishigami (1984, 138) perceives the Clean Government Party as serving two important functions in the development of opposition cooperation: (1) Party efforts reduced the opposition's number of dead votes, and (2) the party used the incentive of electoral cooperation to modify radicalism within the Socialist Party.

51. Morimoto Kōji (1991), a Clean Government Party representative from Nara prefecture, stated that the breakdown of Socialist-centrist relations after the 1990 election was a relief because the party had finally gained complete policy independence. No longer would it have to consult with its Socialist allies on every policy position. The Assistant Secretary General of the Clean Government Party, Futami Nobuaki (1991), seconded these sentiments. He said that it was much easier in 1991 now that decision making in the party was no longer constrained by Socialist Party positions.

52. "Rengō" is the abbreviated name for the full Japanese title "Zen nihon minkan rōdō kumiai rengōkai," translated into English as the "Japanese Private Sector Trade Union Confederation." With the addition of the public sector unions in 1989, Rengō's full name changed to the "Japanese Trade Union Confederation."

53. Sōhyō's promise to join Rengō in the fall of 1989 caused most of Sōhyō's Communist affiliates to pull out of the Sōhyō unions and form their own competing unions and labor federation. This split weakened the new Rengō federation, but it also ensured that the remaining Rengō unions would clearly favor continued cooperation with the centrist parties.

54. The LDP candidates won in only Toyama, Wakayama, and Saga prefectures.

55. For a brief summary of Ishibashi's proposal and its rejection by the Socialist leadership, see Nagata Saburō [pseud.] (1989, 130–132), and Ishibashi Masashi (1990, 104–105). The Rengō union leader Yamagishi Akira (1989, 121) criticized Ishibashi's proposal as being motivated only by Ishibashi's desire to facilitate his own reelection by having one, rather than two, Socialist candidates in his district. Though Yamagishi's criticisms are unsupported by the evidence, they do illustrate Ishibashi's proposal being summarily dismissed.

56. In Gumma 3, the Socialists, the Clean Government Party, and the Democratic Socialists backed a Rengō candidate. They cooperated in Gumma 3 because it is former Prime Minister Nakasone's home district, and his reelection to the Diet was assured because the only serious candidates competing for the four seats were the four incumbents (one Socialist and three LDP or LDP-affiliated). Pressure for the opposition parties to put up a fifth candidate became very intense, since one of their campaign issues was Nakasone's corruption. In three other districts, Hyogo 5, Osaka 6, and Osaka 1, the Socialists and the Democratic Socialists jointly backed independent or Rengō candidates with strong union affiliations. In all three districts, it was clear that neither party could elect a candidate on its own power.

57. In a 1989 interview, the Rengō leader, Yamagishi Akira (1989, 123), laid out his vision for a political reformulation by the mid-1990s. Though he stated that Rengō would give support to Clean Government Party candidates, the inclusion of the party in the political reorganization was "difficult" (in the careful language of Japanese public pronouncements, this is best interpreted as "absolutely impossible"). Rather, he preferred a new party composed of the Socialists, the Democratic Socialists, and the Social Democratic League, which would work closely with the Clean Government Party.

58. Japan severely limits campaign spending through measurable channels,

such as advertising. Massive amounts of money can, however, be distributed through organizations and personal relations. LDP politicians in the House of Representatives spend vast sums building up personal support groups, thus insulating themselves from variations in the overall popularity of the LDP. However, LDP politicians in the House of Councillors would require even larger sums of money to build an equivalent organization for a House of Councillors race. The restrictions on campaign spending prevent them from building candidate identification through the media.

59. Kamijō Sueo (1985, 11), calculating this gap by prefectures, found that in rural areas, the LDP did 11 percentage points better in House of Representatives races. In urban prefectures, the LDP did 1 percent better in the prefectural constituencies of the House of Councillors. Kamijō explains the difference by citing the greater candidate identification of rural conservative voters.

60. In the 1992 House of Councillors election, the LDP rebounded completely from its loss in 1989. However, the weakness of the LDP in the House is shown by the startling success of a new protest party, the Japan New Party (Nihon Shin Tō), which gained 8 percent of the proportional representation vote. In 1995, the LDP again fared poorly, largely as a result of defections from the party, winning only 49 of 126 seats. The party did no better in 1998, winning 45 of 126 seats.

61. For example, in Hyogo 5, an independent was elected with the backing of the Socialist and Democratic Socialist Parties. This joint backing is not listed as formal party cooperation, however, because the candidate ran as an independent.

Chapter 5. Party Cooperation and Strategies of Party Reorganization

1. In a 1985 interview, Secretary General Tanabe of the Socialist Party was asked if recent Clean Government Party criticism of the Socialist Party was motivated by its anger at being left out of the decision-making process. The questioner cited a secret meeting between Tanabe and Kanemaru, in which the Socialists allegedly agreed to end their boycott of the Diet in exchange for LDP concessions on a bill providing year-end income supplements to national railway workers (represented by an important Sōhyō union). Tanabe replied, "There was no such deal. Of course, I did meet Mr. Kanemaru, but we only discussed the supplemental budget [the dispute that had paralyzed the Diet], and it is only natural that the ruling party would want to discuss such an issue with the Socialists." Tanabe then continued, "With regard to the railways issue, I have discussed the reconstruction of the Japan National Railways with Mr. Kanemaru and the leader of the LDP's Policy Affairs Research Council, Mr. Fujio, in the past, but for now there is no linkage of the budget issue and the railways issue." *Shakai Rōdō Hyōron* (1985, 26).

2. Anonymous interview.

3. Tsukamoto Saburō (1990, 150–151) a former Democratic Socialist chairman, says one reason his party lost in the 1990 House of Representatives election was because it was too closely aligned with the Socialists. The party was no

longer seen as a centrist alternative to the LDP, so it forfeited its chance to attract potential defectors from the LDP.

4. Democratic Socialist Yoshida Yukihisa (1991) says that conservative powers in Nara were out to get him because he had played a crucial role in Rengō's victory in Nara during the 1989 House of Councillors election. They wanted him to lose in the 1990 House of Representatives election to pay for the LDP's loss in 1989. Kishimoto Shigenobu (1990, 258–259) also cites this as a partial explanation of Democratic Socialist losses in the 1990 House of Representatives election. Business was giving more than its usual support to the LDP, so it had less support to give Democratic Socialist candidates.

5. Yasumasa Kuroda and Yoshie Kobayashi (1997), however, point out that even the demonstrations in 1960 were scripted in the behind-the-scenes negotiations between party leaders.

6. This discussion of prewar electoral reform is taken largely from Soma Masao (1986, 41–43, 85–86).

7. As an example, consider a hypothetical ten-seat district of the 1900 system. A party could win a seat with only 5 to 10 percent of the vote. The 1925 reform created three- to five-seat districts, in which a party needed from 15 to 30 percent of the vote to win a seat.

8. The Progressive Party (Shimpōtō) later became the Democrat Party (Minshūtō). This party merged with the Liberal Party in 1955 to form the Liberal Democrat Party. These parties are unrelated to the Liberal and Democratic Parties formed in the 1990s.

9. The National Cooperative Party (Kokumin Kyōdotō) eventually became part of the LDP.

10. See Masaru Kohno (1997) and Hayashi Yūmi (1984, 257–293) for detailed descriptions of the bargaining that surrounded the formation of these cabinets.

11. For a thorough description of the events surrounding the union of the Socialist Party in 1955 and its subsequent split in 1960, see Masumi Junnosuke (1985, 489–515).

12. Kenneth Pyle (1992, 86–87) says that Nakasone "had long been an outspoken nationalist." He describes Nakasone as being in opposition to "conservative mainstream policies."

13. Sōka gakkai was politically active well before 1964. They won fifty-four city and prefectural legislative positions in the 1955 unified local elections. In 1956, three of their candidates were elected in the national constituency of the House of Councillors. This trend accelerated in 1962, when they ran a slate of candidates in the House of Councillors election under the name of the Clean Government League (Kōmei seiji renmei).

14. For example, see Naitō Kunio (1970). For the party response to these charges, see *Kōmei* (1970, 18–36).

15. This account of events is taken from Hirakawa Ichirō (1971) and an interview with an anonymous Democratic Socialist official.

16. See *Anarisuto* (1968), which says that the new Democratic Socialist leadership of Nishimura and Kasuga toned down the party's anti-Communism

and showed a greater commitment to the opposition camp. Clean Government Party chairman Takeiri Yoshikatsu (1991) differentiates between Nishimura and his eventual successor, Kasuga. In his opinion, Nishimura was more committed to opposition cooperation because he was willing to merge his party and the Clean Government Party together. Kasuga, however, only wanted to cooperate with the Clean Government Party as he worked to rebuild his party.

17. This attitude was prevalent, as evidenced by a 1967 *Mainichi Shimbun* (Tokyo) editorial calling for the Democratic Socialists to rethink their strategy of close alliance with the LDP. *Mainichi Shimbun* (Tokyo), 19 April 1967.

18. Mainichi Shimbun Seijibu, (1993, 54). See J. A. A. Stockwin (1974) for a more specific account of the shifting alliances surrounding this election. See also Ellis Krauss (1980) for background on the Ninagawa government.

19. A different view of this is provided by Tanabe Makoto (1997), who says that Eda instructed him and other allies to stay within the Socialist Party for their own protection. It seems that Eda planned to risk only his own career to build another vehicle for reform outside the Socialist Party, which his allies could join at a later date.

20. This dissolution was called *bakayarō* because it was sparked by Prime Minister Yoshida's calling an opposition leader a *bakayarō* (jackass) during a session of the Diet.

21. See *Shakai Rōdō Hyōron* (1985, 26–27). In this interview, the third highest official in the Clean Government Party recounts that only Takeiri and Yano knew of Nikaidō's offer. Democratic Socialists, too, were surprised and upset by the plot. See *Ekonomisuto* (1985, 45). For a summary of all the rumors and intrigues surrounding the Nikaidō plot, see Tawara Kōtarō (1985).

Chapter 6. Successes and Failures of the Opposition Parties

1. Quantitative analysis of length-of-service data does not corroborate anecdotal evidence of union leaders serving in the Diet only the minimum time needed to gain a government pension. In a limited analysis of the terms of service of representatives from 1972 to 1993, there was only a slight difference between the terms of service of LDP and Socialist representatives. For example, 5.3 percent of Socialist legislators and 6.4 percent of LDP legislators served only ten years. Those who served only eleven years were 7.2 and 7.5 percent, respectively.

2. The LDP or conservative camp is defined as all members of the LDP and independents who are affiliated with the LDP. The reasons for the latter's inclusion are given in Raymond Christensen (1995, 579–581). Members of the New Liberal Club and its affiliated independents are also included in the LDP camp. The opposition camp is composed of the parties of electoral cooperation—the Socialists, the Democratic Socialists, and the Clean Government Party—independents affiliated with these parties, and members and affiliates of the Social Democratic League. The calculation of winnable seats is based on the actual returns of the other candidates. For example, a camp may have had the votes to elect three people, though in actuality it only won two seats. The third could have been elected if the camp had coordinated its efforts better. This analysis, however, assumes that the possible coordination mistakes of the other camp's

candidates actually occurred. Thus, in a four-seat district, it might be that the LDP could have won three seats and the opposition could have won three seats, for six seats in a four-seat district. The LDP could win three seats if the opposition's mistakes were held constant and the LDP coordinated optimally. Similarly, the opposition could have won three seats if it coordinated optimally and the LDP's mistakes were held constant (see Cox 1997, 243–244).

3. The conservatives outperform the opposition camp in ten of the fifteen paired comparisons for this period.

4. I have also calculated standard deviations and obtained similar results.

5. The formula is given in Cox (1997, 4) and in Arend Lijphart (1994, 67–72).

6. In districts where two seats were winnable, the LDP polled 12, 10, and 13 percent more of the vote than the opposition in years of no cooperation, partial cooperation, and full cooperation, respectively. In districts where three seats were winnable, the LDP advantage was 15, 12, and 14 percent in the three periods. For districts where four seats were winnable, the respective numbers were 10, 6, and 16 percent.

7. Okuno did not run in the district; he ran in a neighboring district.

8. The one exception to this rule was when the union backed an LDP candidate rather than the Democratic Party candidate. It occurred because the LDP candidate's parents were members of the union, so the LDP candidate had very good relations with the union, while the Democratic candidate had no such connections.

Works Cited

Anarisuto. 1968. "Yatō rengō no shōrai" (The future of the opposition alliance). *Anarisuto* 14 (4): 39–42.

Aochi Shin. 1970. "Kōmeitō to 'genron no jiyū' mondai" (The CGP and the "freedom of speech" problem). *Chūō Kōron* 85 (4): 114–129.

Argersinger, P. 1991. *Structure, Process, and Party, Essays in American Political History.* New York: M. E. Sharpe.

Asahi Jānaru. 1971. "Kisei agaranu 'Sha-Kō-Min kyōryoku'" (Unenthusiastic Socialist-CGP-DSP cooperation) *Asahi Jānaru* 13 (23): 127–128.

———. 1972. "Hitasura gisekizō nerau" (Earnestly pursuing an increase in seats). *Asahi Jānaru* 14 (40): 107–108.

———. 1979. "Mizo we ketteiteki ni fukamatta" (The gulf has widened). *Asahi Jānaru* 21 (48): 6–7.

Asahi Shimbun (Tokyo). 27 April; 20, 21, 22, 24 May; 28 June; 4, 8, 15 July 1971. 1 November 1976. 9 Oct. 1979. 27, 29 April; 23 November 1990. 26 March; 28 December 1993. 3, 5, 11, 12, 13, 15, 26, 27, 28 January 1994. 22 October 1996.

Asahi shimbun senkyo hombu (Asahi Newspaper, Election Central). 1993. *Asahi Senkyo Taikan: Dai 40 kai Shūgiin sōsenkyo, dai 16 kai Sangiin tsūjō senkyo* (Asahi Election Overview: The 40th House of Representatives General Election, the 16th House of Councillors Ordinary Election). Tokyo: Asahi Shimbunsha.

Axelrod, Robert. 1970. *A Theory of Divergent Goals with Applications to Politics.* Chicago: Markham Publishing.

———. 1984. *The Evolution of Cooperation.* New York: Basic Books.

Bartolini, Stefano. 1984. "Institutional Constraints and Party Competition in the French Party System." *West European Politics* 7 (4): 103–127.

Bawn, Kathleen. 1993. "The Logic of Institutional Preferences: German Electoral Law as a Social Choice Outcome." *American Journal of Political Science* 37:965–989.

Boyd, Richard. 1986. "The Japanese Communist Party in Local Government." In *Marxist Local Governments in Western Europe and Japan,* edited by Bogdan Szajkowski. Boulder, Colo.: Lynne Rienner Publishers.

Broughton, David, and Emil Kirchner. 1986. "The FDP and Coalitional Behavior in the Federal Republic of Germany: Multi-Dimensional Perspectives on the Role of a Pivotal Party." In *Coalitional Behavior in Theory and Practice,* edited by Geoffrey Pridham. New York: Cambridge University Press.

Calder, Kent E. 1988. *Crisis and Compensation: Public Policy and Political Stability in Japan, 1949–1986.* Princeton: Princeton University Press.

Christensen, Raymond V. 1994. "Electoral Reform in Japan: How It Was Enacted and Changes It May Bring." *Asian Survey* 34 (July): 589–605.

———. 1995. "Toward a Context-Rich Analysis of Electoral Systems: The Japanese Example." *American Journal of Political Science* 39 (August): 575–598.

Cox, Gary W. 1996. "Is the Single Non-Transferable Vote Superproportional?: Evidence from Japan and Taiwan." *American Journal of Political Science* 40 (August): 740–755.

———. 1997. *Making Votes Count: Strategic Coordination in the World's Electoral Systems.* Cambridge, England: Cambridge University Press.

Cox, Gary W., and Emerson Niou. 1994. "Seat Bonuses Under the Single Non-Transferable Vote System: Evidence from Japan and Taiwan." *Comparative Politics* 26:221–236.

Cox, Gary W., and Frances Rosenbluth. 1994. "Reducing Nomination Errors: Factional Competition and Party Strategy in Japan." *Electoral Studies* 13 (1): 4–16.

Cox, Gary W., and Matthew Soberg Shugart. 1995. "In the Absence of Vote Pooling: Nomination and Vote Allocation Errors in Colombia." *Electoral Studies* 14 (4): 441–460.

Cox, Karen, and Len Schoppa. 1998. "The Consequences of 'Sticky Voting' in Mixed-Member Electoral Systems." Presentation at the Annual Meeting of the American Political Science Association, September 3–6. Boston, Massachusetts.

Curtis, Gerald L. 1971. *Election Campaigning Japanese Style.* New York: Columbia University Press.

Duverger, Maurice. 1965. *Political Parties: Their Origin and Activity in the Modern State.* 2d English ed. Translated by Barbara and Robert North. New York: John Wiley and Sons.

———. 1972. *Party Politics and Pressure Groups.* Translated by David Wagoner. New York: Thomas E. Cromwell.

Ekonomisuto. 1973a. "Kakushin sareta zen yatō kyōtō no tadashisa" (The correctness of all opposition cooperation is confirmed). *Ekonomisuto* 51 (49): 38–41.

———. 1973b. "Sōgo fushin no naka no rengō seiken kōsō" (From mutual distrust, proposals for a coalition government). *Ekonomisuto* 51 (49): 50–51.

———. 1985. "Yatō ni seiken e no michi wa aru ka" (Is there a path to power for the opposition parties). *Ekonomisuto* 63 (9): 40–46.

Gilberg, Trond. 1989. "Marxists and Coalitions in Western Europe." In *Coalition Strategies of Marxist Parties,* edited by Trond Gilberg. Durham, N.C.: Duke University Press.

Hayashi Yūmi. 1984. "Sengo Nihon no rengō: Katayama naikaku chūshin ni" (Postwar Japanese coalitions: A focus on the Katayama cabinet). In vol. 1, *Rengō Seiji* (Coalition Politics). Edited by Shinohara Hajime. Tokyo: Iwanami Publishing.

Helander, Voitto. 1997. "Finland." In *Passages to Power, Legislative Recruitment in Advanced Democracies.* Edited by Pippa Norris. New York: Cambridge University Press.

Hirakawa Ichirō. 1971. "'Dai ni hoshutō' wa jitsugen suru ka: seikai no kyogi-kakushin shintō" (Will a second conservative party become a reality: A new progressive party—A political farce). *Asahi Jānaru* 13 (13): 4–10.

Hrebenar, Ronald J., ed. 1986. *The Japanese Party System: From One-Party Rule to Coalition Government.* Boulder, Colo.: Westview Press.

Iizuka Shigetarō. 1973. "Gekitotsu kara kyōtō e no Sha-Kyō kankei" (Socialist-Communist relations, from being at loggerheads to cooperation). *Gekkan Rōdō Mondai,* n.s., 183:10–13.

Indō Kazuo. 1977. "Kyōsantō no kyōtō senryaku to kanōsei" (The possibility and strategy of Communist Party cooperation). *Sekai* 3 (83): 132–144.

Ishibashi Masashi. 1990. "Doi iinchō yo, Kanemaru senryaku wa wana da" (Chairwoman Doi! Kanemaru's proposal is a trap). *Bungei Shunjū* 68 (5): 104–111.

Ishigami Yamato. 1984. "Yatō senkyo kyōryoku—Imi to yakuwari" (Opposition electoral cooperation-its role and significance. In *Nihon no seitō* (Japan's Political Parties). *Jurisuto Zōkan Sōgō Tokushū* 35:132–138.

Ishikawa Masumi. 1979. "Hakuchū to rengō no seiji jōkyō, dai ichibu" (The politics of coalitions and slim LDP majorities, part one). *Gendai no Riron,* n.s., 173:5–21.

Iwai Akira and Shimizu Shinzō. 1973. "Shakyō no yakushin to tōitsu sensen no tenbō" (The advance of the Socialist-Communist coalition and the prospects as seen at the front of the unification battle). *Gekkan Rōdō Mondai,* n.s., 179:16–23.

Johnson, Chalmers. 1982. *Miti and the Japanese Miracle.* Stanford, Calif.: Stanford University Press.

———. 1997. "Preconceptions vs. Observation, or the Contributions of Rational Choice Theory and Area Studies to Contemporary Political Science." *PS: Political Science and Politics* 30 (2): 170–174.

Kabashima Ikuo and Yamada Masahiro. 1994. "Kōenkai to Nihon no seiji" (Kōenkai and politics in Japan). *The Annals of the Japanese Political Science Association, 1994.* Tokyo: Japan Political Science Association.

Kamijō Sueo. 1985. "Senkyo seido to seitō shisutemu" (The electoral and party systems). *Seijigaku Ronshū,* n.s., 22:1–28.

Kawato Sadafumi. 1996. "Hosokawa renritsu seiken to seiji kaikaku hōan no rippō katei" (The Hosokawa coalition government and the passage of political reform legislation). Presentation at the Annual Meeting of Nihon Senkyo Gakkai, May. Tokyo, Japan.

Kishimoto Shigenobu. 1990. "Yatō no shutaiteki arikata o tou" (Questioning the stance of independence of the opposition). *Sekai,* n.s., 539:258–262.

Kitschelt, Herbert. 1994. *The Transformation of European Social Democracy.* Cambridge: Cambridge University Press.

Kohno, Masaru. 1997. *Japan's Postwar Party Politics.* Princeton: Princeton University Press.

Kōmei. 1970. "Kōmeitō ni kuwaerareta chūshō to sono hanron" (Slander of the Clean Government Party and the Party's response). *Kōmei* no. 90: 18–36.

Krauss, Ellis S. 1980. "Opposition in Power: The Development and Maintenance of Leftist Government in Kyoto Prefecture." In *Political Opposition and Local Politics in Japan,* edited by Kurt Steiner, Ellis S. Krauss, and Scott C. Flanagan. Princeton, N.J.: Princeton University Press.

Kujiraoka Hyōsuke, Doi Takako, Den Hideo, and Kunihiro Masao. 1993. *Miki 'seijikaikaku' shian to wa nanika* (A description of Miki's plan to reform politics), Iwanami, no. 290 (Tokyo: Iwanami).

Kuroda, Yasumasa, and Yoshie Kobayashi. 1997. "The Bilayer Theory of Japanese Politics." Presentation at the Annual Meeting of the American Political Science Association, September. Washington, D.C.

Kunimasa Takeshige. 1973. "Kakushin tōitsu seifu kōryō no yakuwari" (The role of proposals for a unified opposition government). *Asahi Jānaru* 15 (43): 102–06.

Laver, Michael, and Michael D. Higgins. 1986. "Coalition or Fianna Fail? The Politics of Inter-Party Government in Ireland." In *Coalitional Behavior in Theory and Practice.* Edited by Geoffrey Pridham. New York: Cambridge University Press.

Laver, Michael, and Norman Schofield. 1990. *Multiparty Government: The Politics of Coalitions in Europe.* New York: Oxford University Press.

Laver, Michael, and Kenneth Shepsle. 1990. "Coalitions and Cabinet Government." *American Political Science Review* 84 (3): 873–890.

Lijphart, Arend. 1994. *Electoral Systems and Party Systems, A Study of Twenty-Seven Democracies, 1945–1990.* New York: Oxford University Press.

Luebbert, Gregory M. 1986. *Comparative Democracy: Policymaking and Governing Coalitions in Europe and Israel.* New York: Columbia University Press.

McCubbins, Mathew D., and Frances McCall Rosenbluth. 1995. "Party Provision for Personal Politics: Dividing the Vote in Japan." In *Structure and Policy in Japan and the United States,* edited by Peter F. Cowhey and Mathew D. McCubbins. New York: Cambridge University Press.

MacDougall, Terry Edward. 1982. "Asukata Ichio and some of the Dilemmas of Socialist Leadership in Japan." In *Political Leadership in Contempo-*

rary Japan, edited by Terry Edward MacDougall. Ann Arbor, Mich.: Center for Japanese Studies, University of Michigan.

Mainichi Shimbun (Tokyo). 3, 13, 17, 19 April 1967; 14 April; 19, 26, 29 June 1971; 13, 28 November 1976; 1 June 1977.

Mainichi Shimbun Seijibu. 1993. *Seinen* (Political Change). Tokyo: Shakai shisōsha.

Masumi Junnosuke. 1985. *Gendai Seiji, ge* (Modern Politics, part 2). Tokyo: Tokyo University Publishers.

Matsuoka Hideo. 1990. *Rengō seiken ga hōkaishita hi* (The day the coalition government fell). Tokyo: Kyōku shinryō shuppankai.

Mayhew, David R. 1975. *Congress, the Electoral Connection.* New Haven, Conn.: Yale University Press.

Mitchell, Richard H. 1996. *Political Bribery in Japan.* Honolulu: University of Hawai'i Press.

Miyakawa Takayoshi. 1982. *Seiji Handobukku, No. 13* (Handbook of politics, no. 13). Tokyo: Seiji Kōhō Senta.

———. 1990. *Seiji Handobukku, No. 25* (Handbook of politics, no. 25). Tokyo: Seiji Kōhō Senta.

Muramatsu Michio, and Ellis S. Krauss. 1987. "The Conservative Policy Line and the Development of Patterned Pluralism." In *The Political Economy of Japan,* vol. 1. Edited by Yamamura Kozo and Yasuba Yasukichi. Stanford, Calif.: Stanford University Press.

Nagata Jirō [pseud.] 1980. "Yanagi no shita ni dojō wa mada iru ka" (Is rich loam still needed underneath the willow tree). *Gekkan Jiyū Minshū* 289: 86–89.

Nagata Saburō [pseud.] 1989. "Ima yatō wa: Ishibashi shi intai hyōmei no shōgeki" (Happenings in the opposition: The shock from Ishibashi's retirement announcement). *Jiyū Minshū* 439:130–132.

Naitō Kunio. 1970. "Sōka gakkai no atsuryoku-Watakushi no baai" (Sōka gakkai pressure–my experiences). *Bungei Shunjū* 48 (4): 94–108.

Naitō Tadashi. 1965. "Saikai sareta Sha-Kyō-Sōhyō no kyōtō" (The revived cooperation between the Socialists, the Communists, and Sōhyō). *Dōmei* 89:39–47.

Najita, Tetsuo. 1967. *Hara Kei in the Politics of Compromise, 1905–1915.* Cambridge: Harvard University Press.

Naka Mamori. 1990. *Kanemaru Shin negishi no kenkyū* (A study of the tactics of Kanemaru Shin). Tokyo: Toyō keizai shimposha.

Nakamura Kenichirō, Uchida Kenzō, and Matsuzaki Minoru. 1990. "Ima koso atarashii seiji no wakugumi o!" (Now is the time for a new political framework!). *Bungei Shunjū* 68 (5): 104–111.

Narita Norihiko. 1996. "Seiji kaikaku hōan no seiritsu katei, kantei to yotō no ugoki o chūshin to shite" (How prime minister's office and coalition parties behaved in political reform legislation—witness of chief assistant to Prime Minister Hosokawa). *Hokkaido Law Review* 46 (6): 405–486.

Nihon Shakaitō. 1983. *Kokumin Seiji Nenkan, 1983* (Citizens' political yearbook, 1983). Tokyo: Nihon Shakaitō.

————. 1986. *Kokumin Seiji Nenkan, 1986* (Citizens political yearbook, 1986). Tokyo: Nihon Shakaitō.

Olson, Mancur. 1982. *The Rise and Decline of Nations: Economics and Growth, Stagflation, and Social Rigidities.* New Haven, Conn.: Yale University Press.

Otake Hideo. 1990. "Defense Controversies and One-Party Dominance: The Opposition in Japan and West Germany." In *Uncommon Democracies, The One- Party Dominant Regimes.* Edited by T. J. Pempel. Ithaca, N. Y.: Cornell University Press.

Pempel, T. J. 1990. "Introduction." In *Uncommon Democracies, The One-Party Dominant Regimes.* Edited by T. J. Pempel. Ithaca, N. Y.: Cornell University Press.

Przeworski, Adam, and John Sprague. 1986. *Paper Stones: A History of Electoral Socialism.* Chicago, Ill.: University of Chicago Press.

Pyle, Kenneth R. 1992. *The Japanese Question: Power and Purpose in a New World Era.* Washington, D.C.: The AEI Press.

Ramseyer, J. Mark, and Frances McCall Rosenbluth. 1993. *Japan's Political Marketplace.* Cambridge: Harvard University Press.

Richardson, Bradley. 1997. *The Japanese Democracy, Power Coordination and Performance.* New Haven, Conn.: Yale University Press.

Riker, William H. 1962. *The Theory of Political Coalitions.* New Haven, Conn.: Yale University Press.

Rochon, Thomas P., and Roy Pierce. 1985. "Coalitions as Rivalries: French Socialists and Communists, 1967–78." *Comparative Politics* 17 (4): 437–451.

Samuels, Richard J. 1987. *The Business of the Japanese State: Energy Markets in Comparative and Historical Perspective.* Ithaca, N.Y.: Cornell University Press.

Sartori, Giovanni. 1990. "A typology of party systems." In *West European Party Systems.* Edited by Peter Mair. Oxford: Oxford University Press.

Sasaki Ryōsaku and Itō Masaya. 1984. "Nijūnen no shūnen, rengō seiken ni kakeru" (Twenty years of tenacity, gambling on a coalition government). *Chūō Kōron* 99 (5): 232–238.

Sasaki Ryōsaku and Kunimasa Takeshige. 1989. *Ippyōsa no jinsei, Sasaki Ryōsaku no shōgen* (A life of one-vote differences, an account by Sasaki Ryōsaku). Tokyo: Asahi shimbunsha.

Satō Sezaburō and Matsuzaki Tetsuhisa. 1984. "Jimintō chōchōki seiken no kaibō" (An examination of the ultra-long LDP regime). *Chūō Kōron* 99 (11): 66–100.

Scalapino, Robert A. 1967. *The Japanese Communist Movement, 1920–1966.* Berkeley: University of California Press.

Schelling, Thomas C. 1980. *The Strategy of Conflict.* Rev. ed. Cambridge, Mass.: Harvard University Press.

Sekai. 1973. "Kakushin kyōtō no kiseki to hōkō" (Opposition cooperation: Where it has been and where it is headed). *Sekai* 331:268–271.

Semba Teruyuki. 1986. "Jun rengō jidai ni okeru Shakaitō no seiji sekinin" (The political responsibility of the Socialist Party in the pre-coalition period). *Gendai no Riron* 224:36–42.

Shakai Rōdō Hyōron. 1985. "Nyū Shakaitō no 80 nendai kōhan no rengō seiken senryaku" (The new Socialist Party's strategy for a coalition government in the latter 1980s). *Shakai Rōdō Hyōron* (May): 25–36.

Shinohara Hajime, Ishikawa Masumi, and Masamura Kimihiro. 1979. "Haku-chū to rengō no seiji jōkyō, dai ni bu" (Razor thin majorities and coalition politics, pt. 2). *Gendai no Riron* 173:22–47.

Shūkan Asahi. 1991. "Ikeda gakkai, hakaen renkinjutsu no zembō" (The full story of how Ikeda's *gakkai* created money out of tombstones). *Shūkan Asahi*, 24 May, 32–34.

Soma Masao. 1986. *Nihon senkyo seido shi* (A history of Japan's election system). Fukuoka, Japan: Kyushu Daigaku Shuppankai.

Stockwin, J. A. A. 1974. "Shifting Alignments in Japanese Party Politics: The April 1974 Election for Governor of Kyoto Prefecture." *Asian Survey* 14 (October): 887–899.

Swaan, Abram de. 1973. *Coalition Theories and Cabinet Formations.* New York: Elsevier Scientific Publishing.

Taagepera, Rein, and Matthew Solberg Shugart. 1989. *Seats and Votes: The Effects and Determinants of Electoral Systems.* New Haven, Conn.: Yale University Press.

Takagi Ikurō. 1989. "Shin Rengō hossoku de seiji chizu wa dō kawaru" (How will the political map change with the new Rengō). *Ekonomisuto, rinji zōkan* 67 (44): 72–77.

Takamune Akitoshi. 1979. "Shin kakushin, chūdō rengō no susume" (The advance of the new progressive, centrist coalition). *Jiyū* 21 (8): 100–113.

Takeuchi Shizuko. 1965. "Sha-Kyō 'tōitsu' undō no yukue" (The progress of the movement for Socialist-communist "unification"). *Ekonomisuto* 43 (7: 46–49.

Tamba Isao. 1998. "Yatō no senkyo undō ni okeru kyōsō to kyōryoku, Tōkai Hokuriku chiku o jirei to shite" (Competition and cooperation in opposition electoral activities). Presentation at annual meeting of the Japan Electoral Studies Association, May. Tokyo, Japan.

Tawara Kōtarō. 1985. "Seikai gyagu geki—Nikaidō yōritsu no kikai" (A political farce—the unseemly Nikaidō plot). *Bungei Shunjū* 63 (1): 134–148.

Tawara Kōtarō, Masamura Kimihiro, and Inoguchi Takashi. 1990. Kore de Kyūjū nendai o norikireru no ka" (Will this allow it to come through the 1990s). *Chūō Kōron* 105 (4): 128–141.

Tominomori Eiji. 1994. *Sengo Hoshin to shi* (A history of the postwar Conservative Party). Tokyo: Shakai shisōsha.

Tsebelis, George. 1990. *Nested Games: Rational Choice in Comparative Politics.* Berkeley: University of California Press.

Tsukamoto Saburō. 1990. "Minshatō wa Minshūtō ni kaimei seyo!" (Change the name of the Democratic Socialist Party to the Democratic Party). *Bungei Shunjū* 68 (6): 150–156.

Ueda Kōichirō. 1971. "Kyō-Sha kyōtō fuseiritsu no shin no gen'in to mondai" (The problems with and real reason that Communist-Socialist cooperation did not occur). *Zen'ei rinji zōkan* 1 (328): 297–304.

Watanabe Masami. 1965. "Chiiki ni okeru Sha-Kyō kyōtō no jōkyō" (The status of Socialist-Communist cooperation at the local level). *Gendai Rōdō Mondai* 90:42–51.

Yamagishi Akira. 1989. "Kyūjū nendai hamba made ni yatō tōitsu o nozomu" (Aiming for a unification of the opposition by the mid-1990s). *Ekonomisuto rinji zōkan* 67 (44): 120–123.

Yanaga Chitoshi. 1956. *Japanese People and Politics*. New York: John Wiley and Sons.

Yano Junya. 1984. "'Yatō rengō' wa seikanchū" (A wait-and-see attitude towards "opposition coalitions"). *Sekai* 463:200–217.

———. 1994. *Nijū Kenryoku, yami no nagare*. Tokyo: Bungei Shunjū.

Yokoyama Taiji. 1971. "Sangiin senkyo ni okeru zen yatō kyōtō ni tsuite" (Concerning all-opposition cooperation in the House of Councillors election). *Shakai Shimpō*, 30 May.

Yomiuri Shimbun (Tokyo). 2, 29 June 1971. 23 June 1980.

Interviews

Futami Nobuaki. Member, House of Representatives; Assistant Secretary General, Clean Government Party. Interview by author, Tokyo. 17 May 1991.

Fukashi Horie. Former Professor of Political Science, Keio University. Interview by author, Tokyo. 6 June 1997.

Ishibashi Masashi. Former Member, House of Representatives; former Chair, Socialist Party. Interview by author, Tokyo. 3 June 1991.

Kunihiro Masao. Interview by author, Tokyo. 22 May 1996.

Matsuda Mitsuyo. Assistant to Representative Kan Naoto, House of Representatives. Interview by author, Yono, Japan. 25 May 1997.

Morimoto Kōji. Former member, House of Councilors; member, House of Representatives. Interview by author, Tokyo. 16 May 1991.

Nishikawa Nirō. Office Manager, Nara City office of Representative Tsuji Daiichi, House of Representatives; former Communist candidate for the House of Councillors. Interview by author, Nara, Japan. 7 February 1991.

Sakata Katsumi. Office Manager, Prefectural office of Representative Tsukata Enjū, House of Representatives; former Chair, Dōmei labor federation in Ibaragi Prefecture. Interview by author, Mito, Japan. 22 May 1997.

Sasaki Ryōsaku. Former Chair, Democratic Socialist Party; former member, House of Representatives. Interview by author, Tokyo. 9 May 1991.

Sasaki Takeshi. Professor, Tokyo University Faculty of Law. Interview by author, Tokyo. 24 January, 20 June, 1991.

Takaichi Sanae. Member, House of Representatives. Interview by author, Tokyo. 5 June 1997.

Takeiri Yoshikatsu. Former member, House of Representatives; former chair, Clean Government Party. Interview by author, Tokyo. 22 May 1991.

Tanabe Makoto. Former Chairman of Japan Socialist Party. Interview by author, Maebashi, Japan. 23 May 1997.

Yoshida Yukihisa. Member, House of Representatives; member, House of Councillors; member, Central Committee of the Democratic Socialist Party. Interview by author, Nara, Japan. 8 February 1991.

Yoshioka Yoshinori. Member, House of Councillors; Chief Editor, *Akahata*. Interview by author, Tokyo. 17 June 1991.

Index

advisory council, 32–33
Ainori. See bandwagon
Akahata, 71, 92
Akamatsu Hirotaka, 27
Allied Occupation. *See* Occupation
ambition, 124, 140. *See also* leadership
    struggle
Aochi Shin, 127
Argersinger, P., 64
Ashida Hitoshi, 134–136
associational effects, 46–47, 55–56, 61, 63,
    71, 76–77, 194, 199n. 4 (56).
    See also coalition governments;
    electoral cooperation
Asukata Ichio, 204 n. 44 (103)
Axelrod, Robert, 49, 57, 67

bakayarō, 146, 208 n. 20 (146)
ballots: fusion, 63–64; joint, 62–66. *See*
    also electoral systems
bandwagon, 80–82
bargaining: costs, 43; model, 41–45. *See*
    also coalition governments;
    Liberal Democratic Party
barter coalitions, 47–48
Bartolini, Stefano, 50, 59
Bawn, Kathleen, 157
boycott of Diet. *See* delay of legislation
Boyd, Richard, 133
Broughton, David, 53
Buraku Liberation League, 94
bureaucrats, 22, 82, 116–117, 130–132,
    137, 156
business influence, 133, 136, 198 n. 8 (23)

Calder, Kent E., 22
campaign: agriculture, 112, 182; business
    support, 126, 182, 207 n. 4
    (126); costs, 10–12; effects on
    cooperation, 56–57, 59, 67–68,
    200 n. 6 (59); fund-raising, 9,
    24–25; issue-oriented, 12, 115,
    182; regulations, 182–183, 185,
    205 n. 58 (115). *See also* media;
    organizations
candidates: women, 112. *See also* inde-
    pendents; unions
caretaker leader, 144
centrist, 19, 27; fear of isolation, 84, 140,
    201 nn. 11, 12, 13 (84). *See also*
    Clean Government Party;
    Democratic Socialist Party
Clean Government Party: Book Publish-
    ing Scandal, 127, 139–141; as
    cooperative partner, 95, 98,
    103, 119–121, 151, 194–195,
    201 n. 7 (80), 202 n. 29 (93),
    204 n. 46 (105), 204 n. 50
    (111), 205 n. 51 (111),
    205 n. 57 (115), 207 n. 16
    (140); Clean Government
    League, 91–94, 106–108,
    207 n. 13 (138); elections, 14,
    185, 188–190, 194–195,
    206 n. 1 (125); founding,
    138–139; organizational
    strength, 95, 151; policy mod-
    eration, 27; relations with
    Democratic Socialist Party,

About the Author

RAY CHRISTENSEN, who holds a Ph.D. from Harvard University, is an assistant professor of political science at Brigham Young University. He previously taught at the University of Kansas and was a visiting researcher at Tokyo University. His work on Japanese elections, specifically campaigning and electoral reform, has appeared in the *American Journal of Political Science, Comparative Political Studies,* and *Asian Survey.* This is his first book.